Organization   *nt*

For Walker and Jennie Graham

Organizational Behaviour for Hospitality Management

Roy C. Wood

Butterworth-Heinemann Ltd
Linacre House, Jordan Hill, Oxford OX2 8DP

℞ A member of the Reed Elsevier group

OXFORD   LONDON   BOSTON
MUNICH   NEW DELHI   SINGAPORE   SYDNEY
TOKYO   TORONTO   WELLINGTON

First published 1994

British Library Cataloguing in Publication Data
Wood, Roy C.
    Organizational Behaviour for Hospitality Management
    I. Title
    647.94068

ISBN 0 7506 1830 2

Typeset by Scribe Design, Gillingham, Kent
Printed and bound in Great Britain by Martins the Printers,
Berwick-upon-Tweed

Contents

Preface

This book is intended for students who require a basic introduction to the key concepts of organizational behaviour and their potential application in the context of the hospitality industry. The book has been written with BTEC, SCOTVEC, HCIMA and first-year degree students in mind. The expectation is that the text will be used in conjunction with other, more generalist, works on organizational behaviour.

No claim is made here for comprehensive coverage of organizational behaviour themes. Rather the aim has been to convey the essence of the subject by relating key topics to academic research in the hotel and catering field, and supporting this with a number of case studies and exercises. Throughout, the goal has been to keep the book's objectives modest in the hope that this will increase its accessibility.

In each of the four sections, particular themes (which may broadly be summarized as organizational theory, the individual and organizations, management and organizations and issues in organizational behaviour) are developed in topic-centred chapters that, wherever possible, proceed from the general to the (hospitality) specific. This has not been a particularly easy task at times. Despite a growing literature on work-related issues in the hospitality industry, very little research has been conducted from an organizational behaviour perspective. It is hoped that this text will go some small way to stimulating interest in this field.

Roy C. Wood

Acknowledgements

I should like to thank Jacqui Shanahan of Butterworth-Heinemann for her support in the writing of the book. My colleagues at The Scottish Hotel School, University of Strathclyde, have exercised their usual tolerance of my preoccupation with writing and, more importantly, my absence on a 6-month sabbatical during which much of the text was prepared. Mona Clark of the School of Food and Accommodation Management, University of Dundee, read and commented on parts of the manuscript and I have benefited from her advice, guidance and support, as indeed I have from the general support and encouragement of Dr Mike Riley of the University of Surrey. I should also like to thank Dr Riley for his permission to use a modified version of the case study 'The Leisure Corporation'. Similar dues are also owed to Addison-Wesley Publishing Co. Inc. for permission to reproduce a modified version of the case study 'Lost in the Desert' from G. Anderson and R. Evenden (1992) *Management Skills: Making the Most of People* (© Addison-Wesley Publishing Co. Inc.); to Carol Marlow, Marketing Director of Forte Posthouse, who allowed the use of company materials in the case study 'Hotels and Organizational Culture'; and to Eric Brown, General Manager of the Criagendarroch Hotel and Country Club for supplying organization charts.

In helping me to keep a sense of proportion, as well as ensuring my social life did not stop entirely during the preparation of the text, I owe a debt of gratitude to Arnaud Frapin-Beaugé, Joseph Fattorini and Donald Sloan. The most significant contribution to the production of a book comes from those who type and otherwise prepare the production manuscript: for this I am indebted to Hazel MacDonald who typed the main draft and Sandra Miller who edited it. Their professionalism and good humour at all times made the composition of the text many times easier. All views expressed herein are those of the author alone. All errors can, and should, be laid at the same door.

1 The nature of organizational behaviour – an introduction

Organizational behaviour is the study of the relations between people and organizations, of the part people play in the design, construction, maintenance and management of organizations. Organizational behaviour or some close variant is present as a subject of study in many business and management courses, including courses in hospitality management. The value in studying organizational behaviour is usually perceived as deriving from a special managerial relevance the subject brings to an understanding of work organizations. Organizations consist of people, and good and effective managers must not only be able to interpret and understand people's behaviour in organizational settings, but, where relevant, manipulate such behaviour in order to ensure the attainment of organizational goals, whether this be in positive ways, e.g. building teamwork and a corporate culture and consensus, or negative ways (e.g. resolving interpersonal conflicts). Organizational behaviour is thus conceived of as a largely positive and vital subject of study, combining managerial directedness with a tinge of altruism.

This is reflected in the form taken by organizational behaviour as a field of study. The term 'field of study' is important here, for in the conventional academic sense organizational behaviour is not a discipline in its own right. Rather, it is eclectic and inter-disciplinary, drawing on a range of subject disciplines, most notably psychology and sociology but also, *inter alia*, political science, history and economics. This borrowing of concepts from other disciplines is not, however, random, but biased towards an understanding of the primary interests of organizational behaviour, which, in the words of Thompson and McHugh (1990, p. 2) are '...social behaviour in the enterprise, directed chiefly towards problems of motivation and the performance of individuals and groups in relation to different structures and practices'.

It is at this point that a recurring criticism of organizational behaviour must be dealt with. This is that, as a field of study, organizational behaviour by the definitions of its own practitioners is highly fragmented, or, put another way, unsystematic and 'bitty'. In this view the only systematic aspect of the subject area is the pursuit of its own 'prime directive', namely the looting of concepts and methods from other disciplines for the purposes of constituting a form of knowledge that, while analytic, is directed to the manipulation of people, comprising knowledge, skills and methods of value to managers in the pursuit of organizational objectives,

objectives which may not be in the interests of anyone other than organizational leaders and may be actively hostile to non-managerial workers, 'ordinary people', and society more generally.

There is no easy way round such charges. On the issue of fragmentation, it is certainly the case that in emphasizing the focus of study (organizational behaviour) as opposed to the concepts of analysis drawn from the variety of disciplines utilized, two common problems arise in the majority of textbooks devoted to the subject. These are, as Thompson and McHugh (1990, p. 46) note:

- The tendency for organizational behaviour texts to comprise a confusing and often convoluted mixture of analysis and prescription.
- The existence of an uneasy relationship between the two principal sources of concepts – sociology and psychology – in that the usual concerns of the latter in the organizational behaviour context, e.g. personality, perception, psychological testing, are rarely, if at all, related explicitly to organizational life or to the sociological material that deals primarily with organizational structure, change and management.

How such difficulties can be resolved is a matter of some debate and centres principally on how an adequate concept of the individual can be integrated within forms of analysis centrally concerned with collective forms of behaviour – a problem that is probably as old as social science (and certainly sociology) itself. This problem is closely related to the second charge levelled against organizational behaviour and its variants – that eclecticism in the choice of 'relevant' concepts from other disciplines obscures the fact that organizational behaviour is not a wholly valid area of study in its own right, but is instead an unappealing mongrel concerned primarily with imposing an uncritical and esentially managerial perspective on human behaviour, one that serves managerial interests but the interests of few others.

It would be presumptuous to suggest that such issues, exercising many in the field of organizational behaviour, can be resolved here – if at all. Awareness of, and some sensitivity to, such criticisms is, however, essential. There is an all too easy tendency in some quarters to present organizational behaviour (and other subjects and approaches) as a universal panacea for personnel and other problems in the workplace. Organizational behaviour is an easy target for the criticisms of the kind mentioned above precisely because of academic suspicions that it is a 'magpie' field of study with no real substance of its own, and one that has developed a too easy and partial relationship with the interests of business and management. In recognizing the legitimacy of this view it is necessary to guard against the academic prejudices and snobberies that can be all too easily dismissive of practitioners in fields that seek to apply knowledge to real situations in an attempt to eliminate and ameliorate phenomena that are regarded as problematic or undesirable. Organizational behaviour is no more a cure-all for organizational problems than aspirin is for a bad head cold. All knowledge is to some extent ideological, i.e. it serves the interests of some individuals or groups. The best guard against the uncritical acceptance of ideas – any ideas – is constant intellectual vigilance and cultivated scepticism.

As a field of study, organizational behaviour focuses on a particular area of social life – organizations and the people who work within them. As such, perhaps the greatest problem to guard against is that of insularity, of failing to locate the study of organizations in an adequate social context. This is the view adopted here, and the whole of the text focuses on the social/sociological dimensions to organizations. This is not to deny the importance of the psychological contribution to organizational behaviour but to recognize the view, both actual and implied, of Thompson and McHugh (1990) that few if any textbooks in the field articulate the two areas competently, or perhaps ever could. In focusing on the one (and historically, it must be said, most important) contributing discipline, the intention is to provide a coherent discussion of the main issues in organizational behaviour that are both integrated and sensitive to the more concrete and 'measurable' social contexts that generate such behaviour. There are, however, three other good reasons for concentrating on the sociological dimensions to organizational behaviour: the insularity of the hospitality industry itself, the existing status of organizational behaviour research in hotel and catering organizations, and the nature of employment in hospitality services.

Insularity of the hospitality industry

Few academic commentators now dispute the point that the hospitality industry is exceptionally insular in its values and outlook – conservative with a small 'c' – and this insularity extends to associated institutions such as hospitality management education, where the majority of students continue to be educated separately from their peers on general management and business studies courses. Insularity in this sense embraces a range of characteristics, including resistance to change; a belief that the hospitality industry is different from other industries to the extent that many of the management practices and procedures of the latter are of little relevance or use to the needs of hospitality organizations; and a tendency to a 'unitary' perspective on the part of management – seeing management as the single source of authority and initiative in organizations, with all that implies for decision-making.

The consequences of the industry's insularity are difficult to define precisely. Principally, however, two features are worthy of note. First, the management of hospitality organizations tends to be prescriptive rather than analytic, drawing heavily on what has traditionally been the response or responses to situations not only in a particular unit but in the industry as a whole. Second, there has been a tendency for managers and some academics (a tendency that in the latter case at least has begun to diminish in recent years) to appeal to psychologistic explanations for human behaviour in organizations, i.e. in accounting for the way in which individuals or groups act in particular situations, or in explaining particular phenomena, emphasis has been placed on individual motivations. For example, it is common for managers in the industry to explain high labour turnover in terms of the characteristics of the individuals who make up the workforce – hotel and catering employees are regarded as 'nomadic' and 'non-conforming' (Mars, Bryant and Mitchell, 1979). Research demonstrates however that labour turnover is better explained not in terms of the collective psychological characteristics of industry workers but in terms of the nature of work in the industry and the nature of skills acquisition (see Wood, 1992, for a review). The fact that social and structural features of the industry are important in influencing organizational behaviour and organizational decisions thus emphasizes the importance of the social over the psychological.

The status of organizational behaviour research in hotels and catering

Employment issues in the hotel and catering industry have always been on the agenda of both operators and educators. Further, the period since 1980 has seen in both the UK and USA an enormous growth in academic research on employment in hospitality services. Much of this research – perhaps the majority – has been from a sociological perspective, broadly defined, yet little has focused on conventional organizational behaviour concerns. Instead, the focus has tended to be on the occupational structure in hotels and catering and, in addition, particular labour problems such as high turnover of staff, low pay and the role of trade unions in the industry (Lennon and Wood, 1989; Wood, 1992).

The absence of extensive 'hard data' on organizational behaviour issues in the hospitality industry necessarily makes a book on the subject difficult to write – or at least difficult to illustrate! As noted earlier, however, organizational behaviour is a field of study eclectic in the sources on which it draws and much of the research on industry employment conducted to date can easily be accommodated within an organizational behaviour framework – a further reason for emphasizing the sociological tradition in organizational behaviour, as some continuity is ensured not only within the field of industrial behaviour more generally, but in terms of the employment issues that have dominated hospitality research.

The nature of employment in hospitality services

The fact that many researchers in the hotel and catering field have found the industry to be characterized by insularity, an insularity that leads workplace and organizational behaviour to be explained by managers and workers in highly individualistic terms, is a further reason for adopting a primarily sociological approach to organizational behaviour. Both social psychological and sociological perspectives on human behaviour encourage a more systematic approach to exploring people's actions, in particular those actions that arise as a result of people's involvement in organizations. Psychological factors are not unimportant in explaining either individual or group behaviour, but much previous research has demonstrated that social and socio-economic factors are crucial to understanding the nature of hotel and catering employment (Wood, 1992).

For example, the industry employs a very large number of so-called 'marginal' workers – women, young people, ethnic minorities – people whose bargaining power in the labour market is limited by the stigma with which society more generally invests them. In looking at the position of one of these groups – women – it is found that in order to earn a family or individual living wage, many women need to work. Often child-care responsibilities limit their employment opportunities to part-time work. The hotel and catering industry is a major source of part-time employment and to a degree facilitates female participation in the workforce, allowing women to 'match' domestic and employment responsibilities. The incidence of female part-time employment in the industry cannot thus be explained by reference to personal or 'industry' factors alone, but must take on board an understanding of the wider social circumstances in which many women find themselves.

A broadly sociological approach to individual and organizational behaviour encourages a systematic approach to explaining such behaviour, a searching out of patterns of regularity that locate work and organization firmly within the community and wider society. This might be considered particularly important in the case of the hospitality industry, which is often an important aspect of community life, serving the everyday needs of local populations as well as those of tourists. This last point leads to consideration of the nature of the hospitality industry and hospitality organizations.

The nature of the hospitality industry

What kind of industry, then, is the hospitality industry? The short (and conventional) answer to this question is to point out that hotels and catering cannot be adequately viewed as a single homogeneous grouping and are better conceptualized as heterogeneous, comprising different sectors all of which have a number of features in common, all of which complement one another, but all of which are in some way distinctive. One of the most helpful definitions of the industry, or at least one that sets easy parameters, is that of the Hotel and Catering Training Board (1987), which differentiates between main activity centres and subsidiary activity centres in an effort to characterize employment in the hospitality industry. In summary:

- Main activity centres include hotels, guesthouses, other tourist accommodation, restaurants, cafés, snackbars, public houses, bars, nightclubs, licensed clubs, and canteens and messes operated by contract caterers.
- Subsidiary activity centres include employees working in tourism and travel catering, public service catering (e.g. the National Health Service, School Meal Services and public administration), retail distribution, office catering and personal and domestic services.

Main activity centres crudely approximate to the principal, private, commercial, 'for profit' sectors of the industry, whereas subsidiary activity centres cover areas where catering may or may not be for profit but is nearly always secondary to the main function of an organization.

Table 1.1   Employment in the UK commercial hospitality industry, 1992, by sector

Sector	Number employed	As percentage of total
Restaurants, snackbars, cafés, etc.	294,800	25.7
Public houses and bars	329,100	28.6
Nightclubs and licensed clubs	137,300	11.9
Canteens and messes	117,700	10.2
Hotel trade	251,000	21.8
Other short-stay accommodation	20,300	1.8
All sectors	1,150,200	100

Source: Department of Employment, *Employment Gazette*, May 1993.

From the point of view of the study of organizational behaviour, then, hospitality organizations come in many different forms. The provision of catering services within an organization like a hospital can have different implications for both individuals within the organization and the organization itself than the provision of catering in a high-street fast-food restaurant.

Other definitional problems arise from variations in organizational form *within* sectors. The most significant issue here is the size of the units. Despite the growth of chains and multiples in the last two decades, certain sectors of the industry – most notably the hotels, guesthouses and other tourist accommodation sector; and the restaurants, cafés and snackbars sector – are dominated by small, usually owner-managed units, employing family labour and a small number of 'helpers'. The nature and quality of small organizations such as these are thus a potential source of difference and are unlikely to be analytically comparable to large, chain-owned units. Indeed, to return to the concept of commercial or 'for profit' catering, it is probably fair to say that the motives of the owner–manager of a small hotel or guesthouse diverge from those who run large chains. For the latter, profit is revenue-generated and is then channelled into the wider organization after the payment of taxes, dividends to shareholders and other costs and obligatory payments. For the former, making a profit can be construed differently and may be better termed 'making a living'. Here the business goal is not expansion or maintenance of a large organization but the generation of a comfortable revenue to sustain a particular lifestyle (see Seymour, 1985, and Lowe, 1987, for interesting perspectives on these issues).

Table 1.1 shows employment by sector in the commercial hospitality industry: here the Department of Employment's figures are used and these produce yet another classification for the industry. When combined with all catering services, total employment in hospitality services is around the 2 million mark.

Any analyst of employment in hospitality services has to contend with the many different classifications of the industry's activities. Problems in attaining a sectorally based definition of the hospitality industry have long been recognized by academic commentators (Medlik and Airey, 1978; Hughes, 1986). Whether a comprehensive and universally acceptable definition of this type is either ultimately useful or attainable is also an important issue. One response to the inadequacy of business and economically oriented definitions of the industry has been to concentrate on the qualitative assessment and definition of hospitality services. For the purposes of this discussion, the most commonly defined issues can be operationalized under four headings: demand, operational, personnel and supply factors.

Demand factors

The demand for hotel and catering products and services can usefully be characterized as:

- Variable and unpredictable – there are often fluctuations in short-term demand and this has consequences for the operation and staffing of hotel and catering units (see below, under 'Operational' and 'Personnel' factors).
- Diverse – hospitality organizations within the limits of their own product specialisms are required to satisfy a variety of needs, wants and expectations.
- Highly localized – except in major tourist centres, or centres whose business is highly seasonal, the demand for hotel and catering services is generally confined to a discrete geographical area (the same is true of the demand for labour in most occupational grades, the highly skilled grades being the most obvious exception).

Operational factors

The operational and production features of hotel and catering organizations differ from those found in manufacturing and many other service industries. Specifically:

- Hotel and catering organizations combine both production *and* service elements – the production of a meal is not widely different to the production of other material goods and in certain types of operation, most noticeably fast-food operations, can entail a high level of investment in capital goods (technology) (see Pine, 1987, and Wood, 1992 – see also Braverman, 1974, pp. 359–62, who takes this argument to extremes in suggesting that the work of room-cleaning staff in preparing rooms for occupation can be likened to the production of goods).
- The production of goods and services frequently calls for a combination of a range of operations, both mechanical and physical, and these require a high degree of co-ordination if they are to be delivered efficiently.
- Hotel and catering organizations function to service the leisure and business needs of others, often with long and unsocial hours for employees – many organizations, particularly hotels, can be 24-hour a day operations, requiring sound administrative skills on the part of managers and flexibility in employment practices.

Personnel factors

The nature of employment in the hospitality industry was touched upon in the previous section. To the observations there can be added the following.

- While the hospitality industry employs many so-called marginal workers – women, members of ethnic minorities and young persons – and much employment is on a casual and part-time basis, unionization in the hotel and catering industry, where conditions might be thought to be ideal to the development of such associations, is in fact very low.
- The occupational range of the hospitality industry embraces skilled, semi-skilled and unskilled jobs, though there is some evidence that the increasing use of technology in the industry is reducing skill requirements among those occupations traditionally requiring high levels of technical expertise, e.g. among chefs and cooks.
- The hospitality industry is both capital- *and* labour-intensive – the latter is widely recognized but the former is often ignored.
- Managers in the industry are expected to demonstrate a much wider range of skills than their counterparts in most other industries. Specifically, they are required to demonstrate an ability to master technical and craft skills as well as possessing managerial competencies.

Supply factors

Just as the demand for hotel and catering services possesses some untypical features, so does the supply of these services. Most important are the observations that:

- Most hotel and catering services are supplied direct to the customer on the premises of the organization. The consumers' purchase of products and services is such that they leave the hospitality establishment with no tangible end result or at the very most a tangible product that is inherently ephemeral and will be rapidly consumed.
- Hotel and catering products are highly perishable, not only in a physical sense, as with food, but in a more abstract sense, e.g. a hotel room that is not sold on a particular night cannot be sold again, and *that* sale is lost forever.
- The hospitality consumer is an integral part of the production and service process – the customer is always at least partially (and often more than partially) responsible for initiating the activation of production and service within the organization.

To a greater or lesser extent all industries are faced with a combination of interrelated external and internal circumstances that are unique. At the same time the uniqueness of any sector should not disguise the features it shares with other industries. The same is true of business organizations *within* a particular industrial sector. Theoretically there are many different forms an organization can take, but to a very great degree the structure, practices and human-resource strategies of individual organizations within an industry will exhibit broadly similar characteristics, and these will be to some extent determined by the interaction of the external and internal forces that act on the organization.

The point being made here is a simple one. It is that external forces do not determine in any *direct* sense the internal (organizational) response to such forces. The variability of demand for hotel and catering services does not mean that high levels of part-time and casual employment are a necessary or inevitable precondition of supplying these services. Rather, once a decision has been taken to provide goods and services in a particular way, e.g. by opening a restaurant rather than operating a mobile hot-dog stand, then the form taken by the organization is a matter of choice, and usually a matter of proprietorial or managerial choice.

Thus, in any organization, a number of questions have to be asked by organizational controllers, questions based on their understanding of the circumstances in which they find themselves. The hospitality industry is often regarded as a 'traditional' industry in the sense of being relatively unchanging over time. It is often the case that organizational practices are justified or validated on the basis that such tasks have always been performed in a particular way. Claims like these reflect, however, the fact that certain choices have been made – the choice, say, to continue performing a task in one way rather than another. The 'availability of choice' in this context means that however conservative an organization may be, there is always a potential for dynamism and change. Indeed most organizations – even those in the hotel and catering industry – are dynamic, changing all the time, if only in small ways.

The questions that have to be addressed by organizational decision-makers tend, then, to be enduring and universal. They are:

- How can the efforts of each individual be harnessed to the goals of the organization?
- Given the external forces acting on the organization and the limitations these place on the organization in meeting its goals, what is the best organizational structure to adopt in seeking to realize these goals?
- What forms of managerial control are necessary to maximize the organization's success, and what types of leadership and management styles are best suited to achieving organizational goals?
- How can all human resources in the organization be motivated and brought together to produce the necessary organizational culture for success?
- What mechanisms are best suited to identifying the need for organizational change and developing strategies to initiate such change?

Organizational behaviour in a hospitality context

So far, the nature of organizational behaviour has been described and the character of the hospitality industry outlined. What remains to be discussed in this chapter is the nature of organizational behaviour 'problems' and 'issues' in the hospitality industry. As suggested at the end of the previous section, most organizations face similar, *general* tasks. It is at this point that a note of caution must be sounded, for definition of what constitutes a 'problem' or 'issue' is, in any context, something of a difficulty in itself, and to a large extent dependent on who defines phenomena as problematic.

Organizational behaviour has often been criticized as a field of study that too readily accepts managerial and proprietorial definitions of what constitutes a 'problem'. For example, in capitalist societies a prime objective of the business organization is to make a profit and to do so at least cost. For the capitalist therefore, organizational problems may thus centre on how best to exploit the workforce. This instance is, in itself, a crude example of what might be termed a 'vulgar Marxist' position, with bosses seen as exploiting workers mercilessly in order to make the highest profits. Reality is more complex. For example, it has been demonstrated on many occasions that employers and managers often adopt strategies that might reduce productivity and profitability from its actual potential in order to realize other benefits, such as a stable workforce. It is therefore important to note that some sensitivity is required in defining what is or is not an organizational 'problem'.

To engage in a meaningful discussion of organizational behaviour and to create a positive organizational environment requires analytical and practical skills that can be brought to bear on creating a true organizational synergy that recognizes the needs of all members of the organization. The problems most commonly identified as hampering organizational efficiency and success in the hospitality industry, and which will surface in many forms throughout this book, can be summarized as follows.

The culture of organizations

To talk about organizational culture is to talk about the attitudes, values and practices that are particular (but not necessarily exclusive) to individual organizations and that derive from features shared in common with organizations in a similar position. While it is difficult to make generalizations about an industry as diverse as hotels and catering, the following points are generally accepted as pertinent.

First is the *culture of informal rewards*. Basic pay in the hospitality industry is generally low and many (though by no means all) workers often 'make up' the rewards paid by employers with tips (from clients), 'fiddles' and 'knock-offs' (acts of petty theft of small monies and comestibles), and in addition receive benefits in kind from subsidized food (meals on duty) and accommodation. In many hotel and catering organizations management tolerates a certain amount of petty theft, such acts being seen as a normal part of industry culture. However, in tipped occupations, competition can be stiff as employees compete with one another to give the 'best service' and therefore enhance the level of their reward. This can give rise to inter-departmental conflict or conflict within a single occupational group (Mars and Nicod, 1984, note how certain items of useful equipment were hidden by waiting staff to ensure a supply of such items at busy periods). In terms of inter-departmental conflict (the classic example of which is that which often occurs between kitchen and restaurant), the speed essential to waiting staff giving good service often leads to a transfer of pressure from waiting staff to kitchen staff, who resent such pressures, and this leads to subsequent conflict.

Second, and related, is the *culture of individualism*. The hospitality industry has the reputation of being a highly competitive industry in which to work and one which contains large numbers of individualistic and even idiosyncratic proprietors, managers and operative workers. Further, this competitiveness is reinforced by the isolated conditions under which many employees undertake their work, e.g. relative 'geographical' isolation (the room attendants working on their own to prepare hotel bedrooms) or isolation within the group engendered by competition (as among waiting staff seeking to enhance their rewards through tips). In its most extreme form isolation of individuals within the hospitality industry can extend to groups and departments. Shamir (1981) has noted that, in many hotels, departments and the workers within them behave on occasion as if they were autonomous units, with little regard for what is happening elsewhere in the hotel. This presents particular problems of integration for managers in the industry.

Finally, in this discussion, comes the *culture of managerial autonomy*. Managers in the hotel and catering industry tend to achieve senior posts at a relatively young age and are given a great deal of latitude in the running of their units. Furthermore, the responsibility of managers is conceived of in terms of styles of management that emphasize individual and personal control of a unit. Unlike the position in many other industries therefore, hospitality managers often exercise 'hands on' control, regularly engaging in 'shop floor' work and enjoying frequent contact with clients and employees. This has important implications for the ways in which 'good' and 'bad' managers are differentiated in the eyes of superiors, colleagues and their subordinates, and the manner in which hospitality organizations are structured.

Poorly motivated workers

Many operational jobs in the hospitality industry are low in skill content and poorly paid. Workers complain of monotony and drudgery and are not regarded as highly motivated. Nor do they feel that they enjoy the respect of their fellow staff, managers or society at large. One female catering worker in a study by Gabriel (1988, p. 85) commented that 'Working in catering you feel sometimes that your job lacks dignity. Kitchen ladies and catering staff generally are treated as inferior people by everyone'. In a survey of Scottish hotel and catering workers by Macaulay and Wood (1992) 60 per cent of employees interviewed frequently complained that others viewed them as 'different', usually negatively so. The biggest complaint, cited by over a quarter of these, was that other people treated them as 'servants or skivvies'.

Labour turnover

Lack of motivation and self-esteem can lead to high labour turnover in hotel and catering organizations. However, labour turnover is a good example of how different perspectives on an issue can generate different definitions of what is problematic. High labour turnover is mainly regarded as problematic by some academics, but other academics, and, more importantly, managers and proprietors in the industry, do not regard labour turnover as a problem. For the latter, labour turnover is viewed as a pathological feature of the industry, as a phenomenon over which they have little control and to which they are therefore resigned. High labour turnover is also seen as conferring certain advantages on the organization, specifically flexibility in staffing arrangements, something highly valued in a sector where demand for services and products can be unpredictable (see Mars, Bryant and Mitchell, 1979). For other commentators, high labour turnover is a blight that costs the organization large amounts of money (see Wood, 1992, for a fuller review of the issues).

In addition to the motivational problems identified earlier, reasons advanced to explain the phenomenon of high labour turnover in the hospitality industry include the following:

- *The nature of the workforce itself*: the hotel and catering workforce is seen as comprising large numbers of psychologically deviant persons and 'misfits' who enjoy changing jobs frequently (Wood, 1992; 1992a).
- *The abdication of managerial responsibility for the workforce*: as noted earlier, the industry pays low wages, often justified on the basis that many workers make up their income from tips. This creates a situation whereby employees often feel they are working as much or more for customers than for the organization, with the result that the competition between workers generates stress, and workers change jobs in the hope of finding a position with fewer pressures.

The problem of motivation of the workforce and of the management of staff as revealed by discussions of labour turnover leads to the third and final main issue in organizational behaviour as it applies to the hospitality industry: that of management style and leadership.

Management style and leadership

It is easy to cite management style and leadership as the root of the problems faced by any organization. Management must, after all, take responsibility for its actions and for proper leadership. Certainly hospitality industry managers have a *reputation* for high- and heavy-handedness, and are often perceived as arbitrary in the decisions they take and authoritarian in style. It is necessary to understand both the appearance and substance of such views, though it must be said at the outset that management is an easy target when it comes to attributing blame for organizational difficulties: a proper understanding is also required of the industrial and organizational context in which managers are required to operate. Managers are employees also and face many of the difficulties in performing their tasks experienced by other industry workers.

Summary

Many of the issues identified in this chapter recur and will be developed throughout the text. The main points of the discussion so far can be summarized as follows:

- Organizational behaviour as a subject of study is concerned with behaviour and actions in organizations. It draws on a variety of disciplines in analysing organizations, though sociology dominates in conceptualizing the structure and functioning of organizations.
- The hotel and catering industry is a heterogeneous industry and one characterized by a high degree of differentiation. Yet all hotel and catering organizations share many features in common. In applying the concepts of organizational behaviour to the study of the hospitality industry, the aim is to identify key features in the operation of hotel and catering organizations and to analyse these with a view to improving organizational performance and clarifying the duties and responsibilities of the organization to its employees and the wider community.
- As with all industries, hospitality organizations have a number of highly individual features, which require sensitivity of analysis. In particular, hospitality organizations are production- and service-oriented and the customer is an integral part of both. Demand for products and services can be erratic, and requires organizational controllers to manage in a reactive and flexible manner. Hotel and catering organizations also face a number of problems, and these are reflected in the relatively poor image of the industry that is held by the general public.

Discussion questions

1 Identify some of the key problems attendant on defining organizational behaviour and consider their relevance for the study of hospitality organizations.
2 What key influences affect the character of hospitality organizations?
3 Explain how diverse hospitality organizations may come to exhibit common cultural characteristics.
4 In organizational terms, why is it important to reject the view that the hospitality industry is unique?

Part One
Work, the Organization and Organizational Design

2 Theoretical perspectives on work and organizations

Organizational behaviour is more than just the sociology of organizations, though that is perhaps its most important constituent component. Here, however, the commentator faces a slight problem. The sociology of organizations is one of those many specialisms that make up what is more broadly termed the 'sociology of work and industry' or 'industrial sociology', and, in point of fact, organizational behaviour draws widely on industrial sociology or, perhaps more precisely, cuts across it, not being confined simply to one of the many specialisms that have evolved within the field. What is there in a name? Perhaps very little, but it is important to be clear about the range of sociological material on work and industry that organizational behaviour draws on.

Figure 2.1 models the field of industrial sociology, showing the various specialisms. There are few of these that organizational behaviour does not draw upon as well as, increasingly, concepts and theories drawn from

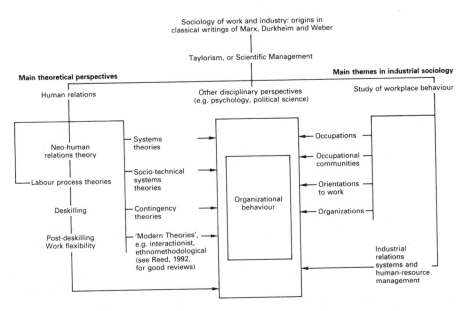

Figure 2.1 The fields of industrial sociology and organizational behaviour

politics, psychology and other disciplines (see Chapter 1). The objective of the discussion that follows is to summarize those theoretical perspectives that are commonly represented as of importance to the field of organizational behaviour.

Classical theories

In the organizational behaviour context the term 'classical' is usually appended to the work of a group of disparate writers active in the latter half of the nineteenth century and at the beginning of the twentieth (some commentators have, however, quite properly pointed to the operation of at least implicit theories of work organization in antiquity: see, for example, Tyson and Jackson, 1992). Many so-called 'classical' authors have little in common other than the period in which they were writing, which was characterized by the rise of industrialization, and a concern to elaborate, with varying degrees of caution, universally applicable guidelines for efficient management.

Undoubtedly the two most important writers in terms of their enduring contribution to the theory and practice of industrial organizations are Max Weber and F.W. Taylor. The two men could not have been more different. Max Weber, one of the founding fathers of modern sociology, along with Karl Marx, Emile Durkheim and Auguste Comte, was an academic social scientist. Indeed, in terms of the commonly accepted list of classical writers on organizations, Weber sticks out like a sore thumb. Furthermore, the contrast with Taylor verges on the bizarre. Taylor was an engineer, a crusader for what became known as 'scientific management'. He exhibited none of the academic sense of investigation and impartiality of Weber, nor any of that writer's intellectual training. Rather, Taylor was a man who sought academic respectability for his ideas and was mainly concerned with the practical implications of work organization. Organizational behaviour as a field of study often makes for strange bedfellows.

Max Weber

Max Weber (1864–1920) was a lawyer by training and spent most of his life in academe, but his sheer breadth of scholarship makes it necessary to recognize that his contribution to the study of organizations was only a small part of his lifetime achievement and interest. In the field of organizational studies Weber is credited with elaborating the concept of the bureaucratic organization, with all that conjures up in contemporary commonsense understandings of organizational inefficiency and waste, red tape and impersonality. For Weber, however, the bureaucratic organization was technically superior to other organizational forms, and was the most pervasive type of organization in modern industrial societies, being entirely rational in the sense that it entailed all parts of the organization being designed for the achievement of organizational goals.

The principal features of Weber's ideal bureaucratic organization were as follows:

- *The organization is constructed hierarchically.* Each position in the organization reports to a position one step higher in the hierarchy.
- *The functions of the organization are bound by rules.* The functions, offices and tasks to be performed by office-holders are circumscribed by detailed rules and regulations that define proper and appropriate procedures, actions and duties of organizational members. In respect of the latter, this often means that bureaucratic organizations are characterized by a high degree of specialization and the division of labour.
- *There is a separation of personal and business affairs, of ownership and control.* Authority in the organization derives from the qualities of the office (position) rather than the office-holder. Office-holders, particularly managerial office-holders, should not have an ownership stake in the organization, to ensure decisions are taken that are best for the organization rather than individuals or groups of individuals within it.
- *Duties, responsibilities and decisions are undertaken in an impartial fashion.* Following from the preceding point, duties and responsibilities (and, ultimately, decisions) are assumed to be undertaken impartially. This is possible because these actions are not motivated by self-interest or personal interests but are functions of the office. Office-holders are selected and promoted solely on the basis of technical qualifications and competence.
- *Uniformity of decisions.* Bureaucratic organizations ensure uniformity and consistency of decision-making over time, not only because of the foregoing characteristics, but because all administrative decisions, rules and procedures are recorded in writing, providing a continuous record of organizational activities.

Criticisms of the bureaucratic model have been well rehearsed. They can be summarized as follows.

First, although the bureaucratic form ideally emphasizes logic and rationality through impartiality and impersonality, this can make bureaucratic organizations resistant to change. As such, the organization, its rules, procedures and ethos become a barrier to change: the organization itself, its preservation and perpetuation, become more important than the efficient discharge of its duties, or its efficient performance.

Second, the emphasis on continuity in record-keeping and paperwork and on impersonality in decision-taking can lead to sluggishness and red tape. It has been argued that bureaucratic organizations by definition enable office-holders to avoid and delay decision-making. Further, initiative and creativity are stifled as organizational members subordinate themselves to the procedures of the organization.

Third, the hierarchical nature of bureaucratic organizations can also significantly slow the decision-making process. At the same time, the dependency on written rules and procedures and rigid definition of individual office-holding responsibilities can lead to inefficient and incompetent organizational members going undetected.

Fourth, because the organization in its own right is considered an important entity, members of the organization can develop an over-reverence of, and dependence on, bureaucratic status symbols and rules. The trappings of office become a desirable thing in their own right and can displace the sense of obligation to duty supposedly integral to the bureaucratic form.

Fifth, Weber's model of the ideal bureaucracy ignores the influence of informal groups and leaders within the organization. The capacity for bureaucratic organizations to be subverted by informal relationships and procedures is underestimated (see Chapter 6 below).

Finally, in proposing the bureaucratic model of organization as the most rational and efficient in an ideal sense, Weber assumes that highly centralized organizational forms are superior to decentralized ones without any real reference to empirical evidence.

The 'ideal' bureaucracy proposed by Weber rarely, if at all, exists in reality, but the majority of organizations exhibit bureaucratic characteristics. Vestiges of the bureaucratic organizational form remain with us today, though they are usually far from Weber's ideal. Weber was at least right in proposing that bureaucratic organizations – or at least some of their characteristics – were enduring in modern societies. The same is true of the principles of work organization advanced by F.W. Taylor.

F.W. Taylor

Frederick Winslow Taylor (1856–1917), who trained as an engineer at night school while a working craftsman (Rose, 1988) is famous for the development of 'scientific management', also commonly termed 'Taylorism'. In Taylor's view the objective of management was to maximize the rewards of both employers and workers. This view was harnessed to another, namely that the level of attainable rewards was necessarily linked to the development of workers to the highest level of employment for which their abilities suited them (Pugh and Hickson, 1989, p. 91). The potential to attain such a state was hampered, according to Taylor, by the ignorance of management of the production process; workers' attempts to protect against the possibility of unemployment that might be engendered by higher productivity (and that led them to restrict output by working more slowly – 'soldiering' as Taylor called it); and the lack of precision in working methods, which relied on too great a degree of arbitrariness, and too little control by managers of how workers performed their tasks.

In Taylor's view scientific management would overcome these difficulties because it was based on a number of important premises that would eliminate bad practices. The first of these was that work, including managerial work, should be studied systematically in order to identify the most efficient forms of task performance and task control. At the Midvale Steel Company in Philadelphia he developed standardized methods for performing work tasks and introduced piece-rate payments, both of which increased productivity.

Second, scientific management was based on the view that, having established appropriate production and productivity standards for each task, workers would have to be scientifically selected to ensure that the 'right' person (in terms of strength, skill and abilities) was matched to the right job. There is more than an element of social Darwinism here, as, clearly, some workers would be deemed suitable for certain types of higher grade, better rewarded jobs, whereas others would not.

Third, scientific management would be most successful only if a change of attitude on the part of both management and workforce was effected. Higher productivity was to be viewed as a common interest, as it ensured not only the expansion of wealth but guaranteed rewards to the workforce. Taylor believed in a 'fair day's pay for a fair day's work' and, further, that there should be few limits to the rewards of a highly productive worker. As Rose (1988, pp. 31–2) puts it:

> A 'fair day's work', Taylor insisted, must be laid down by production engineers after work study. He seems genuinely to have believed this would make it a matter not of opinion but science. A 'fair day's pay' is more elusive, Taylor conceded, but it should be set substantially higher than the going rate for similar kinds of work in the locality. The level of reward should be tied closely to output through the mechanism of the differential piece-rate system. Under this system, a worker who failed to produce a 'fair day's work' should suffer a disproportionate loss of earnings, but if he exceeded the target, he would receive a bonus so adjusted as to reach a ceiling between 30 per cent and 100 per cent above standard earnings.

Relatedly here, in addition to agreeing common goals in terms of productivity, Taylor argued that both management and workforce must accept a division between mental and manual work, the former being the rightful province of management in determining how work should be organized and performed. Workers would be relieved of the responsibility of thinking, allowing their energies to be channelled into the production process.

Two last points should be noted concerning related concepts Taylor introduced in his disquisition upon management. The first is his notion of 'functional management', the application of scientific management to management itself. Rather than managers and supervisors performing a variety of functions, acting as rounded individuals or, if preferred, Jacks and Jills of all trades, Taylor believed that the functions performed by these personnel should be separated and performed by specialists. In terms of the conduct of management Taylor also introduced the idea of the 'exception principle', whereby management reports would be short and concise except in identifying, in detail, exceptions to previous standards and averages of production – both good and bad. This would allow managers to pinpoint exactly how current production was progressing, enabling the identification of action points and, in the case of negative developments, corrective action to be taken.

Many organizational behaviour texts give the impression that scientific management is dead and gone, a thing of the past. It is not. Like Weber's theory of bureaucracy, substantial traces of scientific management thinking can still be found in work organization, so pervasive has been the influence of Taylor's work. Rarely perhaps have his principles and prescriptions in reality ever been thoroughly applied. Rather, like Weber's model of bureaucracy, adoption of Taylorist techniques has been haphazard and patchy.

Harry Braverman

Over the past 20 years interest in Taylor's work has been revived in academic circles, largely as a result of the publication in 1974 of Harry Braverman's *Labor and Monopoly Capital*. Braverman, an American crafts-man turned academic, sought to illustrate the validity of Karl Marx's views on the capitalist exploitation of labour, by claiming to show how, in the twentieth century, the widespread adoption of Taylorism has led to the degradation of work. According to Braverman, the 'labour process' – human activity directed towards work, the objects on which work is performed, and the instruments of work – has been cheapened, largely as a result of the separation of mental and manual labour, or the separation of conception and execution of work. Work has been deskilled (a term Braverman never uses but which has nevertheless been applied to the debate that has followed on his work) with the ultimate aim of depriving employees of their one bargaining counter in the employer–worker relationship – their skill. The process of deskilling has often been harnessed, when economic to do so, to the application of technology to labour processes, so that skill is further eradicated and the financial cost of labour to the employer reduced, with workers being relegated to the status of machine-minders.

Labor and Monopoly Capital is perhaps one of the most significant social scientific works to be published in the post-war period. It has generated discussion and research of almost unprecedented proportions, leading one commentator to describe such activity as 'Bravermania' (Salaman, 1986, p. 24). On balance, Braverman's view of the impact of scientific management has been found substantially wanting. Three criticisms are of particular importance:

- *Braverman's view of skill is a very narrow one, based on the romantic idea of the skilled artisan.* Various historical studies have shown that artisan skills were generally confined to a minority of workers in pre-industrial society. Further, most pre-industrial employment was in agricultural labouring and domestic service. Certainly, Taylor was clear as to the different levels of skilled work that existed in any given context and operates a much broader definition of skilled work than Braverman.
- *The application of scientific management techniques in industry and other organizations has never been universal or unproblematic.* Managers in organizations pursue different strategies, calling for different levels of control. Many varied forms of autonomy are allowed to organizational members. Different levels of capital investment in technology are evident. A variety of organizational forms are adopted when structuring administration, and many of these do not conform to the prescriptions of scientific management. Similarly, where elements of the scientific management approach have been employed, or where organizational leaders have attempted to implement such techniques, these have often been resisted by individuals and organized labour (notably trade unions) and the worst excesses of Taylorism thus avoided or ameliorated.
- *Braverman fails to acknowledge counter-tendencies to deskilling.* In particular, it has been alleged that Braverman fails to recognize that in many forms

of work reskilling and enskilling can occur. Attewell (1987, p. 325) gives good examples of this in his study of the American insurance industry. During his research, management reorganized tasks in the company under study and transferred many of the simpler tasks of insurance examiners, such as coding bills and identifying methods of payment, to lower paid data-processing and entry clerks. The result was that the examiners were left with a higher skill mix of tasks, but the removal of their less complex tasks enlivened and enskilled the otherwise monotonous and repetitious work of the data-processing and entry clerks.

Human relations theories

The criticisms of Braverman's views of the application of scientific management to work organization in contemporary society were in many respects prefigured by the work of the human relations movement. Again, it is not always wise to regard the human relations movement as representing a universally coherent intellectual position, but most of those normally associated with human relations did share a number of assumptions about the nature of work and people's attitudes towards it.

Principal among these was the view that Taylorism and other 'classical' management writings took a misplaced view of human nature, in which people were seen as being motivated primarily by money – 'greedy robots' as Rose (1988) aptly puts it. Exponents of the human relations approach did not regard economic factors as being necessarily the prime motivator in the workplace. Non-economic rewards could, it was felt, be more important. In particular, the social conditions of employment, the human need for sociability and enjoyment of personal relationships, and the need for security could all be equally as significant as, or more significant than, wages for positive and motivated experiences of work. Job satisfaction was regarded as being as important to productivity as financial rewards by human relations specialists – a happy worker was a productive worker!

The most frequently cited study of the human relations period is that of the Hawthorne experiments. Conducted by a team from Harvard University at the Western Electric Company's Hawthorne plant in Chicago, these experiments were designed to assess, *inter alia*, the effects of variations in working conditions and technology on productivity and work experience. A key element in these experiments was the study of six female workers in the 'Relay Assembly Room', who were isolated from the rest of the workforce for the purposes of the research. Over a 2-year period some thirteen changes in conditions, hours, and incentive schemes were implemented. The results of this study, together with others in the company, were revealing.

- Productivity increases were noted during periods when conditions remained unaltered, and output often increased when conditions were worsened.
- The very fact of participating in the experiments led many of the workers in the study to work as a team.

- It appeared that work group organization and the norms of the work group were most influential in determining behaviour – not managerial control or directives, or financial incentives.

Of the foregoing, the second point is undoubtedly the most important. The 'experimenter effect' – taking part in the experiment and desiring to please the researchers – was crucial to the results of the Hawthorne studies. It is common to present the Hawthorne experiments as a model study of the greatest significance within the human relations 'movement', despite the fact that many other research projects during the era contributed considerably to the growing intellectual base of the field. Indeed the Hawthorne experiments themselves are not uncontroversial. At a general level, however, the fact of the Hawthorne experiments' elevation to model status sounds the alert as to criticisms of that research that have wider implications for human relations theories.

First of course is the inevitable danger in generalizing the observations on small groups to human behaviour *in toto*. There is some evidence that the human relations credo was excessively influenced by Hawthorne and related experiments to the extent that the concepts of 'sociability' and the need for group 'belongingness' have been grossly exaggerated (Rose, 1988). Indeed, for a period from the 1940s until the 1970s, human relations theory was distinctly unfashionable, a key criticism being that its exponents positioned themselves at the opposite theoretical extreme to Taylor and other classical writers, over-emphasizing human and organizational factors in work over financial reward.

A second criticism of the human relations approach is that it ignores both the effects of organizational design and structure *and* external political, economic and social factors on the experience of work, viewing organizations as closed systems (see the section on 'Systems theory' below, p. 25). Individuals bring to their employment in organizations many different attitudes, interests and experiences. Furthermore, not all individuals confront the organization in an equal or similar manner, because wider social inequalities are an important determinant of labour market position (see Chapter 5).

A final negative view of the human relations school centres on the tendency to overestimate the extent to which individuals seek to exercise control over their own work. Some people are happy 'ploughing their own furrow' and following the lead of others. A corollary of this view is that the influence of the work group on individual behaviour can be overestimated and ignore wider social–structural factors, such as the external influences on behaviour mentioned above.

Neo-human relations

Despite (or perhaps because of) criticisms of human relations that developed from the 1940s onwards, the kinds of approach typified by the movement declined in popularity and influence. However, just as manifestations of Taylorism are still to be found in industry, and just as surely as the bureaucratic organization of sorts persists as an archetype, then so have the forms into which the human relations world-view has mutated sustained both academic and industrial interest. From the 1940s to the 1970s the so-called neo-human relations school of writers exercised enormous influence on management education through their writings on motivation (detailed in Chapter 10). Two key points should be noted. The first is that, like the human relations school from which they derived their inspiration, the neo-human relations writers were hostile to the claims of Taylorism. They were also deeply concerned with the issue of how workers could best be motivated. In the best traditions of the human relations movement their writings focused on theorizing about the nature of human motivations and experiences of work in an effort to prescribe ways in which performance could be improved with due regard to these factors.

The second point to note is that, unlike many in the human relations movement, neo-human relations writers were as much (if not more) concerned with the applicability of their work to the employment situation in organizations than with the academic depth of their reasoning. This is not to challenge the integrity of these writers, but merely to indicate that they seemed more interested in the 'doing value' of their work than its academic foundations. The point is made less sympathetically by Watson (1980; p. 38):

> A psychologistic concern with some notion of 'human nature' as the basis for understanding human aspects of work is clearly seen in what is proving to be one of the most influential contributions of social scientists to managerial thinking to date. This is the work of those writers frequently seen as comprising a neo-Human Relations school and whom I like to label *behavioural science entrepreneurs*. These writers include...McGregor, Likert, Argyris, Gellerman, Blake, Herzberg and Reddin. I refer to them as entrepreneurs because their work is designed to sell, whether in the form of books, management seminars, training films or consultancies. Like the task-splitting scientific management with whom they so passionately take issue, their work is reductionist, partial, evangelistic and sociologically highly inadequate on the explanatory level...It is ultimately simplistic but by a judicious mixing of simplistic assumptions and pseudo-scientific jargon it has made itself highly marketable.

Watson's severity is a salutary reminder of the greater or lesser extent to which all social scientific knowledge is underpinned by the motives of its practitioners. Nothing is fixed and every claim and theory must be scrutinized with care. However, there is a harshness in Watson's remarks that detracts from an appreciation of the extent to which neo-human relations writers were seeking, whatever their motives, to propose intellectual strategies for the management of people at work.

Systems theory

Just as human relations theory had its origins in a reaction against Taylorism, so did systems theory come to supplant human relations as the dominant approach to the study of organizations, predicated on the view that it offered an avoidance of the weaknesses of that perspective. Systems theory derives its main impetus from the functionalist school of social theory. Functionalism is a form of social theory that views society as analogous to a biological organism, as a self-regulating entity tending towards a state of coordination, balance and order. Each part of the system functions towards these objectives so that, in societal terms, social institutions, e.g. the family, education, the political system, operate naturally towards the creation of stability.

The functionalist view of society can be traced at least as far back as the work of the French sociologist Durkheim, one of the acknowledged 'founding fathers' of sociology. From the 1940s onwards, however, the functionalist perspective was most closely associated with the work of the American sociologists Talcott Parsons and Robert K. Merton.

In the context of organizational behaviour, systems theory evolved, rather than emerged overnight, as an alternative to previous perspectives. Its most important form – open system theory – rested on a rejection of the 'closed system' approaches of scientific management and human relations, the term 'closed system' being applied retrospectively (and with growing acceptance, see Clegg and Dunkerley, 1980, pp. 191–6) and signalling a specific rejection of the conceptualization of organizations as self-sufficient entities. The nub of the critique advanced by open systems theorists in rejecting earlier approaches to the study of work and organization was, then, that there was a tendency in these perspectives to view the organization as being isolated from the rest of society. Earlier perspectives, so the argument went, were insular, inward-looking, and failed to take into account the effects on the organization of its constant interaction with the outside world.

The characteristics of an open system include a constant functioning of the system's parts or components (and thus the whole) towards environmental adaptation in order to attain organizational goals and maintain balance and stability within the organization. A corollary of this is that organizations operate in conditions of uncertainty and develop mechanisms (sub-systems) to cope with these conditions. Also of importance in open system theory are the concepts of inputs and outputs. By virtue of being an open system, of interacting with the external environment, an organization is a *processor*: it takes inputs, e.g. raw materials, technology, human resources, from the physical and social environment and transforms these into outputs, which are then returned to the external environment as goods and services. As in most systems, feedback is then received from the external environment and channelled into the organizational system, to provide one of the principal mainsprings to adaptation of the organization. That is, responses to the organization's outputs are a primary source of motivation to change and adaptation.

Socio-technical systems

Socio-technical systems theory is a derivative of the open system approach and has its origins in the work of the Tavistock Institute of Human Relations, London, and in particular, the investigations of Eric Trist and his colleague K.W. Bamforth. Trist and Bamforth analysed the effects of mechanization on the British coalmining industry. The social integration of work groups was disrupted with the introduction of new, mechanized methods of working, which fundamentally altered the process of coal-getting. The stress engendered as a result led to a decline in harmony among workers and an increase in absenteeism. One of the principal conclusions of Trist and Bamforth's study was that effective work organization entailed the integration of social and technical sub-systems within the organization. The social and technical systems in organizations are independent but interrelated, each constraining the other.

This concept of the socio-technical system has perhaps been the most visibly important development of systems theory. The two sub-systems – social and technical – are seen as the most vital. Socio-technical systems theory has also had a fairly wide-ranging impact on industry, influencing many managers. It is not hard to see why. As a theory, the socio-technical systems approach is both humane and practical. Writers such as Trist and Bamforth suggested on the basis of empirical research that improved performance can result from work that is organized in such a way as to actively allow for the integration of organizational sub-systems. In short, socio-technical systems theory seems to be that most attractive thing – a theory with enough evidence to suggest it works!

The most important method for achieving integration deriving from the work of Trist and Bamforth is the idea of the autonomous work group. These authors argue that harmony in the face of technological imperatives can best be achieved by allowing workers a measure of control over the organization of their own work. Jobs in autonomous work groups are structured in such a way as to design work for the group rather than the individual. The group is then allowed varying amounts of discretion in scheduling work and, in some circumstances, determining who should be hired to join the group and what form the apportionment of pay increases should take (Moorhead and Griffin, 1989).

Systems theory, and in particular socio-technical systems theory, thus emphasizes the reconciliation of individual and production needs. The central issue to arise from the work of socio-technical systems theorists is that of the availability of *organization choice*. To a large extent the human relations approach took the organizational form for granted. The quasi-bureaucratic Taylorist style organization typical of much mass-production manufacturing industry and pen-pushing service organizations was not necessarily either the most efficient (in technical and production terms) or desirable (in social terms) but human relations theorists sought primarily to deal with the human consequences of work organization. In the socio-technical systems scenario, management has a responsibility to seek integration of social and technical systems of work organization.

The attractiveness of this approach lies in increased productivity and performance and so may be justified in terms of economic rationality. Systems theory and the socio-technical systems approach still accept implicitly that all organizational members tacitly share organizational goals, and the essential problem is to ensure that through positive management practices this consensus is sustained. Conflict is therefore viewed as pathological. However, as Taylor found, there may well be a conflict of interest between management and workforce, and the assumption of shared interests on the part of labour and capital can be misplaced. Indeed it is a tenet of the contrary Marxist position that this must be true, since conflict is inherent to capital–labour relations, which are predicated on exploitation (Braverman, 1974).

A final point is worth noting here. In many ways systems theory can be seen to be the first 'true' organization theory in the sense that it explicitly addresses issues of organizational form and behaviour. Previous theories and perspectives undoubtedly did this but the issue of organizations (except in Weber's study of bureaucracy) was integral to wider discourse upon employment and management practices. Systems theory very much belongs to organizational analysts and is concerned centrally with the relation of the organization to the environment.

Like all theories, the systems approach also has its limitations. The two most important of these are, first, the emphasis placed on *process* over *people* and, second, the inherent tendency of systems theory to embrace a *reification* of organizations, i.e. treat organizations as if they had an existence of their own independent of the human actors who work in them. Treating the organization as a system subject to certain regulating processes brings the danger that human activity is relegated to just another variable in the organizational equation. More importantly, imputing the facility of self-regulation to organizations does not deal with the problem that conflict is obscured or viewed as anomalous and dysfunctional. In short, a systems approach has to guard against too easily assuming a uniformity of interests in the organization. Different groups within the organization may well view the organizational system in different ways, and their behaviour may regularly be competitive and conflictual, with either beneficial or negative effect. In emphasizing uniformity of purpose the systems approach can draw attention away from the role of these influences in actually encouraging stability or creating instability.

Contingency theories

In most discussions of organizational behaviour contingency theories are treated as separate from and successive to the systems approach, though, in many respects, they are a developed manifestation of the latter. The essence of contingency theories of organization is the observation that it is impossible to legislate universal forms of organizational design and 'appropriate' management styles. These must be flexible if organizations are to be successful in achieving their goals. This flexibility will to a large extent be determined by the kind of environment in which an organization functions. Unlike systems theory, which despite its many differences from previous theories retained strong orientations to prescribing 'one best way' for understanding and managing organizations, contingency theory accepts the inevitability of an organization system being best constructed in response to the constraints placed upon it by the type of business it is, relative to the external environment in which it operates.

A key influence on the development of contingency theory is the work of Burns and Stalker (1961). Having implicitly accepted a socio-technical

Table 2.1 Characteristics of mechanistic and organic organizational structures

Characteristic	Mechanistic	Organic
Organizational structure	Hierarchical, often rigidly so	Fewer layers of authority; groups in organization may be small, comprising interrelated networks
Communication styles	Mainly vertical, flowing from top to bottom and vice versa through clearly defined channels and offices	Mainly lateral, consensual rather than directive, within parameters of goals set by organizational leaders
Work orders, directions and instructions	From formally empowered supervisor or manager	From within task groups, consensually, within boundaries laid down by organization
Possession and use of information and knowledge	Knowledge concentrated at apex of organization and disseminated mainly on a 'need to know' basis	Knowledge and information widely distributed throughout organization; fewer restrictions on dissemination
Employee involvement with organization	Employees required to have loyalty, dedication, but above all obedience to instructions of empowered officials	Employees much more widely involved in decision-taking and required to have commitment, responsibility and ownership

systems view of industrial organizations as comprising both social and material elements, they went further and insisted that in order to understand the nature of an organization at a given point in time, it was necessary to examine the degree to which that organization faced predictability/unpredictability and stability/instability in its environment. An important element of this assessment was thus a historical understanding of the organization and its markets. Organizational structures do not simply appear; most evolve over time in response to their environment and through the actions they take to mould that environment.

Burns and Stalker found in their study of firms in the textile, engineering and electronics industries that organizations operating in an environment characterized by relatively stable and predictable markets and technology tended to have what they termed *mechanistic* forms. In more uncertain environments, with relatively unstable and unpredictable markets and complex technology, where innovation was important to business success, firms appeared to employ a more *organic* organizational form. Table 2.1 compares the main features of each type of structure. The mechanistic organization generally resembles a bureaucratic organization, where there is clear demarcation of position, authority and task specialization and responsibility. The organic type of organization is altogether less rigid in form.

The central thesis of Burns and Stalker's work is that different organizational forms are not only a reality but entirely reasonable and rational. Two American writers, Lawrence and Lorsch (1967), extended this view to show that *within* single organizations different sub-units can and do adopt varied organizational forms and structures, and this be crucial for overall organizational success. The problem for management in such circumstances becomes one of establishing mechanisms for ensuring a balance between differentiation and integration. Further important observations on the contingency of organizational success were made by Woodward (1958; 1965), who shifted the focus from the markets in which business organizations operated to the technologies they utilized. Woodward found that technological complexity and the type of production system operated by firms were significant in influencing organizational structure and decision-making processes, thus reinforcing the findings of Burns and Stalker.

Summary

The theoretical perspectives discussed in this chapter are summaries of often complex debates about the nature of organizations. The intention has been to give merely a flavour of the key issues: a brief survey of some basics. Organizational theory does not stop with contingency theory. However, since the mid-1970s, debates within the organizational field have tended to become increasingly fragmented, with the 'grand' theories described here acting as a reference point and source of inspiration for more sophisticated analyses of organizations (see Brown, 1992, Thompson and McHugh, 1990, and Reed, 1992, for good reviews of recent developments in organizational theory). The main points of this chapter can be summarized as follows:

- Organizational theory is a developing area of enquiry that evidences a growth away from 'one right way' prescriptive approaches to understanding organizations, to more contingent and pluralist perspectives.
- The process of development of organizational theory has been closely related to research in industrial sociology more generally, although in the period since the 1950s the more distinctive perspectives emerging take their major reference point from the study of organizations *per se*.
- Despite the growth of a distinctive field of organizational behaviour, validated against concepts and methods evolved within the field, the dominant theoretical perspectives evidence a primary concern with the relation of organizations to the wider environment, and the extent to which organizations interact with and respond to the environment in which they find themselves.

Discussion questions

1 Relative to personal experience and knowledge, assess which of the theoretical perspectives presented in this chapter best explains the nature of work in hospitality organizations.
2 Consider advantages and disadvantages that might be associated with the adoption, by hotels, of bureaucratic forms of organization.

3 Given the oft-stated view that the hospitality industry is a 'people industry', might this suggest that the human relations perspective has most to contribute to an understanding of hotel and catering organizations?

4 Conceptualize a hospitality organization of your choice as a system and identify the component sub-systems of that organization. Does a systems view of hospitality organizations offer a practical way of describing such organizations?

3 Organizational structure and design

Central to any discussion of theory in organizational behaviour is consideration of the issues of organizational structure and design. Both of these are integral to organizational theory and practice. Many early organizational theories were concerned with the 'best way' to organize and manage work, where 'the best' usually constituted the most profitable and productive, given some due concern for the motivation of workers. Organizational structure is generally understood to mean the formal structure of the organization as determined, or designed, by its senior personnel or owners. As Mullins (1992, p. 52) puts it, the purpose of organizational structure is to define the division of work, tasks and responsibilities, channels of communication and roles within the organization.

Of course the structure of organizations can evolve and develop in a non-directed way such that the form of any organization's structure at a given moment in time may only partially reflect, if at all, the actions of organizational decision-makers. This is a point to bear in mind, because the idea that structure can simply be designed by senior personnel and left to function as they intended does not account for the realities of day-to-day life in many organizations. Some conscious design elements are usually present in organizations' structures, however, though in certain types of operation – notably here hotel and catering organizations, as will be shown later – the conscious elements of structure and design can be fluid and ambiguous.

There have been many efforts to classify different types of organizational structure at both the abstract, theoretical, level and by reference to real-world examples. Most commentators are seemingly agreed upon the point that few organizations represent a pure example of one type of structure, though all organizational structures to a greater or lesser extent are influenced by the traditions and concerns that have their origins in the early stages of industrialism and the growth of large-scale organizations. Thompson and McHugh (1990) note that the correct organizational structure has, historically, been seen to be the key to the best performance. Accordingly, emphasis has been placed on design techniques, and these may be broadly grouped under four headings:

- The degree of the division of labour and job specialization.
- The organizational superstructure: whether or not the organization is 'tall' or 'flat' in terms of the number of levels of management, the span

of control enjoyed by managers over each other and the workforce, and the extent to which decision-making structures are centralized or decentralized.

- The criteria (function, size, product) by which units and activities within the organization are grouped.
- The types of integrative mechanisms employed by the organization to ensure coherence.

It should be noted that all these concerns are related, with varying degrees of explicitness, to the design of more or less bureaucratic organizations. The ubiquity of the bureaucratic organization is inescapable, though in recent years increasing attention has been paid to ways in which organizational design can produce less bureaucratic forms. It is testimony to his original analysis that much organizational theory and work on organizational structure and design has been directed in various ways to improving upon Max Weber's idealized bureaucratic type.

The degree of division of labour and job specialization

As might be deduced from academic commentaries, personal observation and the pronouncements of those like F.W. Taylor, the history of work organization is to a very large extent the history of ever-increasing specialization – at least in manufacturing organizations. The breaking down of jobs into specialized functions and the distribution of these functions among different workers has traditionally offered employers a number of advantages, such as (*a*) greater control over the ways in which work is performed (the labour process), (*b*) improved productivity, and (*c*) labour cost savings resulting from the ease in finding and training employees to perform highly specific and limited tasks.

It should be noted, however, that there are many types of organization and occupations that have neither employed nor experienced extensive division of labour and specialization of the kind that might be encountered, for example, on a motor car assembly line. It is also possible for different levels of division of labour and specialization to co-exist within single organizations or organization types. For example, in a hotel the kitchen department can be bureaucratically organized with fairly rigidly enforced division of labour and specialization, whereas in the housekeeping department room attendants require a range of skills as they perform a 'whole task' in cleaning and preparing a room for occupation.

While division of labour and specialization bring many advantages to organizations, it is widely recognized that productivity can actually be increased if employees are engaged in a greater variety of tasks. This is particularly so in settings such as the autonomous work group, where team work and task variety can increase motivation and hence performance. In recent years debates about the relevance of division of labour and specialization have advanced in the form of discussions over the flexible firm and flexible working; the latter centres on various forms of measures to improve the 'quality of working life' through job enrichment (Hales, 1987), an issue that will be examined further in Chapter 12.

The organizational superstructure

One aspect of the division of labour and specialization that is often forgotten is that which exists among management and supervisory staff. To a very large extent the forms this takes are determined as a result of decisions over the organizational superstructure.

Tallness, flatness and span of control

'Tallness' and 'flatness' in this context refer to the number of levels of authority in the organization and its sub-units – in other words, to the size of the hierarchy. The size of an organizational hierarchy is necessarily determined by the number of people who work for the organization, the complexity of the organization's tasks, the kinds of activities it is engaged in and the desired levels of centralization or decentralization of decision-making processes, i.e. the span of decision-making and other forms of control.

Large span of control

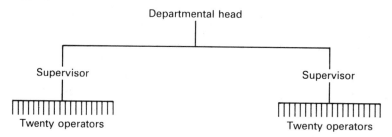

Note: In this example there are two managerial/supervisory levels in the hierarchy and the departmental head has a span of control of two compared to the supervisors' twenty

Small span of control

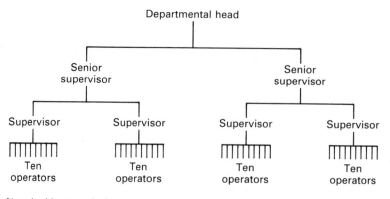

Note: In this example there are three managerial/supervisory levels in the hierarchy and the departmental head has a span of control of two, as do the senior supervisors

Figure 3.1   Organizational spans of control

The span of control is defined as the number of persons who report directly to a single official – manager or supervisor – in the organization (Mullins, 1992, p. 65). Small spans of control mean that a manager or supervisor can maintain a very close watch and control over the employees for whom s/he is responsible. Conversely, a large span of control implies less scope for direct supervision. Figure 3.1 shows two contrasting spans of control.

In theory large spans of control yield savings in management salaries (because there are fewer managers), information flows more quickly between levels in the organization, there are fewer opportunities for confusion over accountability (over who is accountable to whom) and bureaucratic delays are reduced because decision-making is restricted to fewer levels of management (Tyson and Jackson, 1992). According to Robbins (1992), more and more organizations are increasing their span of control, and many are achieving this effectively, without detriment to organizational efficiency, by improving the training of subordinates so that they may function effectively with less supervision. This sometimes takes the form of 'empowerment' (see Chapter 13).

Another point is worth noting here. It is the argument that as managers ascend the organizational hierarchy, they encounter more complex problems, and in order to release time for dealing with these, a smaller span of control is required than would be the case with managers lower in the hierarchy. A uniform span of control throughout the organization may not be an effective way of managing people, since the span of control enjoyed by managers in these contexts is the same as those lower in the organizational hierarchy, leaving less time for strategic planning and creative functions.

Centralization and decentralization

The structure of the organization and the span of control within it will be influenced by the views of senior organizational decision-makers as to the desirable level of centralization of authority. In highly centralized organizations decisions are made at the highest levels of the organization by a small core of senior officials, and then transmitted downwards. The capacity for those lower in the organization to ignore, misunderstand or modify these decisions is thus reduced, unless, as is often the case even in the most centralized organizations, some responsibility for implementing decisions is delegated to relatively junior post-holders in the hierarchy.

There are a number of evident advantages to highly centralized organizational structures. All members of the organization are subject to rapid control processes, and conflict between individual and departmental views in the organization can be reduced. A unified decision-making process centred on a small group of senior decision-makers allows for rapid responses to changing situations. New strategies and policies can be rapidly implemented, with the minimum of disruption and with due regard for the achievement of organizational goals. Centralization also allows for an overview of organizational functions: in taking decisions, a core of senior officials can appraise how they will affect the organization as a whole and devise procedures for their implementation throughout the organization.

The disadvantages of highly centralized organizational structures are that, because information flows downwards, there is little scope for members lower down in the hierarchy to make a contribution to decision-making. Thus the organization's talent, or human capital, may not be fully utilized. Highly centralized organizations can also be extremely inflexible and resistant to change. They may also be reasonably easy to subvert, as authoritarian-like 'dictats' from the higher echelons of the organization are circumvented by resentful organizational members who prefer to operate according to their own traditions and methods, often through informal structures.

Decentralization also generates disadvantages. If decisions in centralized organizations can be taken with only limited reference to those possessing expertise and insight positioned elsewhere in the organization, then a decentralized structure can encourage the divorce of the senior officers from the operating units of the organization. At the same time, however, decentralization may encourage greater responsiveness and serve to motivate managers of the organization's operating units by giving them greater freedom in decision-making.

Criteria by which organizational units and activities are structured

Central to the determinate form of the organizational superstructure is the construction of the constituent elements of the organization. The organizational hierarchy, span of control and degree of centralization/decentralization will all be affected in turn by the structuring of activities and component units of the organization. Activities and units in organizations can be grouped together – departmentalized or divisionalized – on the basis of one or a combination of features (Moorhead and Griffin, 1989; Tyson and Jackson, 1992). Principal among these are grouping by business function, e.g. personnel department, finance department and so on; by product, e.g. soap powders, washing-up liquids, lavatory cleaners; by geographical region; by process, e.g. wood stripping, sanding, priming and painting; and by customer, e.g. domestic clients, commercial clients, overseas clients. These are all illustrated in Figure 3.2, which shows a hypothetical and exaggerated instance of the combination of all the aforementioned methods of grouping. In reality one company or organization may well operate a combination of groupings, though it is unlikely that they would appear as shown in Figure 3.2! However, this fictitious instance does lead to consideration of how activity groupings within an organization can be integrated. For example, if a manufacturing organization has a head office division of business functions as shown in Table 3.2, how would these be represented in the company's manufacturing unit? Would they be serviced separately, with a small management staff in each of the units, or would each unit have a mini-version of the head office structure? Such considerations have acquired particular salience over the last 30 years in the work of systems and contingency theorists, who have laid the groundwork for a number of potential solutions to the problem of integration.

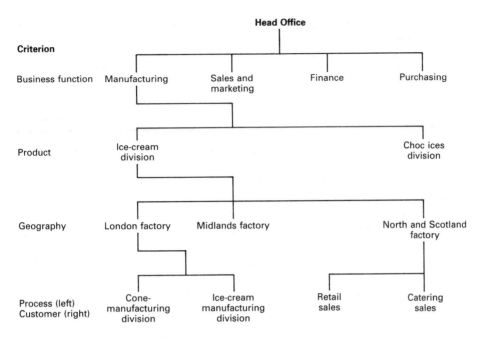

Figure 3.2 Hypothetical model of the structure of organizations by various criteria (Ice Cream plc)

Integrating the organization's activities

Inherent in perspectives on organizations such as systems and contingency theory is a view of organizations as functioning towards integration. Integration, however, cannot be taken for granted and is a proactive process. Lawrence and Lorsch (1967) noted that in highly complex organizations there was a tendency towards increasing differentiation such that individual sub-units within the organization often exhibited their own collective ethos, approaching tasks differently to other units in the organization, according to the demands made of them in meeting the requirements of the external environment. Lawrence and Lorsch found that overall organizational effectiveness was best where the need for differentiation and integration was explicitly recognized and organizational leaders had established mechanisms for reducing internal conflict, such as the appointment of senior managers explicitly responsible for the integration of the organization's functions, and the creation of committees that cut across departmental and divisional boundaries.

Of related interest here is the work of Likert (1961; 1967), who proposed that organizational integration could be achieved by a process whereby managers acted as 'linking pins' between different sub-units. All but the most senior managers are, in this system, members of two groups, the work group or unit that s/he supervises and controls and a group that comprises similarly placed managers in the organization and *their* immediate superior(s). In recent years other developments designed to improve integration and coordination within organizations have included task forces and project teams, quality circles, and matrix approaches.

Task forces and project teams are created on an *ad hoc* basis within the organization to tackle a particular issue or problem. Membership is drawn from across the organization and from different levels in the hierarchy, including, for example, operative workers as well as managers. Task forces and project teams are usually temporary in nature (unless, in the case of the latter, as will be shown below, they form part of a matrix structure) and therefore have limited potential for long-term integration. Quality circles are similarly constituted and normally have responsibility for identifying improvements in the organization's products and services. They can be temporary or permanent, and if their membership is selected astutely, can play a significant role in cutting across sub-unit boundaries and contributing towards integration at the level of product/service design and delivery.

Matrix structures of organizational design have increased in popularity in recent years. A matrix structure combines functional and product departmentalization by superimposing the latter on the former. Thus functional departments exist within the organization primarily for the purpose of grouping together like skills and competencies in a specialist unit, e.g. the marketing department, personnel department, finance department, but cutting across these boundaries are a number of project teams with specific responsibilities for particular products and services. Both functional departments and project teams have a manager/leader and almost all members of the organization are members of both a department and a project team. This creates a dual chain of command, for each employee technically has two bosses – a potential source of conflict that also breaches the idea of *unity of command*, a treasured concept in classical organization theory and practice where there is a unilinear chain of reporting and responsibility for each organizational member, who is answerable to only one supervisor (as implied in the notion of 'span of control').

Matrix systems therefore need to be carefully designed, specifying ultimate individual authority–responsibility relationships, and this is not always easy. One way of resolving the problem is to make departmental heads responsible for matters of professional development and discipline while allowing project managers full responsibility for employees' behaviour and contribution to a particular project (cf. Knight, 1976; also Tyson and Jackson 1992). Provided both managers and supervisors clearly understand the basis of *their* relationship, then a very positive system of management can be developed by means of a matrix system.

A matrix form of organization can offer a high degree of flexibility as it is easy to introduce and disband project teams as required while retaining a permanent departmental structure with which individuals can fully identify. A matrix structure might also allow employees at all levels to participate more widely in organizational decisions and developments by virtue of the fact that project teams provide a more democratic balance of participation than conventionally structured, hierarchical, departments.

The downside of matrix structures includes the possibility of senior managers becoming over-burdened, particularly if their role requires a high degree of liaison and negotiation responsibilities with similarly placed

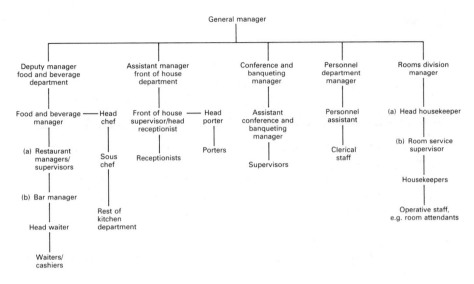

Figure 3.3   Hypothetical organization chart for a large three-star hotel

managers for what are, in effect, overlapping resources, e.g. a manager may be working on one programme as well as having departmental responsibilities. Further, participation in a range of product/service teams can produce a feeling of 'unbelonging', because the range of responsibilities held by an individual restricts scope for the development of specialist interests and skills.

A note on organization charts

Whatever structure of authority exists within an organization, the chances are that this is formally mapped in an organization chart. The concept of the traditional organization chart was encountered in the earlier discussion on span of control. An organization chart is a diagram that can illustrate one or more of the locations of (*a*) individuals, (*b*) departments, and (*c*) jobs, within the structure of the organization (see Figure 3.3). For the knowledgeable organizational decision-taker, an organization chart serves more than an illustrative purpose, for s/he can combine knowledge of the formal structure of the organization with knowledge of the informal structure. In this way the organization chart forms a useful basis for organizational redesign. As a historical document, the organizational chart is similarly useful in tracing the development of a particular structure through time. The 'time' element is important here, for an organizational chart is merely a snapshot of the organization at a particular moment in its history. Furthermore, it shows only what is *supposed* to happen in terms of accountability within the organization. Many people are surprised on encountering their first 'real life' organization chart to find that it often bears little resemblance to what actually goes on in an organization.

Summary

- Traditionally, organization theorists have seen the design of organizations as crucial to functional and economic success. This has led to a largely prescriptive approach to organizational design closely modelled on classical bureaucratic lines and designed to ensure substantial control over organizational members.
- Theories of organizational design and structure emphasize the options for organizational *choice*. Despite the potential for appeals to traditional or previous practice, there is nothing immutable about the choice of organization structure: structures can be changed or different types of structure can be adopted within different sub-systems of a single organization.
- Recent developments in organization design emphasize the weaknesses of classical methods in terms of motivating employees and securing optimal productivity. Looser, more fluid forms of organization design are seen as more appropriate in certain circumstances, and it is possible to combine the traditional with the new, provided organizational leadership is strong and the responsibilities of organizational members are clearly specified.

Discussion questions

1 Consider the nature and extent of specialization and division of labour in a range of hospitality organizations.
2 To what extent is it possible to describe occupations such as chef, room attendant and receptionist as 'specialized'?
3 Why might matrix structures of organization be deemed inappropriate to hospitality organizations?
4 What arguments can be advanced to justify the proposition that hospitality organizations must, by definition, adopt a contingent approach to operational management of staff and facilities?

4 Work, organization and the hospitality industry

The previous chapters examined the development of organizational theory and perspectives on organizational design. The tendency of organizational behaviour texts to treat these areas separately for the purposes of clarity is useful, but in this chapter the two have been integrated in an examination of key applications of the material covered earlier to organizations in the hospitality industry.

What type of organization? Bureaucracy and beyond

Dominated as it is by small, often owner-managed, firms, and character-ized by great diversity in the different types of operation that are present (hotels, restaurants, pubs and so on), the first thing to note is that it is almost impossible to generalize about the organizational structure of units within the hospitality industry. Discussions to date have tended to focus on medium to large *hotels*, other types of operation barely getting a look in. Relatively few *units* in the industry are large enough to warrant anything like the kinds of structure discussed earlier.

Indeed, the fact that small firms dominate in nearly all the hospitality industry's sub-sectors is generally attributed to the fact that an attraction of entering the industry is the *direct control* afforded proprietors and managers over the operation. Macro-organizational structures in the context of large, multi-unit companies have received virtually no attention at all. All these points have to be kept in mind in reviewing the academic research on hospitality organization structure and theory, the question to be kept in mind at all times being 'How far do statements x, y and z apply *generally* to organizations in the industry?'

The hotel bureaucracy

To a very large extent any organization of some size tends to have a bureaucratic or quasi-bureaucratic structure. Much has been made of the extent to which hotels tend to be structured in a classically bureaucratic and *mechanistic* way. Lockwood and Jones (1984, p. 173) write:

On looking at organisation structures within hotels, we find an emphasis on a mechanistic or bureaucratic format, such as the classical kitchen brigade. This structure is based on tradition, with a breakdown of the operations into specialist occupational areas. It is also influenced by the need for a formal framework within which the uncertainty and instability of the guest input can be handled – all staff know their respective roles and positions and therefore the basis of their reactions to customers' requests.

It is important to note that Lockwood and Jones are talking of two levels of bureaucratic organization here: that of the hotel unit and that of departments within the hotel (specifically, the kitchen). In large hotels it is sometimes the case that the bureaucratic principle of departmentalization is present – the food and beverage department, the housekeeping department and so on. However, Figure 4.1 shows the organization chart for a large luxury hotel conceptualized in terms of the lines of accountability of hotel personnel (also a common format of organization charts).

In hospitality organizations in general, departments rarely exist in the discrete sense that they do in other types of organization. Departments tend not to occupy a particular space or location and are often synonymous with occupational groups (an exception to this spatial dispersement being the kitchen department). Staff, and in particular management staff, are often cross-functional in role, e.g. the food and beverage manager may also have responsibility for personnel where no specialist department exists (Croney, 1988; Aslan and Wood, 1993). The nature and flow of work in hotels and other hospitality organizations means that hard and fast divisions within hotels and among the staff in terms of functional responsibility are often absent or, at the very best, fluid.

This point is underpinned by the work of Shamir (1978), who studied hotels from the perspective of contingency theories of organizations. He found that while many large hotels formally exhibited the properties of bureaucratic and mechanistic organizations, in reality they tended to have an organic structure.

Shamir (1978, p. 286) applies the precepts of contingency theories of organization to the study of hotels, suggesting that, in order to succeed, business enterprises 'adopt their structure and mode of operation to the nature of their specific tasks, to the technology available for the execution of those tasks and to various environmental constraints'. Shamir argues that the outward appearance of hotels' organization structures is mechanistic in the sense defined by Burns and Stalker (1961, see Chapter 2 above), with a high level of differentiation and division of labour. This division of labour is largely according to function, i.e. according to the priorities of the organization, and the main environmental influence on hotels – their customers – has little effect on the way in which work is organized and services delivered. Another mechanistic feature of hotel organization is 'hierarchy', which in formal terms at least is highly structured, with many different levels of authority and responsibility.

Behind the formal structure, however, lies an informal structure, which is 'organic' in nature. The main characteristics of this informal structure include:

• Verbal and lateral communication (rather than written and vertically flowing communication).

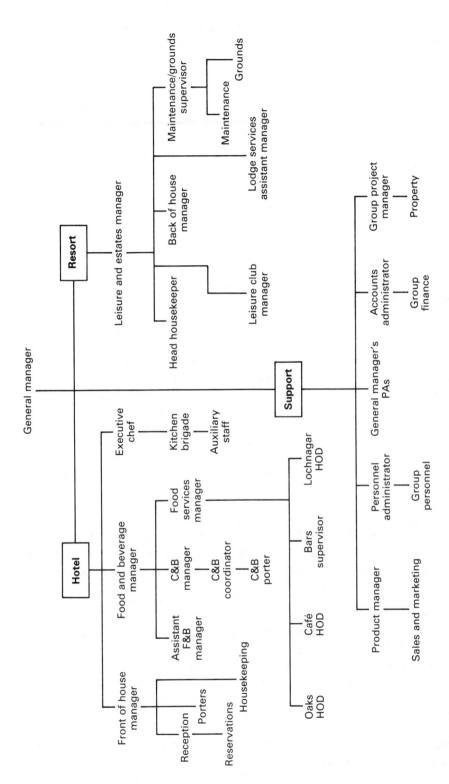

Figure 4.1 Organization chart for the Craigendarroch Hotel and Country Club (reproduced by permission)

- A division of labour that nevertheless allows the easy and rapid transfer of human resources from one department to another.
- The maintenance of reserves of labour in the form of casual employees or the flexible use of live-in employees.

Shamir suggests that the ostensibly mechanistic structure of hotels may be attributed to the power of tradition, in particular the traditional imitation of hierarchical models of domestic service employment. However, another factor of importance is the role played by superficially bureaucratic organizational forms in reassuring customers of the ability of the hotel organization to meet their needs in an effective manner while retaining the flexibility of organization actually necessary to supplying commercial hospitality in conditions of demand uncertainty.

Tallness, flatness and span of control

One of the principal observations that flows from Shamir's revelation of the organic structure behind the formal, mechanistic organizational design of most hotels is that the 'height' of the organization and the span of control, as defined by the typical bureaucratic chart, may be more fluid than would appear. Except in the very largest hotels, the expectation might be that lines of authority are somewhat more blurred than is implied by the formal structure. In terms of span of control there must be an element of truth in this. Some hotel departments by necessity have very large staffs, employing many part-time and casual workers as demand for hotel services dictates. In this sense span of control is likely to vary considerably between departments. This point is lent emphasis by the 'hands on', 'being there' style of management characteristic of hotel and catering organizations, where the emphasis on functional divisions, e.g. food and beverage, front office, rooms, banqueting, is complemented by an equal if not greater emphasis on managerial skills and in particular on managers and supervisors 'coping'.

At the same time it is worth noting that the greater or lesser rigidity of the organizational structure, its 'tallness' or 'flatness', is affected by the extent to which the existence of functional divisions is divorced from single-manager control. As noted above, this is particularly important in organizations where members of the management team may have multiple cross-functional responsibilities. In such cases departmental managers may have to delegate large amounts of work to supervisors, thus diluting their control. The multiple responsibilities of some managers are not unlike an imperfect, informal matrix system of organization, with duties cross-cutting the unit. The limited number of managers (as opposed to supervisory positions) suggests that while on paper hospitality organizations may look like 'tall' classical bureaucracies, many are in point of fact relatively 'flat'. This view is supported by the evidence on managerial work in the hospitality industry, which emphasizes the role of unit managers in direct supervision of their units (see Chapter 8).

As a rider to these observations, it is important to consider large hospitality organizations in the corporate sense, i.e. those with multiple outlets.

As previously noted, individual unit managers in the hospitality industry tend to have a great deal of flexibility in the running of their units. Non-unit management levels tend to be quite small within the industry, even in large companies. Some companies, however, do practise forms of division-alization reminiscent of large manufacturing organizations, though the principles of divisionalization may vary. *Forte plc* organizes its hotels according to brand, and this is true also of other hospitality industry companies.

Centralization, decentralization and integration

While the view of hospitality organizations as essentially 'organic' in nature is one supported by a good deal of research evidence and is easily appreciated in small units (even though it does not always detract from managers and proprietors often having very fixed ideas about how the organization should be run!), organicism it is a little more difficult to appreciate in larger organizational contexts. In a study of hotel companies Dann (1991) clearly differentiates between centralized and decentralized companies. In decentralized companies the manager is often treated by superiors as an entrepreneur, and is expected to use his or her powers and authority accordingly. Such an approach is often supported by strong incentive schemes to encourage high performance. In centralized companies the manager tends to be regarded as a cost controller. S/he may be relatively insulated from operational matters within the hotel, instead being required to focus attention on sales and cost control, seeking to attain the targets set by the company's senior executive managers.

Whether centralized or decentralized, hospitality organizations place great emphasis on the role of managers in integrating the various sub-systems within a unit. The importance of managerial roles in this respect derives from the environmental instability facing most hotels and restaurants. These require managers to make regular short-term adjustments in inputs (labour, materials) to match 'outputs' in the form of consumer needs and wants. The environment in which hotel and catering units operate is, as noted in Chapter 1, relatively unpredictable, and this can lead to a situation of *ad hoc* management whereby managers are required to respond in a systematically unsystematic – arbitary – manner. Certainly there are many different responses that managers can and do make to shifting demand and operational circumstances. The responsibility for such decisions is deeply felt, which is why so many hotel and catering general managers have a poor reputation for delegation. Often their role is oriented primarily to integrative functions, leaving little time for issues of longer-term strategy, and this role is taken extremely seriously even where a substantial number of junior managerial staff may be assigned to the team that runs a unit.

Division of labour and job specialization

The 'figurehead' role of the unit general manager, and the unwillingness to delegate too much to junior management, suggest a very limited division of labour in hospitality organizations. At management level in all but the largest units this is often the case. Not only do many assistant managers have a number of functional responsibilities, but they may, in addition, be required to undertake unit-wide duty management responsibilities in the absence of the general manager. Hospitality management is nothing if not diverse.

There are, however, varied views on the degree of specialization and division of labour that characterizes operative jobs in the industry. Riley (1991a, p. 237) argues that 'By and large hotel work is not single-task monotony. It is a bundle of low-level tasks requiring a degree of self-organization'. He is undoubtedly correct in so far as some jobs tradition-ally regarded as unskilled, e.g. that of a hotel-bedroom cleaner, do require a mixture of fairly complex skills. There is a tendency (for men in particu-lar) to dismiss such jobs as relatively unimportant in skill terms because they require forms of domestic skill, and both domestic skills and hotel-room cleaning are roles associated with women and accorded relatively low status. Such views seriously underestimate the complexity of skills needed in these and other tasks. However, some jobs in the industry *do* call for fewer skills, and, far from constituting a 'bundle' of low level tasks, embrace a limited number of routine manipulative and social skills that lead to monotonous jobs, though this is not to say that such work is any less valuable to the organization.

It is doubtful, though whether the organization of hotel and catering work has ever approached (or ever could approach) the level of special-ization and division of labour advocated by F.W. Taylor and perceived in modern work by Braverman (see Chapter 2 above). Clearly both division of labour and specialization are evident in hotel and catering jobs to varying degrees. This does not mean, however, that hotel and catering work has been deskilled. There is considerable debate among hotel and catering labour analysts as to the nature and extent of deskilling in hospi-tality services (see Wood, 1992, for a detailed summary of the debate). There seems to be some measure of agreement on two points, namely:

- Any deskilling that has taken place in the industry has been patchy and uneven and more characteristic of large multi-unit organizations than the small firms sector.
- *Some* deskilling has taken place in *some* occupational groups, but this has often been accompanied by a degree of enskilling, i.e. the incorporation of new skills within the boundaries of the occupation. A case in point would be front-office staff whose clerical and organizational skills have been to some extent diluted by the introduction of information technol-ogy, which at the same time has, however, required personnel to acquire new skills relevant to the operation of such technology.

Human relations in hospitality organizations

The human relations movement generated the first important study of work organization in the hotel and catering industry. To this day, W.F.

Whyte's *Human Relations in the Restaurant Industry*, first published in 1948, remains an underrated classic whose influence is felt, though often implicitly, in much subsequent organizational research in the hospitality field. According to Rose (1988), Whyte's work *in general* is important, not primarily because it was a product of the human relations school by virtue of Whyte's association with some of the key American researchers in the field, but because it embodied an advance on the conventional human resource perspectives of the time and laid the foundations for the later research on the role of technology in organizations, including socio-technical systems theory and contingency theory.

In point of fact, Rose (1988, p. 162) is rather dismissive of *Human Relations in the Restaurant Industry*, describing it as 'a popularly written work, with much advice to restaurant managers on keeping employees happy, containing little systematic theorizing'. Rose prefers an article published in the *American Journal of Sociology* in the following year as an example of Whyte's contribution to intellectual change in the human relations area (Whyte, 1949). Both works are important and offer certain insights which as Rose (1988, p. 163) again puts it 'before Joanne Woodward...had begun to throw doubt on the generality of classical principles of organization...even suggesting that human relations skills were a less valid method than organization restructuring for improving co-operation and performance'.

Whyte's primary research was undertaken in Chicago in 1944–5 and supplemented by interviews with managers and supervisors in a number of establishments in other cities. The main features of his work can be summarized as follows (Rose, 1988; Saunders and Pullen, 1987; Wood, 1992). First, restaurants as social systems embrace a complex of social relations that to a large extent arise from status differences between workers. These status differences more often than not arise from a division of labour that separates production and service functions. Though restaurants are both production and service organizations, the tendency for real or supposed differences in skill to be reflected in production (generally more skilled) and service (generally less skilled) generates status consciousness and conflict between workers. Whyte found that skill status differences frequently coincided with gender and ethnic differences, with women and non-whites found in lower skill positions. To some extent the social system of the restaurant thus reflected the social status differences to be found in wider society.

Second, because consumers tend to be integral to the hospitality product and because demand for products and services can be unpredictable, the tempo of work can change dramatically in any given time period. Depending on the size of the restaurant, the extent of departmentalization and division of labour, this can add to the complexity of human relations in the organization, requiring managers and supervisors to demonstrate high levels of coordinating skill. However, more often than not, operative workers labour under conditions of high stress. The demands made of service staff by customers, and ultimately of cooks and chefs by the service staff, can cause individual and inter-departmental conflict not only because of the pressure but because lower status staff are calling for action from higher status staff. Whyte found that many managers viewed such conflict as an inevitable feature of 'human nature', over which they had little scope for control. Coordination of restaurant operations suffered as a consequence.

Third, these characteristics of restaurant organizations led Whyte to conclude that pressures and conflict in organizations arose from problems centring on the nature and quality of communication processes and on who was doing the communicating. Whyte recognized that relations between people often improved when interaction was reduced (a variation on the 'absence makes the heart grow fonder' principle). The best way to improve human relations in restaurants was therefore to reconcile the superficially seemingly inevitable factors of necessary and frequent communication between personnel, and limited interaction between staff. This was to be achieved by the use of communication devices such as internal telephones and public address systems, which preserved personal contact between staff but reduced the need for face-to-face contact.

In summary therefore, Whyte raised a number of important issues that have formed the basis for many subsequent investigations. They are:

- The relation between status differences in the organization and wider social status differences on relations between staff (see Wood, 1993, for further discussion of this aspect of hospitality work).
- The effect of pressure of work on stress levels and conflict between individuals and departments.
- The importance of the supervisor and manager in coordinating complex operations within the restaurant – an inefficient and negative approach to such coordination was reflected in a belief on the part of supervisory staff that conflict was unavoidable, with concomitant negative implications for restaurant operation.
- The role of communication, social interaction and technology in managing human relations – although as far as Whyte's strictures on the use of communication devices for reducing face-to-face contact are concrned, these seem impracticable in all but the largest operations with multi-service points.

Whyte's subsequent influence has been most keenly felt among those writers who work in the area dubbed by Dann (1990) as 'hospitality anthropology'. This field includes detailed studies of particular occupations and includes Mars and Nicod's (1984) examination of waiters in hotels, where Nicod posed covertly as a waiter in order to acquire information on the actions and attitudes of his fellow workers. Many of Mars and Nicod's findings echo those of Whyte, particularly in respect of highlighting the conflict that can occur in the workplace as a result of relatively low status waiters initiating action for higher status chefs and the pressures that arise from uneven work flow. In a similar vein is the work of Saunders (1981), who illuminated the role of status in hospitality organizations by studying kitchen porters. Elsewhere, Saunders (1985) turns this study to advantage in true 'human relations' style by offering a number of recommendations to managers for the dignified treatment of kitchen porters, including (*a*) bringing porters into the work of the kitchen, (*b*) encouraging other kitchen staff to take an interest in the work of the porters, and (*c*) ensuring porters are allowed to help decide how their work is performed.

There are many other British and American studies of hotel and catering occupations that are in the anthropological style, though not all reflect any explicit concern with 'human relations'. In point of fact it is a little unfair to class the work of Mars and Nicod and Saunders in this vein, as they are heavily influenced by other traditions in organizational behaviour, notably systems theory.

Systems and socio-technical systems

The concept of socio-technical systems was implicit to the early work of Mars and his colleagues on hotel and catering organizations (Mars and Mitchell, 1976; Mars, Bryant and Mitchell, 1979). In the latter Mars, Bryant (who was associated with the Tavistock Institute – the book draws on several pieces of research by the Institute) and Mitchell identify five problematic aspects of the socio-technical systems of hospitality organizations that require attention if organizational design and structure is to be successful.

First is *the problem of transition*. Hotel and catering organizations are transitional communities particularly in respect of the relation between products, services and customers. The transitional nature of customers places strains on product and service delivery, particularly as demand is erratic and uneven. The need to employ significant numbers of casual, part-time and seasonal staff in many operations in order to cope with this erratic demand can also contribute to the pressures on the workforce, leading to high levels of labour turnover, i.e. transience among the workforce. The problem for the organization is thus adequately to integrate staff and customers in a systematic way. Of particular importance to achieving this goal is the role of permanent full-time core staff, who in their relations with part-time and casual employees and with customers need to feel secure and valued in their work, thus ensuring identification with the organization's aims.

Second is *the problem of the industry's service role*. Mars, Bryant and Mitchell argue that customers' needs are essentially dependency needs and can give rise to expectations of personal service that go beyond what the organization is geared to providing (one example of this would be guests who stay in a one-star hotel and expect five-star service). The difficulty here rests in part on the observation that guests expect service to be rendered to them personally while the goal of the hotel or restaurant is to meet collective customer needs by largely impersonal means (cf. Mars and Nicod, 1984). These dependency needs can rub off on staff, who, in an effort to cope with customer demands, become dominated by them, leading to inefficiency and low productivity. According to Mars, Bryant and Mitchell (1979, pp. 113–14):

> Establishments with a strong dependency orientation among staff fail to delegate effectively; staff are not given and do not take responsibility of which they should be personally capable. Staff are likely to demand excessive 'perks' or if they are not given them to try to take them.

Third here is *the problem of underemployment of time and capacity*. Mars, Bryant and Mitchell remark that the hotel and catering industry seems to face a permanent shortage of general and skilled labour and yet can seem overstaffed, with many employees having much 'idle time' on their hands. This, the authors suggest, reflects an ineffective socio-technical system, one that fails to utilize labour properly. To a large extent this failure derives from a combination of (once again) erratic demand and the maintenance of traditional modes of working, such as split shifts, which call for excessive specialization. As a solution to this problem, Mars, Bryant and Mitchell suggest that multi-skilling might be employed, giving the example of chambermaids who may double as waitresses. The objective of such a strategy is to reduce the total staff in the unit and improve effective utilization of a smaller number of employees. Moreover, ineffective use of staff time and efforts may lose the organization much talent as personal capacities are not fully utilized. The idea of multi-skilling has been a recurring theme in the study of hotel and catering work organization, though it has never really caught on in large organizations. It is generally very near the norm, however, in small owner-managed units (see Chapter 12).

Fourth, the *problem of the quality of labour* may reflect the operation of an inappropriate socio-technical system. A frequent complaint of managers in the industry is that good quality staff are hard to find. Mars, Bryant and Mitchell argue that this may in part reflect a failure of the socio-technical system to provide opportunities for personal development and for employees to earn financial rewards commensurate with such development. Many hotel and catering organizations do not develop internal labour markets whereby skills can be developed maximally through internal promotion and upgrading. Indeed, more recently, authors such as Riley (1991) have argued that it is not in the interests of management to do so, as reliance on the external labour market is cheaper because labour is plentiful. Nevertheless, very large organizations can develop internal labour markets, and some do.

Conventional approaches to human resource management in the industry embody the notion that high turnover and the absence of career opportunities and development within a single organization is damaging in cost and efficiency terms. Furthermore, as Mars, Bryant and Mitchell themselves note, low wages and the absence of opportunities for advancement advertise to the outside world that jobs are of poor quality, and this leads to low quality staff being attracted. At the same time, however, high wages are perceived as a burden by employers, many of whom regard even the relatively low rates set by Wages Councils (see Table 4.1) as detrimental to business. Overcoming these problems can only be achieved by adopting new approaches to pay, rewards and organizational design, but except in times of crisis (such as periods of labour shortage) hospitality industry employers have so far shown little interest in these ideas, and it must therefore be assumed that they are yet to be persuaded of their relevance and effectiveness.

Finally, Mars, Bryant and Mitchell's assessment reaches *the problem of managing change*. Because the character of a hotel and catering organization is to a large extent defined by its customers and other factors extraneous to the organization, and because by definition these elements shift and

Third here is *the problem of underemployment of time and capacity*. Mars, Bryant and Mitchell remark that the hotel and catering industry seems to face a permanent shortage of general and skilled labour and yet can seem overstaffed, with many employees having much 'idle time' on their hands. This, the authors suggest, reflects an ineffective socio-technical system, one that fails to utilize labour properly. To a large extent this failure derives from a combination of (once again) erratic demand and the maintenance of traditional modes of working, such as split shifts, which call for excessive specialization. As a solution to this problem, Mars, Bryant and Mitchell suggest that multi-skilling might be employed, giving the example of chambermaids who may double as waitresses. The objective of such a strategy is to reduce the total staff in the unit and improve effective utilization of a smaller number of employees. Moreover, ineffective use of staff time and efforts may lose the organization much talent as personal capacities are not fully utilized. The idea of multi-skilling has been a recurring theme in the study of hotel and catering work organization, though it has never really caught on in large organizations. It is generally very near the norm, however, in small owner-managed units (see Chapter 12).

Fourth, the *problem of the quality of labour* may reflect the operation of an inappropriate socio-technical system. A frequent complaint of managers in the industry is that good quality staff are hard to find. Mars, Bryant and Mitchell argue that this may in part reflect a failure of the socio-technical system to provide opportunities for personal development and for employees to earn financial rewards commensurate with such development. Many hotel and catering organizations do not develop internal labour markets whereby skills can be developed maximally through internal promotion and upgrading. Indeed, more recently, authors such as Riley (1991) have argued that it is not in the interests of management to do so, as reliance on the external labour market is cheaper because labour is plentiful. Nevertheless, very large organizations can develop internal labour markets, and some do.

Conventional approaches to human resource management in the industry embody the notion that high turnover and the absence of career opportunities and development within a single organization is damaging in cost and efficiency terms. Furthermore, as Mars, Bryant and Mitchell themselves note, low wages and the absence of opportunities for advancement advertise to the outside world that jobs are of poor quality, and this leads to low quality staff being attracted. At the same time, however, high wages are perceived as a burden by employers, many of whom regard even the relatively low rates set by Wages Councils (see Table 4.1) as detrimental to business. Overcoming these problems can only be achieved by adopting new approaches to pay, rewards and organizational design, but except in times of crisis (such as periods of labour shortage) hospitality industry employers have so far shown little interest in these ideas, and it must therefore be assumed that they are yet to be persuaded of their relevance and effectiveness.

Finally, Mars, Bryant and Mitchell's assessment reaches *the problem of managing change*. Because the character of a hotel and catering organization is to a large extent defined by its customers and other factors extraneous to the organization, and because by definition these elements shift and

Whyte's *Human Relations in the Restaurant Industry*, first published in 1948, remains an underrated classic whose influence is felt, though often implicitly, in much subsequent organizational research in the hospitality field. According to Rose (1988), Whyte's work *in general* is important, not primarily because it was a product of the human relations school by virtue of Whyte's association with some of the key American researchers in the field, but because it embodied an advance on the conventional human resource perspectives of the time and laid the foundations for the later research on the role of technology in organizations, including socio-technical systems theory and contingency theory.

In point of fact, Rose (1988, p. 162) is rather dismissive of *Human Relations in the Restaurant Industry*, describing it as 'a popularly written work, with much advice to restaurant managers on keeping employees happy, containing little systematic theorizing'. Rose prefers an article published in the *American Journal of Sociology* in the following year as an example of Whyte's contribution to intellectual change in the human relations area (Whyte, 1949). Both works are important and offer certain insights which as Rose (1988, p. 163) again puts it 'before Joanne Woodward...had begun to throw doubt on the generality of classical principles of organization...even suggesting that human relations skills were a less valid method than organization restructuring for improving co-operation and performance'.

Whyte's primary research was undertaken in Chicago in 1944–5 and supplemented by interviews with managers and supervisors in a number of establishments in other cities. The main features of his work can be summarized as follows (Rose, 1988; Saunders and Pullen, 1987; Wood, 1992). First, restaurants as social systems embrace a complex of social relations that to a large extent arise from status differences between workers. These status differences more often than not arise from a division of labour that separates production and service functions. Though restaurants are both production and service organizations, the tendency for real or supposed differences in skill to be reflected in production (generally more skilled) and service (generally less skilled) generates status consciousness and conflict between workers. Whyte found that skill status differences frequently coincided with gender and ethnic differences, with women and non-whites found in lower skill positions. To some extent the social system of the restaurant thus reflected the social status differences to be found in wider society.

Second, because consumers tend to be integral to the hospitality product and because demand for products and services can be unpredictable, the tempo of work can change dramatically in any given time period. Depending on the size of the restaurant, the extent of departmentalization and division of labour, this can add to the complexity of human relations in the organization, requiring managers and supervisors to demonstrate high levels of coordinating skill. However, more often than not, operative workers labour under conditions of high stress. The demands made of service staff by customers, and ultimately of cooks and chefs by the service staff, can cause individual and inter-departmental conflict not only because of the pressure but because lower status staff are calling for action from higher status staff. Whyte found that many managers viewed such conflict as an inevitable feature of 'human nature', over which they had little scope for control. Coordination of restaurant operations suffered as a consequence.

Third, these characteristics of restaurant organizations led Whyte to conclude that pressures and conflict in organizations arose from problems centring on the nature and quality of communication processes and on who was doing the communicating. Whyte recognized that relations between people often improved when interaction was reduced (a variation on the 'absence makes the heart grow fonder' principle). The best way to improve human relations in restaurants was therefore to reconcile the superficially seemingly inevitable factors of necessary and frequent communication between personnel, and limited interaction between staff. This was to be achieved by the use of communication devices such as internal telephones and public address systems, which preserved personal contact between staff but reduced the need for face-to-face contact.

In summary therefore, Whyte raised a number of important issues that have formed the basis for many subsequent investigations. They are:

- The relation between status differences in the organization and wider social status differences on relations between staff (see Wood, 1993, for further discussion of this aspect of hospitality work).
- The effect of pressure of work on stress levels and conflict between individuals and departments.
- The importance of the supervisor and manager in coordinating complex operations within the restaurant – an inefficient and negative approach to such coordination was reflected in a belief on the part of supervisory staff that conflict was unavoidable, with concomitant negative implications for restaurant operation.
- The role of communication, social interaction and technology in managing human relations – although as far as Whyte's strictures on the use of communication devices for reducing face-to-face contact are concrned, these seem impracticable in all but the largest operations with multi-service points.

Whyte's subsequent influence has been most keenly felt among those writers who work in the area dubbed by Dann (1990) as 'hospitality anthropology'. This field includes detailed studies of particular occupations and includes Mars and Nicod's (1984) examination of waiters in hotels, where Nicod posed covertly as a waiter in order to acquire information on the actions and attitudes of his fellow workers. Many of Mars and Nicod's findings echo those of Whyte, particularly in respect of highlighting the conflict that can occur in the workplace as a result of relatively low status waiters initiating action for higher status chefs and the pressures that arise from uneven work flow. In a similar vein is the work of Saunders (1981), who illuminated the role of status in hospitality organizations by studying kitchen porters. Elsewhere, Saunders (1985) turns this study to advantage in true 'human relations' style by offering a number of recommendations to managers for the dignified treatment of kitchen porters, including (a) bringing porters into the work of the kitchen, (b) encouraging other kitchen staff to take an interest in the work of the porters, and (c) ensuring porters are allowed to help decide how their work is performed.

There are many other British and American studies of l occupations that are in the anthropological style, though explicit concern with 'human relations'. In point of fact i to class the work of Mars and Nicod and Saunders in thi heavily influenced by other traditions in organizational b systems theory.

Systems and socio-technical systems

The concept of socio-technical systems was implicit to Mars and his colleagues on hotel and catering organiz Mitchell, 1976; Mars, Bryant and Mitchell, 1979). In the l (who was associated with the Tavistock Institute – th several pieces of research by the Institute) and Mitc problematic aspects of the socio-technical systems of hos tions that require attention if organizational design and successful.

First is *the problem of transition*. Hotel and catering transitional communities particularly in respect of the products, services and customers. The transitional nat places strains on product and service delivery, particula erratic and uneven. The need to employ significant numb(time and seasonal staff in many operations in order to cof demand can also contribute to the pressures on the wor high levels of labour turnover, i.e. transience among th problem for the organization is thus adequately to ir customers in a systematic way. Of particular importance goal is the role of permanent full-time core staff, who in tl part-time and casual employees and with customers need valued in their work, thus ensuring identification with aims.

Second is *the problem of the industry's service role*. Mitchell argue that customers' needs are essentially depe can give rise to expectations of personal service that go organization is geared to providing (one example of thi: who stay in a one-star hotel and expect five-star service). rests in part on the observation that guests expect servi to them personally while the goal of the hotel or restaurar tive customer needs by largely impersonal means (cf. 1984). These dependency needs can rub off on staff, wl cope with customer demands, become dominated by inefficiency and low productivity. According to Mars, Bi (1979, pp. 113–14):

Establishments with a strong dependency orientation am delegate effectively; staff are not given and do not take respo they should be personally capable. Staff are likely to d 'perks' or if they are not given them to try to take them.

Table 4.1   Wages Councils' rates, 1992, hotel and catering industry

	£ *Hourly rate*	£ *Overtime rate (after 39 hours)*	*Date effective*
Licensed Residential Establishment and Licensed Restaurants Wages Council	2.80	4.20	1 May 1992
Licensed Non-Residential Places of Refreshment Wages Council	2.91	4.365	15 January 1992
Unlicensed Places of Refreshment Wages Council	2.92	4.38	8 June 1992

Note: In late 1992 the Government announced its intention to abolish wages councils and therefore minimum wage protection. Wages councils were formally abolished at the end of August, 1993.

change over time, managers have to be responsive to such potentialities and be experimental in their style of organizational control, e.g. in being prepared to modify their own role in terms of delegation and other management skills.

In many ways the prescriptions advanced by Mars and his various colleagues may seem a little naive, even idealistic. However, they do point to the importance of the interaction between technological and social systems in hospitality organizations, and contribute the only explicit consideration given to the theoretical applications of socio-technical systems theory in the hotel and catering research literature (but see Mullins, 1992, who offers a useful general discussion, which is not, however, illuminated by reference to empirical research).

Contingency theory

If it is not apparent already, then it is necessary to state at this point that organizational behaviour research in the hospitality industry is fairly thin on the ground. The reasons for this have been explored elsewhere (see Wood, 1992, Chapter 1) but can in general be attributed to the fact that studies of industrial behaviour in hotel and catering services has only recently developed as a systematic field of enquiry, corresponding to the professionalization of hospitality studies education in higher education institutions. Little useful has been written on contingency theory as applied to the hospitality industry but one important study, by Bowey (1976), deserves mention.

Bowey offers an 'action' theory of hotel and catering organizations. While action theory is conventionally regarded as distinct from other theories of organizational behaviour, Bowey argues that by fusing the best elements of systems and contingency perspectives together in an 'action frame of reference' then it is possible to reconcile elements of structural and individual behaviour in organizations. To illustrate this, Bowey outlines four principles of action theory. They are the principles of role, relationships, structure and process:

- *Role.* Individuals view their own behaviour and that of others as comprising coherent patterns of meaningful actions and tend to react in systematic ways, according to how they perceive their own and others' roles. Behaviour is not random and people tend to conform to patterns of role behaviour: the concept is thus useful in classifying certain types of individual behaviour and reactions to such behaviour.
- *Relationships.* To a very large extent the relationships between two people are based on the perceptions each has of the other's role, and when this is extended to significant numbers of other persons, patterns of behaviour and responses can be observed, classified and analysed. Of particular importance, however, is the view that the relationship any one person in an organization has with any other is often derived from at least an implicit assessment by the first person of his or her relationships not only with the second but with others in the organization. Thus relationships with superiors may be characterized by relative formality and reserve, but with workmates by informality and relative intimacy, because of the sense of collective group-interest, of *esprit de corps*, that is expected of such relationships. An operative worker who develops a less formal and warmer personal relationship with a superior might invite a negative response from workmates whose goodwill and cooperation it is essential to maintain for the successful performance and experience of work.
- *Structure.* So far in this book structure has been discussed in mainly abstract, impersonal terms. Any organizational structure is, however, also a social structure. Bowey argues that social structures are not static but may change over time, reflecting shifting power relationships – both formal and informal – within the organization and its sub-systems. Any form the social structure takes lasts only for so long as organizational members' perceptions of that structure persist. Further, one part of the organization can undergo changes in the social structure while other parts remain stable. For example, the structure of relationships between key players in an organization or part of an organization can change, with ramifications for that system or sub-system. Inter-departmental conflict may be limited between kitchen and restaurant departments if a head chef and head waiter enjoy a friendly personal relationship. Thus Bowey's structure principle points to the importance of individual relationships within organizational structure but without resorting to abstract psychological generalizations about individual behaviour.
- *Process.* The way in which structures change is rarely radical in nature. Rather, structures change as a result of cumulative processes that derive from the actions of organizational members in response to internal and external pressures. Clearly some organizational members (senior officials) are in a better position to initiate such change than those lower down the organization. Internal pressures to change structure may arise from senior officers' desire to change practices and behaviour through- out the organization (Bowey gives the example of breaking up a conveyor belt production system into cells – see the earlier discussion of autonomous work groups in Chapter 2). External pressures might include those that derive from the competitive behaviour of other organizations, developments in technology or legislation and so on.

Process is thus a useful concept for explaining change from one organizational state to another but it must not be assumed that only senior organizational members are capable of initiating such change. First, it is important to recognize that in addition to the formal structure of the organization, the informal structure of relationships is important and much more within the control of groups with limited formal authority. This point is examined further in Chapters 6 and 7. Second, many organizations make provision for members to suggest improvements to structure and functioning, e.g. through such means as 'quality circles' or, more crudely and at the other extreme, such simple devices as suggestion boxes. Third, formal relationships between parties in organizations, such as those between management and trade unions, can lead to changes in organizational structure.

Though Bowey's concepts are ostensibly couched in the language of action theory, a strong contingency orientation can be discerned. Much of the organization of units in the hotel and catering industry derives from tradition (Saunders, 1981), but, as Shamir (1978) shows, behind formal mechanistic structures that superficially maintain this tradition an organic organizational tradition is also well established. Bowey's contribution to the understanding of organizations lies in the extent to which discussion of organizational structures is linked to the role of groups and individuals. The emphasis is placed on individual action and behaviour in a group, social and structural context, on the meanings that individuals bring to their work, and the meanings, values and attitudes that they formulate while they are at work. It is these values, attitudes and actions and their formulation that are the subject of closer scrutiny in Part Two of this book.

Summary

- A recurring theme in the literature on hospitality organizations is the erratic and unpredictable nature of the environment in which such organizations function. In many ways hospitality organizations can be viewed as the archetypal contingent organizations, constantly interacting with the external environment and having to make adjustments to it. However, most hotel and catering organizations have a clearly definable socio-technical system, and this is important in analytic terms to an understanding of patterns of organizational behaviour.
- Socio-technical systems are complex in hotel and catering organizations. General features can, historically, be traced back in time a long way. The human relations work of Whyte demonstrates the extent to which relations between people in hospitality contexts are influenced heavily by status differences within the organization; it also shows the extent to which communication and technology play an important role in formulating people's experience of work and also individual and collective performance.
- Studies of organizational behaviour in hotels and catering have a long tradition of seeking to reconcile individual and group behaviour aspects

of employment with structural imperatives. Socio-technical systems theory and contingency and action approaches demonstrate the importance of locating individual and group behaviour in a social and structural context without appealing to crude psychologisms.

Discussion questions

1 Why do hotels often exhibit a formal 'bureaucratic' structure when in practice they tend towards the 'organic'?
2 Discuss the proposition that the people-orientation of the hospitality industry always creates a tension between satisfying the needs of clients and those of organizational members.
3 To what extent do hospitality organizations engender a 'dependency orientation' among staff?
4 Consider how Bowey's axioms of action theory apply to hospitality organizations.

Part Two
The Individual and the Organization

5 Individuals and work organization

Part One of this book examined some of the precepts of organizational behaviour and sought to illustrate these by reference to examples drawn from the hospitality industry. Part Two begins with this chapter on individuals and work organizations and proceeds to examine the social dimensions to individuality and to affiliations, i.e. the nature of relationships between individuals as manifest in social behaviour. To this end, the concept of role is examined as a means of linking an understanding of the concept of the individual to that of the 'group' or 'team', of linking the individual in the wider society to the individual in the organization.

Work and instrumentalism

From discussion in the preceding chapters, it is evident that for many people both financial and social factors are important in work, and the lack of opportunity for working, e.g. as when people are unemployed, can have serious consequences. Work lends meaning to life. Paid employment is particularly significant in this respect. One of the first questions we ask (or would like to ask!) when we meet a new person is 'What do you do?' A person's line of work helps us as individuals to locate him/her in a social context.

This is not to say that all people enjoy their work. Over the past 30 years or so there has been a growing school of thought that has identified increasing *instrumentalism* among certain sections of the working population. That is, more people are working not for the intrinsic enjoyment of their labours or, indeed, for the social dimensions of their work, but instead work primarily for money, which is then used to generate a lifestyle that itself confers status on persons and lends meaning to their life. This is not the same as saying that people work for money alone, although it is easy to underrate the extent to which financial rewards are paramount or at least predominant in the motivation to work. The financial/social dimensions to motivation in employment are examined in greater detail in Chapter 10.

To a large extent, then, instrumentalism leads people to give greater meaning to work in an abstract sense: work is not necessarily good in itself but for what it can buy. The social significance of work to individuals is a derived rather than a direct consequence of the work they perform. For the most part, increased instrumentalism in attitudes to work has had its most pronounced effect among those people who work in highly routinized jobs.

In particular, the growth of mass-production-type jobs with a high technology content in the manufacturing sectors during the 1950s and 1960s has, in the view of some commentators, led to increased monotony and alienation at work, for work has become less intrinsically interesting and perhaps less skilled. Many of the criteria that used to differentiate workers from each other – skill labels, length of training and so on – have been displaced, with a concomitant displacement of those factors that confer status and give meaning to life. For some workers at least, what work one does has become less important than what one does with the financial rewards from employment.

An instrumental attitude to work is not exclusive to any particular level of employment or confined to manual and operative jobs alone. However, instrumental attitudes to work usually arise more in employment contexts where work has become routinized or monotonous. In addition, an instrumental attitude to work can arise in cases of genuine financial need – a job is taken because the job-holder needs the money in order to sustain basic needs. However, it is important to recognize that the kind of work a person does is still crucial to determining status (the social esteem that a person enjoys). It is therefore clearly important to have some understanding of the social factors and processes that influence the choice of work itself. It is also important to recognize that the concept of choice in this sense does not necessarily imply a totally free choice. Rather, the social system embraces a number of enabling and constraining influences on human choices – any choices – and the interplay between these have to be clearly defined and appreciated.

Getting work

Full employment is temporarily, if not forever, a thing of the past. Society quite simply no longer owes us a job (if in fact it ever did). Changing economic circumstances have made work harder to find. Talk of 'social security scroungers' and 'the idle poor' are still with us, and such insensitivity itself reflects a failure to come to terms with the values of an earlier era in which work was not only seen as a duty but very much a right. Unemployment was seen as a scourge. To a large extent it still is, though the 1980s have demonstrated that in the UK at least, high levels of unemployment are accepted as a fact of life. Another fact of life is, however, that most people want to work, not only for financial reasons, but because work gives meaning to life.

The work ethic is still strong. However, for many young people who have never had work, it remains to be seen whether the strength of the work ethic will be inter-generationally transmitted. The value that society as a whole places on paid employment suggests that the work ethic will remain strong, perpetuating, for so long as high unemployment persists, an underclass of people who will feel frustrated and alienated from society because of the non-availability of work.

One reason for this is the socialization process. From an early age, young people are socialized into belief in the value of paid employment. The

school is a major influence here, as the major task of the school is education, not only for its own benefits but in its mission to educate for work.
Perhaps ironically, in the last decade and a half, the commitment of government to vocationally relevant education has increased the employment
expectations of the young. The kinds of job people end up doing (or not
doing!) are determined by a variety of interrelated factors, which can be
summarized as follows.

Scholastic achievement

Many lines of work require some kind of formal qualifications – GCSEs,
'A' levels, highers, a degree or diploma, and so on. We live in an increasingly credentialist society where paper certification of levels of achievement
– both general and specific – are an important determinant of the kinds of
work available to people as well as to the prospects for promotion that exist
in any given line of work.

Personal and parental values

Different types of work are almost always viewed in a hierarchical way.
Some people may refuse certain kinds of work because these are seen as
demeaning, 'not good enough', inadequately rewarded or offering inadequate scope for personal development.

The supply of jobs

The number of jobs alone is not the only important factor influencing the
kind of work people do. To a great degree, many people are not mobile,
and so their career opportunities are limited by the nature of the local
economy. Many local economies are highly specialized in nature. At one
extreme are occupational communities built around one, or at most two,
key industries, and where work and social life are inseparable, e.g. fishing,
coalmining and agricultural communities. The decline of an industry in
areas like these can have a devastating effect not only on the quantity of
jobs in that industry but on the community as a whole. Specific examples
would include the decline of steelmaking in Motherwell, Scotland, and
coalmining in South Wales.

Other local economies, though less specialized, are composed of interrelated industries with one or two dominant, where changes in the fortune
of these affect the supply of jobs throughout the local economy. Examples
would include the decline of motor manufacturing in such areas as
Coventry and Birmingham, which has had a widespread effect on jobs, not
only in related industries but in the local economy as a whole. The retail
trade is particularly susceptible to such changes, being sensitive to a decline
in the spending power of the local population.

At the other extreme to the examples given above are those areas that are
highly differentiated in terms of the range of employment opportunities, but

where these opportunities are limited. These include many suburban areas of large towns and cities, where significant communities have grown up and where there is a measure of service employment e.g. in retail trades. For the most part, people live in such communities and require a certain level of services, but residents find work in a nearby town or city.

The availability of training opportunities

The choice of subjects at school is an important facilitator of access to job opportunities. More important, however, is the age of prospective employees relative to training opportunities. For school-leavers, lack of work experience can be an important barrier to obtaining employment in an economy where unemployment is high. However, because of the latter, work experience is often difficult or impossible to gain, thus creating a cycle of disadvantage. In many areas in the past local industries provided apprenticeships as a means of bridging the gap between school education and the world of work. Apprenticeship schemes have declined dramatically in recent years. Government-financed training schemes have plugged the gap to some extent, but most are unattached to specific industries and of course do not guarantee jobs upon completion of a course of training.

Social class

The United Kingdom is a class society. Sociologists have conventionally asserted that class differences continue to be perpetuated and there is little progress to an open society based on individual meritocratic achievement. Recently this position has come under increasing attack from that rare (thought not as rare as might be thought) species the rightist or libertarian sociologist. For example, Saunders (1990) in a lucid account has excoriated traditional sociological views of class and suggested that, though far from being a meritocratic society, Britain is much more open in terms of social mobility than sociologists have often suggested.

The debate is an interesting one and cannot be ignored. Writers like Saunders are undoubtedly correct in pointing to the greater fluidity of the class system. However, for many, social class is still an important determinant of life chances and, most important here, career and job opportunities. Cultural dimensions and determinants of class (values, attitudes, beliefs) as well as technical dimensions (income, wealth, housing standards, education, occupation) are remarkably resistant to change, and if classlessness is equated with eradication of inequality of opportunity, then there is some way to go before the classless society is achieved, and even further to go if classlessness is equated with an end to absolute inequality.

Gender

People's gender is an important determinant of the job opportunities available to them. Indeed gender is an important influence on life chances in general. Social psychologists have long recognized that male and female children are socialized differently. Their parents and others channel them towards socially accepted 'male' and 'female' behaviours, values and attitudes. Young boys are encouraged to be independent, aggressive and oriented away from the home, while young girls are encouraged into a role aligned with domesticity and the rendering of domestic services to men. In terms of employment opportunities women can be encouraged towards occupations that are held to be socially appropriate as 'feminine' or 'womanly': caring professions (nursing, teaching), occupations calling for the public performance of a domestic role (cleaning, food service roles) or jobs entailing the supportive servicing of male needs (secretarial positions).

This so-called 'pink blanket' theory of socialization (Howe, 1977) is something of a generalization but retains much explanatory force. Despite a widespread commonsense belief that we live in an age of greater equality, few women achieve high positions in paid employment. This is not simply because women are directly discriminated against by men (although this is often true) but because women themselves often lower their own sights in order to survive within an organization, or because they are channelled into stereotyped roles within the organization, i.e. 'acceptable' female jobs. Whatever the case, high quality employment experiences for many women are restricted, and discriminatory practices must be regarded as leading to a loss to the organization of talent and creativity.

Ethnicity

If the diminishing inequalities between male and female opportunities remains an enduring myth, then so does the view that discrimination against members of ethnic minorities is a thing of the past. Deeply embedded racist attitudes remain in British society. Though both direct and indirect discrimination in employment against people on the grounds of race and ethnicity is technically illegal, there is little doubt that such discrimination occurs. The Commission for Racial Equality (1991) found that their code of practice on employment, issued in 1984 and offering practical advice in implementing effective equal opportunity policies, had met with little response from hospitality industry employers. In the hotel sector in particular, they noted, the reputation of the industry for giving low priority to personnel matters was reflected in an almost universal disregard of the code's recommendations. Further, the diverse recruitment methods used by the industry for the many different levels of jobs, when combined with a lack of systematic personnel strategy, was seen by the Commission as detrimental to the recruitment of ethnic minority employees.

Discrimination is a complex phenomenon, and while the ethnic origin of a person can be an important determinant of employment opportunities, then gender and class together with ethnicity can also have a bearing on life chances. In other words, no single variable considered so far in this section necessarily operates in isolation to enable or constrain employment opportunities.

Individuals in hotel and catering organizations

The hospitality industry is widely recognized as embracing a very large number of low-grade unskilled jobs. According to Riley (1991), a reasonable estimate of 'skill' distribution in any one hospitality unit would be 64 per cent operative workers (semi-skilled and unskilled), 22 per cent craft (skilled), 8 per cent supervisory, and 6 per cent managerial. There is, however, an important point to be noted here. It is that skill is notoriously difficult to define. Defining a person as 'skilled' is rarely problematic – there would be little hesitation in defining, say, a chef as a skilled worker. It is in the semi-skilled area that genuine difficulties arise. Traditionally, semi-skilled workers would include receptionists and waiting staff. But in what sense are, for example, waiting staff skilled? In being able to demonstrate silver service skills? Or follow mechanical routines for laying up tables? If so, then the label semi-skilled could equally be applied to people who clean rooms or who wash pans in a kitchen. Each requires a level of skill in work and routine task organization, in the application of elementary technical knowledge to tasks. More often than not, however, such jobs are classified as unskilled.

The skill definition problem is one that has yet to be adequately addressed in the hotel and catering (and other) industries. The central issue is that skills are normally *socially constructed*. That is, the processes by which work is defined as skilled, semi-skilled and unskilled rely less on objective, scientific analysis than on social processes, on who is doing the defining, on particular industry and organizational factors and traditions, and who interprets these (see Thompson, 1989, for a more detailed discussion of these issues).

Gender is an important influence here. For example, it is conventional to regard cleaning work as 'unskilled' despite the fact that an argument could be made for regarding such work as requiring a complex balance of task organization, the application of (though low-level) technology and technological processes, and the knowledge of these processes. Sociologists have shown that many jobs performed by women, whether in the home or in paid employment, are defined as low skilled, semi-skilled or unskilled because, historically, what has been defined as skilled reflects a male view of what is valuable. Cleaning work in the home is not usually valued by men, being taken for granted or viewed as a wife's duty, a view that has arguably been transferred to the public performance of cleaning in paid employment.

Gender is not the only important factor in determining how work comes to be defined (or not defined) as skilled. This can depend on the power of organized labour and its ability to persuade or otherwise cajole management into accepting artificial skill distinctions in order to maintain pay and status differentials for its members. Organization and industry tradition can also influence definitions of skill. Job content alone therefore is not the primary means of determining skill levels.

Individuals together

The problem of definition aside, how persons are classified in terms of skill has implications for their experience of work inside the organization, and for their ability to acquire experience and skills that may enhance their position in the labour market and thus life chances. The relative arbitariness of skill definitions is important here in denying many people in different industries the necessary validation of their abilities. The result is that large groups of workers and would-be workers are effectively confined to a pool defined as 'unskilled', and thus unable to command high wages and sophisticated terms and conditions of employment. The principal groups that fall into this category are women, ethnic minorities and young people. Thus while it is proper to talk of individuals and individual needs, for analytic purposes it is also necessary to recognize that, in understanding labour markets, the properties of individuals in groups, as with people who have features in common, are important to appraising the nature of organizational processes.

The hotel and catering industry is extremely reliant on women, the young and members of ethnic minorities to fill operative positions, and it repays study to consider in turn the role of each within the hospitality labour market.

Women

The vast majority of employees in the hospitality industry are women. Estimates vary but a figure of between 65 and 75 per cent is generally accepted. The proportion of women in different sectors of the industry varies, being usually lower in hotels than in other sectors, for example. The proportion of women in the hospitality workforce is not the only important statistical dimension to female employment in the industry, however. The majority of women (approximately 70 per cent) are employed in operative grades, and while the industry has one of the highest proportions of female managers in any industry at 47 per cent, this is much lower than both the proportion of women studying hotel management in colleges (75 per cent) and the proportion of women in the total hospitality workforce (for further statistical dimensions see Hotel and Catering Training Board, 1987; Wood, 1992, 1992b). Further, in the commercial sectors the 1989 Census of Employment suggests that of 720,000 part-time jobs, 75 per cent were performed by women.

Young workers

The three categories of employee – 'women', 'young workers' and 'ethnic minority employees' – are not mutually exclusive. The industry employs large numbers of young female workers for example. Figures for the number of young workers in the hospitality labour force are imprecise however, and until recently Byrne's (1986) estimate of 150,000 young workers in the commercial sector was the only reference point.

However, Lucas (1991) has inferred from a study of Wages Council data that since under-21s were removed from the scope of wages protection in 1986, the number of workers covered by the main commercial hospitality industry wages council, the Licensed Residential Establishment and Licensed Restaurant Wages Council (LRE), was reduced by around 176,000 persons; and Lucas considers this a good indicator of the number of young, under-21s employed in commercial sectors. If she is correct and young workers in other, non-commercial sectors of the industry are included, any estimate of the number of under-21s in hospitality industry employment must be revised upwards. Even then, however, many 'young' workers are older than 21, and at what point a person ceases to be 'young' is impossible to establish! In a study of Scottish hotel and catering employment, Macaulay and Wood (1992) found the majority of workers to be under 30, although there were relatively few under-21s in their sample. Wood (1992c) in his analysis of hotel and catering enquiries to the Scottish Low Pay Unit found that the mean age was 22 years. The number of young workers in the industry, while impossible to establish with any accuracy, is therefore probably very large.

Ethnic minorities

Many ethnic minority workers in hospitality services are employed in the specialist restaurant sectors covering, *inter alia*, Chinese, Indian and Pakistani cuisines. Many, however, are drawn into other sectors. Estimates are again difficult to establish. Byrne (1986) reported that black workers were twice as likely to be employed in hotels and catering compared to white workers. He further estimated that, in addition to an unspecified number of persons drawn from the indigenous ethnic minority groups in Britain, a further 150,000 migrant workers were employed in hotels and catering. Generally speaking, ethnic minority workers are found in lower-grade operative jobs. The study by the Commission for Racial Equality (CRE) (1991) referred to earlier found members of ethnic minorities not only under-represented in management in the hotels sector but also reported colleges as having difficulty in placing ethnic minority students on work experience programmes with employers, difficulties that were attributed to racial discrimination. This corresponds with the findings of Dronfield and Soto (1980), that members of the ethnic minorities they interviewed tended to be in jobs that called for little or no public contact.

'Motivations' to work

A range of explanations have been put forward to explain the presence of large numbers of young, female and ethnic minority workers in the hospitality workforce. Conventionally, a key factor in explaining the presence of women in the workforce has been the part-time nature of much hospitality employment. Part-time employment is a useful device for coping with short-term fluctuations in demand and has traditionally been seen as particularly 'suitable' to women, many of whom have domestic and child-rearing responsibilities that allow them to work only at certain times. Furthermore, as suggested earlier, many of the jobs in the hospitality industry are apparently sex-stereotyped, being regarded as 'women's work', calling for the application of certain domestic skills that have, what is more, been learned as part of the socialization process and therefore cause few training costs to the employer.

Recently some doubts have been cast on the validity (or at least the completeness) of arguments such as these. Three observations are important in this context, namely:

(*a*) In some sectors where demand for products and services is relatively stable, e.g. hotels in certain provincial or seasonal areas, there is a tendency for hospitality organizations to employ a relatively high proportion of full-time workers, who form the core of the workforce;

(*b*) Part-time working has been, in the past, an *organizational choice*: split shifts, one of the main means by which part-time employment has been sustained in the industry, is a traditional mechanism; work could be just as easily organized to facilitate a greater proportion of full-time employment.

(*c*) The crucial feature of part-time and casual employment is that it is cheap, and it is cheapness that determines the sources of labour an employer will seek to utilize.

Propositions (*a*) and (*b*) above are still essentially speculative, though evidence does exist that, dependent on geography and market demand, a stable core of full-time workers can be maintained in some hospitality organizations (see, for example, Guerrier and Lockwood, 1989).

Slightly more evidence exists in support of the third proposition. For example, Crompton and Sanderson (1990, p. 148) claim emphatically that:

> ...lower level work in the hotel trade has not been firmly sex-typed. In this highly competitive industry it is necessary that labour should be cheap, rather than it should be one sex or another. Thus, despite evidence of what may appear to be quite extensive segregation by gender, the realities are more complex. An 'inverse statistical discrimination' operates. Female labour is used because it is both cheap and available at the right time of day and season. If another source of cheap labour becomes available it will be used as well. The economic recession, in combination with central government policies, has made young people such a source. Unemployment rates are particularly high amongst the younger age groups, and the system of benefits has been structured so as to make it more likely that they will accept poorly-paid work. More young people are staying on into the sixth form, and/or going into further education. The declining value of student grants and pressures on parental incomes has further increased the necessity for part-time work of some kind.

Crompton and Sanderson's view is supported by evidence from international comparisons of hospitality industry employment, which show an increased dependence on youth labour (Wood, 1992b) and indirectly by increased interest among hospitality industry commentators in both the labour market problems inherent in the decline of the youth labour pool and the problems of ageism. In respect of the former, there is some limited evidence that certain employers are exploring the possibility of hiring older (often retired) persons in the face of a decline in the number of young workers. The trend is hardly widespread, however, owing to the large supply of youth labour from among the unemployed and student groups. The problem of ageism also to some extent counteracts any inclinations towards employment of older workers. Like many others, the hospitality industry has a 'youthful' image, and employers can be reluctant to hire older persons (see Lucas, 1993). There is thus a good case for arguing that the hospitality workforce has become predominantly youthful as well as female, at least in the commercial sectors of the industry.

Where do members of ethnic minorities fit into this analysis? There is a view that while ethnicity is clearly an important variable in determining employment opportunities, gender and class are more important differentiators. Many members of the ethnic minorities in the UK are constrained by the educational system to (relatively) low attainment and thus find themselves in a 'class position' similar to that of the working class, with all that implies for life chances. In this view, broadly speaking, members of ethnic minorities are discriminated against in the labour marker primarily on class-related educational attainment criteria, and, for women, gender is the determinant constraint on labour market position.

Complacency on questions of race and ethnicity, however, must be avoided. In an industry like hotels and catering, where image is important, it appears that senior managers (who are predominantly male and white) often perceive non-whites as antithetical to a positive image, and this leads to the exclusion of members of ethnic minorities from, in particular, customer contact roles. Clearly such forms of discrimination have implications for individual careers, limiting the opportunities for advancement within the industry.

Workforce composition and the organization

The argument discussed above concerning the importance of the cheapness of labour in employment decisions must not be pressed too far, as evidence on the point is far from conclusive. Nevertheless, even if a significant minority of the hospitality workforce falls into the young/female/part-time categories, then there are significant consequences for the character of hospitality organizations. Two observations are particularly important in this respect: (a) the presence of large numbers of relatively unskilled workers confined to operative positions may engender a lack of commitment to the organization's goals and objectives; and (b) employers' willingness to accept a large proportion of unskilled workers implies a like willingness to forgo attempts to capitalize on the range of talents and skills of organizational members.

Commitment

That many hospitality industry workers have a limited commitment to any single organization or unit is reflected in the relatively high labour turnover that characterizes hotel and catering employment. There are many reasons for this high turnover and they will not be rehearsed here (see Wood, 1992, for a review).

However, there are important differences in emphasis among commentators as to the effects of high turnover. Writers such as Johnson (1981) and Mars, Bryant and Mitchell (1979) see turnover as costly and detrimental to the organization in terms of the provision of consistent quality of service. In contrast, Bowey (1976) and Riley (1992) among others see turnover as a valuable and necessary feature of hotel and catering work, since it allows employers a degree of flexibility in staffing, ensures constant infusions of 'new blood' into a unit, and often reflects positive motivations on the part of workers to improve themselves. This last point can be explained by the fact that in any one unit there is a limit to the skills that a worker can acquire. Since the acquisition of skills is crucially linked to the development of a career, and, more often than not, to pay, this limit serves as a motivating force to workers to move regularly in order to improve their repertoire of skills (Riley, 1991a).

There are problems with both the positions described above. Any necessary link between labour stability and quality of service is difficult to establish, and the cost to employers in the industry of high labour turnover may be exaggerated, given that the supply of labour is plentiful and cheap and many jobs are unskilled – giving rise to a close substitution effect whereby any reasonably competent person can perform the work required. The 'close substitution' effect is also the major objection to the arguments of those like Riley (1992) in that if the majority of the work in the industry is relatively unskilled and access to skilled work is dependent on extra-organizational factors, e.g. paper qualifications, then the potential for skill acquisition is minimal and the motivation to seek out more and better skills accordingly restricted. Riley (1991a) is, however, undoubtedly correct in pointing to the grey area of semi-skilled work, where such access might be gained as a result of job mobility.

Whatever the realities (and they *are* complex and variable), the employment of large numbers of unskilled workers drawn from groups marginal in labour market terms presents employers with a challenge – namely, how to motivate employees and secure their commitment to the organization. There is considerable evidence to suggest that many employers have abandoned this challenge in the past. However, in some quarters at least, there is evident change in the air. There is an increasing emphasis on training. This has been engendered by legislative requirements; government training and education initiatives, as in, for example, National Vocational Qualifications and their Scottish equivalent, which seek to raise work-based competencies and improve standards of training throughout industry (for developments in the hospitality field, see Teare, Adams and Messenger (1992), and Chapter 12 below); or sheer self-interest, e.g. in establishing supremacy in customer handling and sales, as with fast-food chains, or in product and service differentiation, as with 'theatrical' restaurants (on the latter see Gardner and Wood, 1991).

However, while corporate hospitality organizations may be open to innovation and change in organizational management, the bulk of the small firms in the industry are often less easy to convince of the need for training and motivation of the workforce, though this should not be allowed to detract from the need to emphasize the importance of valuing *all* employees. Research on hotel and catering employment is replete with examples of workers feeling 'undervalued', and whatever labour strategy an employer adopts, there are both moral and selfish reasons for creating a positive motivational climate.

Many sociologists tend to sneer at the human relations 'axiom' that a contented worker is a productive worker, or that it is possible to 'humanize' work. However, not only do such views contain kernels of truth, they are also highly suggestive in the hotel and catering context of the need to challenge existing practices. Whatever the labour cost implications, whatever the benefits of a highly flexible workforce, it makes no sense to create either more problems than are necessary, or the potential for inefficiency, by the adoption of a *laissez-faire* approach to labour motivation and retention.

Loss of talent

The loss of talent to an organization that may result from inappropriate strategies for managing organizational members has already been referred to several times in the text. At the lower levels of all organizations, irrespective of industry, there is often a tendency to treat people merely as a resource, and view this resource as contributing only to the maintenance of the organization. This is a mistaken view: over the past 20 years or so it has become clear that all organizational members, whatever their position, can contribute to the organization. In organizations in the hospitality industry, where many personnel are engaged in frequent interaction with customers, the importance of bringing operative staff into decision-making might be regarded as particularly important. Too often, staff are treated as mere 'bodies', performing essentially mechanical functions.

By the same token, staff have little influence on organizational development. Many employers and managers will claim to involve staff, but this is often found to be restricted to such things as 'suggestion boxes', 'new employee bonuses' (where by a member of staff receives a bonus payment for introducing a new member of staff to the organization) or 'staff meetings' (where the agenda is controlled by management and restricted to management 'advising' upon policy and procedure). It is sufficient to note at this point that successful organizations, broadly defined, are those that evolve the procedures and mechanisms for managing the tensions that arise from employees constituting a generic aggregate (and within that aggregate, distinctive sub-groups based on occupation, external labour market factors and so on) and yet requiring leadership and management as both a group or groups, and as *individuals*. It is to this issue that the following discussion is addressed.

Individuals apart

In both theory and practice there is a tendency for management in organizations to perceive employees as comprising broad groups or aggregates of individuals, as chefs and cooks, as chambermaids, as men and women, as young people and so on. Such prescriptions apply not simply to management's gaze within the aggregate(s) or unit(s) but to perceptions of the kinds and qualities of labour available in the labour market, and accordingly affects the way in which management treats employees within the organization. There are often good practical reasons for this in terms of personnel procedures. The problem for organizations and for management is, however, in the expectations of employees that they will be treated as individuals. This is not to say that all members of the organization do not expect at some point to be treated according to particular group characteristics. Most, however, expect their dignity as individuals to govern most of their relations with peers, managers and supervisors.

The concept of the individual is a philosophically problematic one. On too many occasions it is used to divide people and to obscure the interests of powerful groups in society. Former British Prime Minister Margaret Thatcher is credited with the remark that there is no such thing as society. To the social scientist this seems absurd and risible except in so far as such a claim is understandable in the context of the extent to which sociologists in particular have almost eliminated any concept of the individual from sociological analysis.

But if sociologists have been guilty of relegating the individual to the conceptual netherworld, at least they have addressed the individual more seriously than most writers of organizational behaviour textbooks, who serve up a cod psychology that rarely articulates the individual and the social in a meaningful framework (see Chapter 1). Indeed, the 'psychology of the individual' often represented not only does a disservice to psychology and psychologists but is so partial as to beggar belief. For example, many texts on organizational behaviour discuss stereotyping as a feature of perception, and perception in turn is recognized as a primarily psychological process mediated by social factors only in so far as it is recognized that in stereotyping others, individuals tend to draw on shared stereotypes, e.g. Scots are mean, or drunkards, or haggis-eating caber-tossers; the French are inveterate romantics and sex maniacs; the Germans are arrogant, militaristic and untrustworthy.

Such a limited view of stereotyping as a psycho-social process fails to take account of the wider social dimensions to the phenomenon. It is not just that many people share stereotypes, it is that stereotypes serve a purpose. They reinforce prejudice when directed *against* people and support a particular world view or set of interests, often the interests of powerful groups in society. From the crude labelling by tabloid newspapers of the French as 'frogs' and Germans as 'krauts' to the (usually more subtle) questioning of the motives of these nations by politicians, it is possible to mobilize collective and often irrational prejudices. The perception of others and the active process of stereotyping are not merely neutral classification processes but ones that are always tied to erroneous views of others (a view generally acknowledged in organizational behaviour texts) and ones that embrace a set of ideologies that serve some set of wider interests (not always recognized in the same texts).

While acknowledging certain abstract difficulties attendant on the concept of the individual, it is *not* difficult to accept that most people regard themselves as individuals exercising free will. The dictum of the American sociologist W.I. Thomas is as important today as when first mooted: if people define a situation as real, then it will be real in its consequences. For the majority, the society of individuals is a reality. However, lack of any serious consideration of what it is to be an 'individual' means that there is no vocabulary and few strategies for dealing with the individual.

The often optimistic language of the 'new management' literature (see, for example, Peters and Waterman, 1982) frequently couches its prescriptions for personnel and human resource management in what appear as common-sense aphorisms – say, 'Treat everyone with dignity and respect', or 'Recognize that every person has feelings and a view that can contribute to the success of the organization' (these examples are invented for the purpose of the present discussion but reflect well enough the 'philosophy' of 'new management' writing, see Chapter 11). Perhaps ironically, however, 'new management' theory also acknowledges that in subscribing to any concept of the individual it is both deeds and words that are important. Lip service is not enough – actual contact with individuals at the personal level is necessary in an organizational context. What 'hidden agenda' such approaches may disguise or what effect they have in reality is another matter. More pointedly, whether in the abstract world of organizational behaviour textbooks or in the day-to-day, all too real environment of organizations, the tendency to conceive of individuals as constituting elements within groups, networks and aggregates is still common and indeed vital. Individuals themselves can achieve only so much, for within the organization it is groups and teams that advance the organization's goals.

Summary

- Individuals are shaped by their social environment, and their 'life chances' are determined by a range of factors.
- Some of these factors are immutable, e.g. gender and ethnicity can have an often restrictive influence upon life chances.
- Structural factors, e.g. the nature of labour markets, can influence the kinds of employment opportunities available to individuals.
- The hospitality industry relies heavily on young and female workers, many of whom work part-time and have little job security.
- A possible consequence of the confining of organizational members to low-skilled jobs (many hotel and catering jobs are low-skilled or unskilled) is a loss of talent to the organization. Furthermore, the lack of opportunities for advancement and training provide few opportunities for individuals to enhance their labour market position, and this can lead to high labour turnover, based on instrumental values, e.g. the search for incremental increases in remuneration.
- While there is an expectation in our society that people should be treated as individuals, the concept of the individual is a philosophically problematic one, and in organizations the basic administrative unit tends to be the group.

Discussion questions

1 Consider how variables listed in the section 'Getting Work', p. 58, may explain the structure of the hotel and catering workforce.

2 What jobs in the hospitality industry should be considered skilled, semi-skilled and unskilled?

3 Why might some workers in the hospitality industry be viewed as being discriminated against – and by whom?

4 What is meant by the use of the term 'individual differences' and why should caution be exercised in employing the term to describe individuals' motivations to work in the hospitality industry?

6 Roles in the organization

In a broad sense the concept of role links that of the individual to that of the group. The concept of role has three principal elements:

- A role is a *collectivity* (set) of behaviour patterns – people generally have more than one role.
- The behaviour patterns associated with roles are *expected* patterns of behaviour – they are thus to a greater or lesser extent shared by people.
- Roles are defined in relation to a person's position in the social order.

As indicated in the previous chapter, individuals bring to the organization certain experiences and qualities from their wider social experience, including the generalized roles played by individuals outside the organizational context: the roles of husband, wife, father, daughter, son and so on. Many of these roles may be important within the wider community. This is an important point, because it is often the case that organizational behaviour analysts focus only on roles in the organization, with little regard for how these are influenced by extra-organizational roles. An unwritten organizational rule is that people should not bring their personal/domestic problems with them to their work. In many cases, however, this is unavoidable, and not only in extreme circumstances such as family bereavement or individual health circumstances. If a person has a difficulty in his/her home life or fulfils a more important role outside the work organization than inside it, then it might be impossible to exclude their effects from the organizational environment and they may affect an individual's performance.

The key point, then, is that while a good deal is heard about the work ethic and the way it dominates many people's lives (even where an instrumental attitude is the principal motivator), work is just one aspect of life. Organizational careers are influenced by (and influence) other aspects of behaviour and other roles.

Roles and socialization

Roles, like most aspects of human behaviour, are learned as a result of processes of socialization. In early life roles are learned as a result of individuals observing those in their immediate circle – parents, siblings, relatives and the like. As children get older, their social circle widens and expands to include school friends, teachers and others. It is through this process that individuals come to understand role conventions, e.g. about what constitutes appropriate male and female behaviour, how people ought to be treated in particular circumstances and what is expected of a role-holder by others in general. In absorbing these norms and values, people begin to police their own behaviour, to learn self-control and discipline, and to understand what behaviour is acceptable and in what contexts.

Within the organization in which an individual is employed socialization continues: in the words of Handy (1975, p. 134) it is a process by which the organization 'seeks to make the individual more amenable to the prevalent mode of influence'. This means that organizational socialization is also a process of control and constraint, where role definition is primarily a process of delineating parameters of acceptable behaviour. However, socialization is also an enabling process. The hope is that a person will absorb the organizational culture and acquire at least some of the values of the organization and, in particular, a commitment to advancement of the organization's purpose.

Sometimes, these values are quite vague and ill-defined. For example, most academics are not only expected to teach but to undertake research and publish scholarly books and articles. Yet few institutions of higher education specify precisely in contractual terms how much of each activity should be undertaken. A commitment to research is an *implicit value* to which academics are expected to subscribe. In hotels and catering there is often a like expectation that because of the customer-driven nature of the organization, staff will do their best to be polite to customers at all times and anticipate their needs, not merely react to customer demands.

The language of role theory

Organizational behaviour analysts use a variety of special terms to describe different aspects of role behaviour. The purpose of these terms is to identify the facets of such behaviour and potential problems that can arise as a result of individuals' efforts to perform their role(s) in an organizational context.

Role-holding

It has already been established that, at any one time, individuals perform a number of different roles. To a large extent therefore everybody is a multiple-role holder – as employee, boss, father, mother or whatever. The roles played by any individual are, according to Mullins (1992), determined by a combination of situational and personal factors. Situational factors in the organizational context include the organization type, the job tasks of the post-holder, and the nature of organizational structure and leadership. Personal factors are the already alluded to set of characteristics that people bring to the organization from their external lives – values, attitudes, beliefs and norms. It is also important to distinguish between a person's formal and informal roles in particular circumstances. In an organization, a person's formal role may well be defined by a contract of employment and job description. Their informal role will, however, be determined by a confluence of factors such as personality, reputation and track record within the organization.

In many organizations there are formal and informal leaders (see Chapter 9 below). An informal leader is someone who is able to influence opinion and enact policies and other courses of action through both formal and informal channels without necessarily having the *formal* authority. At a lower level most organizations have one or more people who, irrespective of their formal position, act as a focus for emotional and practical support, e.g. so-called 'mother' or 'father' figures, or as 'go-betweens' for different parties in the organization or one of its sub-units. A variety of informal functions may be performed by individuals in organizations, and these individuals often exert great influence on the smooth (or bumpy) running of the organization.

Role set

A role set is the range of interactional associations persons have with other organizational members as a result of the performance of their roles. In any one situation the number of interactional associations may vary greatly. For example, in the hotel and catering context a waiter or waitress includes among their role set customers with whom they come into contact, however temporarily or transiently, as well as fellow workers, supervisors and managers (see Figure 6.1).

Figure 6.1 Possible role set of a waiter/waitress

Role identity

The term role identity refers to those attitudes and behaviours that are consistent with a role. Identification with a role is therefore commensurate with the expression of appropriate attitudes and behaviour. In the hospitality industry this is perhaps most clearly seen in the extent to which employees are expected to adopt a subordinate role to customers.

This has led to debates over whether in servicing the needs of others, hospitality industry employees must, by definition, be servile in their attitude. At a commonsense level it is often held that this need not be so. In some organizations and organizational settings adopting a subordinate position bordering on the servile may be expected by the customer. In some tipped occupations, like waiting on table, this is especially so, and servility may be perceived by waiting staff as a means of increasing the likelihood of customer satisfaction and hence a good tip. However, research has shown that even where servility is expected by the customer, it rarely generates these kinds of reward, as other aspects of employee performance, e.g. speed of service, are regarded as more important by customers (see Mars and Nicod, 1984; Butler and Skipper, 1981). In addition, excessive servility may have the effect of irritating the customer, despite he or she having ambiguous feelings over what they expect from staff. Hospitality industry staff thus walk something of a tightrope in respect of role identity in terms of customers' *expectations* of them, and failure to identify with their role can lead to *role conflict* (both are discussed further below).

Role perceptions and role models

In organizational behaviour theory discussion of roles is usually confined to roles within the organization, i.e. the mutuality of roles among employees. As was indicated in the discussion of role identity, however, hospitality services workers have a dual audience for their role performances. The term 'role perceptions' describes individuals' view of their role and how it should be performed. It is a term that circumscribes the potential actions that may be followed in a given situation.

Individual perceptions of how a role should be performed can come from a variety of sources. Whereas some formal aspects of the role will be legislated for in contracts and job descriptions, other aspects will be learned through training and observation of other workers. Informal aspects of role perception will arise from the individual's own motivations as they combine with the more formal specifications of the role. These motivations will vary according to context. A new employee seeking to make an impression on superiors may behave in an exaggeratedly positive and solicitous manner towards both managers/supervisors and guests if s/he thinks such behaviour is likely to win favour. Alternatively, in order to ensure that they are accepted by their peer group, individuals may behave in a manner likely to maximize the possibility of such acceptance even where this means behaving in a manner unlikely to attract managers' attention to more than a usual degree. To a large extent such behaviour rests on who the individual sees as his or her primary *reference group*, or, put another way, on who are perceived as being the most important 'significant others'.

A reference group is simply a social group with whom a social actor most readily identifies and desires to emulate/be accepted by. The term 'significant others' has a similar if more precise meaning. A 'significant other' is someone who a person regards as a role model. How persons perceive their role(s) is to some degree dependent on which role models and reference groups they adopt. Individuals are not confined to adopting a single role model, and most people absorb elements of behaviour from a variety of sources, whether within similar or different reference groups. They may also utilize characteristics of several role models variously, and in different situations, as they seek to engage in what the American sociologist Erving Goffman (1959) called 'impression management'.

Considering the examples given earlier, individuals may seek to heighten in a positive way their supervisor's perception of their performance while at the same time presenting a different face to their peer group and to customers. A classic example of the impression management technique as it applies to customer–worker relations was recorded by George Orwell in his book *Down and Out in Paris and London* (1933; 1986, pp. 60–1):

> It was amusing to look round the filthy little scullery and think that only a double door was between us and the dining-room. There sat the customers in all their splendour – spotless table-cloths, bowls of flowers, mirrors and gilt cornices and painted cherubim; and here, just a few feet away, we in our disgusting filth. For it really was disgusting filth. There was no time to sweep the floor till evening and we slithered around in a compound of soapy water, lettuce-leaves, torn paper and trampled food. A dozen waiters with their coats off, showing their sweaty armpits, sat at the table mixing salads and sticking their thumbs into the cream pots. The room had a dirty, mixed smell of food and sweat. Everywhere in the cupboards, behind the piles of crockery, were squalid stores of food that the waiters had stolen. There were only two sinks, and no washing basin, and it was nothing unusual for a waiter to wash his face in the water in which clean crockery was rinsing. But the customers saw nothing of this. There were a coco-nut mat and a mirror outside the dining-room door, and the waiters used to preen themselves up and go in looking the picture of cleanliness.

While it is conventional to think of the adoption of role models as an informal process, historically many organizations and professions have adopted a formal *mentoring* policy whereby new members of staff at whatever level of the organization are attached to an experienced employee who 'shows them the ropes', and who acts as an informational source as well as a source of support, counselling and guidance. In a mentoring system there is no guarantee that the mentor will ultimately act as the primary role model, but mentoring schemes do formalize what is often an informal process in organizations, and might reasonably be expected to inculcate appropriate standards and behaviour.

Role expectations

In that people are identified with the role(s) they play, then for each role there are expectations that others will have of a person claiming to 'fill' that role. Mullins (1992) distinguishes three categories of role expectation:

- Formal role expectations are those legislated for by the organization in contracts of employment and job description.
- Informal role expectations are those not normally prescribed but expected as a matter of convention and may be enforced – examples include dress codes and certain forms of polite behaviour.
- Self-established role expectations are those commonly (though by no means exclusively) associated with senior organizational members, where formal role expectations are largely unspecified and a high degree of discretion in role-related behaviour is allowed.

A breakdown in role expectations during interaction with others can be embarrassing and detrimental to the organization, particularly where third parties are affected, as with customers in the hospitality context. Problems for staff may be exacerbated by the often mercurial nature of clients, whose expectations may vary from the conventional to the unreasonable, causing problems for the management of role expectations.

Role conflict, role stress, role overload and role bargaining

When an individual finds that the role(s) s/he is expected to perform do not easily rest together, then role conflict can ensue. Role conflict is the result of finding that compliance with one role requirement is incompatible with fulfilling a second. The important thing to remember in respect of the hospitality industry is that there are probably very few unreasonable demands that can be made of staff but there are many unfortunate ones. Role conflict can occur when an organizational member faces different expectations from different individuals and groups (superiors, subordinates, peer group, clients). Unease and inconsistency in behaviour arises as a result of a failure to specify priorities for action.

Role conflict can give rise to role stress, where difficulties in communication and interpersonal relationships develop into a systematic feature of role performance and limit that performance. This is particularly true in cases of role overload, where a person is given too many responsibilities and this gives rise to conflicting expectations and priorities. In circumstances like these an individual may engage in role bargaining, i.e. seek to negotiate with superiors new boundaries for the role(s) s/he performs. In some cases this may be achieved without reference to superiors when persons make their own decisions as to what priorities they will apply. There are obvious dangers in this approach, as, if unchecked, it is possible that certain responsibilities will not be discharged, to the ultimate detriment of the organization.

Role stress and real stress

Role stress is at one level a pleasantly abstract concept, but employment-related stress is now recognized as a major factor in unhappiness and poor performance among individuals in the workplace. Stress may be defined as both a physiological and psychological response to demands placed upon the individual. To some degree, stress is a useful phenomenon, which, if controlled, can encourage highly motivated performance. However, excessive stress can be damaging to the individual and the organization.

One of the most useful self-contained discussions of stress in a hospitality context is provided by Drummond (1990). Drummond characterizes three groups of stress symptom. Physiological symptoms of stress include nausea and high blood pressure, difficulty in sleeping, susceptibility to illness, and an increase in the number of aches and pains experienced, whether in the form of muscular pain or headaches/earaches and so forth. Psychological symptoms of stress include depression, lowering of self-esteem, excessive concern about other people's opinions and a decline in the ability to concentrate. Performance symptoms of stress embrace avoidance behaviour (people, situations), a decline in the ability to make hard and fast decisions, a reduction in versatility in task performance, and erratic judgements.

Stressors – the things that cause stress – are relative. What is stressful to one person is not necessarily stressful to another. Brymer (1979) argues that all hospitality managers encounter stress at some point in their careers. In general terms stressors fall into one of four categories. First, there are individual stressors, those that arise mainly from self-imposed pressures but may also be attributable to self-doubt. Those who place a lot of pressure on themselves are said to exhibit Type A behaviour (first identified in the 1950s, according to Brymer), typified by the workaholic, highly competitive personality, always racing against time. In contrast, Type B behaviour is more laid back. Brymer (1979, p. 62) argues that Type A behaviour is quite common among hospitality managers, where it is often culturally valued as a norm. He remarks that 'many compulsive workers may be attracted to work in the lodging and food-service fields because of the pace and long hours'.

The second major source of stressors is the family. The family is not always a refuge but may be a source of stress, especially if organizational demands prevent family obligations from being met. The family is also a source of disruption, e.g. through the ill-health of parents, partners or children. In the hospitality management context stress originating in the family may be generated as a result of the frequent relocations that are generally part of hospitality managers' career development.

A third source of stressors is the organization itself. In the hospitality industry unpredictability (of demand, of employees) is a major source of stress, but the high levels of responsibility that many managers bear can also be significant in stress causation, particularly as a sense of isolation may be experienced because of a unit's independence from other units and the larger organization.

Finally, stress may be caused by wider social and environmental factors – those that reside in the infrastructure of society. These include changes in economic affairs, legal matters that bear on the organization, changing consumer preferences and consumption patterns, and public distrust of organizations.

Stress is no longer regarded as a sign of weakness in modern organizations but is a very real phenomenon that can impair individual and organizational performance. This realization underlines the importance of avoiding role stress and conflict by creating an environment conducive to minimizing stress.

Managing role stress

According to Mullins (1992), the responsibility for controlling and reducing role conflict and role stress necessarily lies with management, which can pursue a number of strategies in order to fulfil this responsibility. For the purposes of this discussion, the main points noted by Mullins (1992, p. 245) have here been condensed.

First, there are *structural* solutions to the problems of role stress and conflict. These may entail regular reviews of organizational structure and the definition of existing roles to effect a change in structure and the range and number of roles in the organization. For example, in cases of role overload, jobs and tasks may be redefined at a lower level and elements of a role/task reallocated to other persons. This kind of strategy may well have resource implications. There is a tradition in the hospitality industry of high role expectations, and, in order to control costs, management may well be reluctant to employ extra staff. The possibility of such a dilemma emphasizes the importance of proper human resourcing strategies, in particular the creation of realistic performance standards (Riley, 1991). By way of illustration of this point, Riley (1991, p. 80) suggests that a suitable performance standard for bedroom cleaners is fifteen rooms per person per day. Indeed fourteen or fifteen rooms per day is an industry norm (the provenance of which is, however, uncertain). To what extent this standard is realistic is a matter, like any other performance standard, that needs to be kept under review and related to the nature of the hotel business. It may be an inappropriate standard for certain types of luxury hotel where personal service of a high standard is required. It may also be inappropriate to the environment in which the hotel functions at given points in the calendar. For example, fifteen rooms per cleaner may be reasonable in periods of average occupancy but not for full occupancy during the tourist season or special promotions, e.g. Christmas packages.

A second strategy for reducing role conflict and stress may be termed the *informational and communicative* approach. This entails ensuring (*a*) that roles in the organization at all levels are defined in an unambiguous fashion and there are appropriate mechanisms for clarifying individual and collective instances of such ambiguity; (*b*) that exceptional events likely to lead to uncertainty and apprehension among organization members are notified well in advance and appropriate plans are laid for coping with these events; and (*c*) organizational leaders specify clearly the procedures that will be followed in all aspects of the management of subordinates, and these procedures are detailed and understood by all organizational members.

Point (*c*) above leads to consideration of *personnel solutions* to the problems of role conflict and stress. These include the implementation of carefully considered recruitment strategies, whereby every effort is made to ensure that the skills of individuals hired are appropriate to the job they will be doing. This means more than simply technical skills. It implies that individuals' motivations and aspirations are assessed against the nature of the job(s) on offer. Similarly, induction and training, career development and retention policies may be employed rigorously to ensure that, once within the organization, an individual's skills and aspirations are developed and realized (see Chapter 12).

Roles in the hospitality industry

The concept of role has received very little explicit attention in the literature on hotel and catering work. However, it is possible to make a number of observations from existing research evidence. Foremost among these is the complexity of many hotel and catering workers' role sets. While everybody is, to some extent, a multiple role holder, there are many work organizations in which role relationships are between personnel of the organization alone – between co-workers and workers and managers. For many hospitality industry employees, however, customers can be an important element in the organizational role set, as indicated earlier (see Figure 6.1). This has important implications for the performance of work.

In one of his studies of hotel and catering employment, W.F. Whyte (1949) postulated a three-way grouping of relations between participants in a hospitality organization. The importance of these relations have been subsequently elaborated to suggest that, at least for those workers in customer contact roles, role conflict is inherent to organizational relations because each employee effectively works for two bosses. The customer initiates requests and orders, and the meeting of these demands is essential not only to the satisfaction of the customer's requirements but in some cases in generating additional rewards for service staff – tips and suchlike. At the same time, the employee owes a duty to the employer (as represented by managers and supervisors) to perform in such a way as to meet personal and organizational objectives. Problems arise, however, from the mercurial nature of customers and the pressure of work. The obligations owed to the customer, to the satisfaction of the customer's demands, can lead staff to transfer these pressures to other sectors of the organization.

The most commonly cited instance of such behaviour is the inter-departmental conflict that can arise between restaurant and kitchen. In a busy restaurant speed of service is often perceived by clients and waiting staff alike as essential to a pleasant dining experience. The fact that most clients see service as being rendered to them personally and that such a view is internalized within the organization (despite the fact that the organization is, in reality, offering the collective satisfaction of those demands; see Mars and Nicod, 1984; Wood, 1993, 1994) increases pressure on waiting staff. This pressure may be transferred to the kitchen staff. As Bowey (1976) notes, 'nagging' chefs is one way for waiting staff to ensure speedy service. However, this approach can also generate resentment on the part of kitchen staff, manifest in the creation of hostile personal relationships between employees in both departments or, more seriously, behaviour on the part of kitchen staff hostile to waiters and waitresses – an instance would be by working more slowly to reduce the pace of service delivery.

To some extent, inter-departmental conflict of the kind described above arises out of differing role perceptions. For waiting staff, perceptions of role content derive from the customs and practices of the restaurant in which they work, which is in turn influenced by the general principles and values of service to customers. For kitchen staff, and especially chefs and cooks, the pressure and speed of service may take second place to the production of food consonant with self-perceptions of professional competence. Although both departments are, at the level of the organization's mission, supposed to be engaged in different elements of the same process (satisfaction of consumer demands), differing circumstances, environments, role perceptions and role identities can generate conflict. An intervening variable in this respect is the 'triadic' relation between employer, employee and customer identified by Whyte (1949).

One aspect of this relation is, as already noted, the degree to which staff are dependent for their instructions, their 'orders', on both clients and managers/supervisors. A second aspect is the manner in which management often abdicates responsibility for controlling both the process of communication and satisfaction of client needs. Although in theory both waiting and kitchen staff are often dependent on clients for the initiation of action (service), waiting staff are often dependent on clients for the additional element of remuneration (tips), *and* are responsible for initiating actions for chefs and cooks whose role perceptions characteristically include a view of themselves as higher in status than waiting staff (Wood, 1993). The fact that this process of communication and initiation of action is often left by supervisors to self-management on the part of the workers concerned without any significant control procedures (including, it might be noted, the amelioration of the frequent association of service with servility by encouraging tipping as a means of subsidizing low wages, see Wood, 1992) is where abdication of managerial responsibility bites in this context.

In his study of *Human Relations in the Restaurant Industry*, Whyte (1948) was sufficiently concerned by the phenomenon of inter-departmental conflict to suggest reducing interaction between the major parties to conflict. As noted in Chapter 4, this was to be achieved by the use of technology, and, in particular, communication devices such as internal telephones by which orders could be transmitted to the kitchen from the restaurant. This suggestion, like others of Whyte's, is a little 'fuzzy edged' and it is not always clear as to how inter-role conflict is to be resolved by such means. Yet it is important testimony to the extent of the problems engendered by inter-departmental conflict that impersonal measures seemed to Whyte to be the principal method of resolving these difficulties.

A final point worth considering here is the effect of inter-role conflict on role stress. The hospitality industry's high levels of labour turnover may be attributable in part to the stress encountered by many workers. In public-contact roles, the pressures created by inter-departmental conflict and the tendency for much work to be highly individualized, i.e. performed not always in co-operation with other workers but on an individual, instrumental, basis, means that the attractions of moving job can be considerable on the 'change is as good as a rest' principle. Here the possibility of a new job can be enough to alleviate job and role stress, even if this effect is, in itself, short-lived. That many workers experience stress is not in doubt (see Macaulay and Wood, 1992, 1992a), and although stress is not the only factor contributing to the often phenomenal rates of turnover in hotels and catering, it is one of the more important ones. Although the evidence is slight, writers such as Johnson (1985) have found inverse correlations between hotel star rating and turnover, suggesting that in top quality hotels turnover is lower, a possible reason for this being the staff-to-room ratio of such establishments, i.e. in high quality hotels, there are more staff per room and work is therefore better paced.

Summary

The main points of this chapter can be summarized as follows.

- The concept of role links that of the individual to that of the group.
- A role is a set of behaviour patterns that give rise to expectations on the part of others as to how a person will act.
- Roles are learned through the process of socialization from an early age. Organizational roles are acquired through employment socialization and experience.
- Most people are multiple role holders and the interaction between these roles is important in understanding people's behaviour and the perceptions they bring to bear on a situation.
- Role performance requires self-discipline and the performance of roles is also influenced by perceptions of other role-holders' expectations.
- A common problem in organizations is role stress and role conflict, both of which may arise from a failure of organizational leaders to properly clarify the formal requirements of a role within the organization. This may be particularly problematic for workers in hotel and catering organizations, where roles can sometimes be 'fuzzy edged'.

Discussion questions

1 Consider how the three principal aspects of a social role apply to members of a group with which you are familiar.
2 Identify examples of role stress that may occur in the hospitality industry, and suggest ways in which such stress might be reduced.
3 To what extent can inter-departmental conflict in hospitality organizations be attributed to role conflicts?
4 How do customers' roles affect the organization and performance of work in hospitality organizations?

7   Groups and teams

At first sight, the idea that any difficulties could be encountered in defining the concept of 'group' seems unlikely. Everybody knows what a group is, what a group physically *looks* like. However, as Lockwood and Jones (1984, p. 103) point out, social scientists across a range of disciplines and disciplinary areas, including organizational behaviour, tend to emphasize different aspects of 'groupness'. Lockwood and Jones identify at least seven 'angles' to the definition of the concept of group:

- *Perceptual* (when a number of people think of themselves as a group).
- *Interactive* (a group is a collective of people who communicate regularly over time, and face to face).
- *Purposive* (a group is defined in terms of people who share common interests and/or objectives coming together).
- *Motivational* (where membership of a collective satisfies personal needs for security, protection, advancement and so on).
- *Interdependent* (groups are defined in terms of shared life chances, where events affecting one group member affect others).
- *Mutual* (groups comprise persons who influence one another by virtue of interaction).
- *Structural* (groups are defined in terms of the nature and quality of the relationships between those individuals who share something to the extent that a collective value system emerges to regulate behaviour).

Lockwood and Jones' typology is very useful, covering a range of definitions of groups that have been offered by commentators in various social science disciplines. In sum, the defining features of a group can be identified as follows. First, a group comprises two or more people. Second, these people interact with one another in such a way as to mutually influence opinions and actions: they communicate regularly over time, and often face-to-face. Third, groups share common interests, objectives or aspirations (all or a combination of these). Fourth, groups satisfy individual *and* group needs: individual needs for belonging and sharing, group needs for strength and identity.

These are the essential characteristics of a group. Other characteristics include individual and collective self-perception as a group (usually when the group's existence is centred on some common interest or purpose explicitly recognized or tacitly accepted); interdependency of members, where actions of individuals influence or affect the group as a whole; and structure, where regular, i.e. systematic, patterns of relations within the group can be discerned and these serve some group purpose.

In distinguishing between these features of groups and their four 'essential' characteristics, the objective is to point to the extent to which some features of groups *may* be acquired, whereas others are *necessary* to lend definition to the idea of 'a group'. Thus a group must have members, and members must interact and communicate with one another (and therefore influence one another, however minimally), and they must have something in common – and so on. Groups need not perceive of themselves as constituting a group to be a group, however, nor need they evidence a high level of interdependency. Often both these last features *will* characterize a group, but they are not, by themselves, necessary to a sense of groupness.

Formal and informal groups

Another important reason for distinguishing between the essential features of a group and certain 'optional extras' lies in the tendency of many definitions of the concept to lend great weight to the voluntary nature of groups. That is to say, many definitions of what a group 'is' implicitly reflect the view that group associativeness is largely voluntary and people are relatively free to choose whether or not they join a group. This is, of course, true of many groups that individuals join over a lifetime. It is equally true that many groups exist without their members thinking of themselves as a group, as well as groups becoming formalized as such after a period in which a sense of 'groupness' was tacit and informal.

In the organizational context, and particularly in the context of work organizations, groups are not always voluntarily constituted. *Formal groups* are those deliberately created by organizational leaders for a specific purpose. Leaders are selected by management, and management exerts influence over defining the goals of the group. Some formal groups in the organization are relatively permanent and can be identified with particular divisions or departments of the organization, so-called 'command groups' (see Robbins, 1992, and Moorhead and Griffin, 1989, for elaboration). Other formal groups include task groups, which are relatively impermanent and are usually established to tackle particular problems. Examples would include project management groups, task forces and quality circles (Burton and Michael, 1992; Hales, 1987). Further examples of command groups include autonomous work groups, and of course the day-to-day work groups of which most employees are members and which form the basis for the performance of work, but are often smaller than formal departments or divisions within the organization.

Informal groups, as the term suggests, are not deliberately created by organizational leaders but come about as a result of informal interaction between certain organizational members. The ties that bind members of informal groups together are friendship and sociability. This often means that informal groups are more flexible in their membership than formal groups, and are inclined to greater volatility. It would, however, be a mistake to suppose that informal groups enjoy less status or even authority than formal, organizationally created groups.

It is common to distinguish between two types of informal group – the friendship group and the interest group. The latter is normally regarded as transient and more purposive than the informal friendship group. However, in many ways this is too simplistic. Informal groups within a single organization (as opposed to those that transcend organizational boundaries) may well be based on ties of friendship and sociability but by virtue of shared interests may, regularly or infrequently, act as an interest group or be otherwise influential in the deliberations of the formal organization. This is particularly true of groups composed of people of equal or roughly equal status. For example, in many universities the power of the informal grouping of professors is considerable and can cross-cut the power of formal groups composed of a wide range of people drawn from different status positions in the organization. This is not to say that informal groups arising from single levels of the organization (status levels, functional levels of departments) are more powerful than informal groups that draw their membership from different levels of the organization.

Formation of groups

The distinction between formal and informal groups makes it difficult to generalize common causal factors in group formation, development and structure. Nevertheless, both formal and informal groups share much in common. Even formal groups that are deliberately created for organizational purposes may have few affiliative qualities to begin with, but, as the group develops, may acquire many of the friendship, sociability and common interest features of voluntary groups. Indeed, as the later discussion on teams will demonstrate, if organizational leaders are sensitive to individual and group needs, they can contribute greatly to creating such values in a disparate group of people.

Groups come into being for a variety of reasons, and instead of seeking to differentiate motivations in the context of 'formal' and 'informal' groups, it is more appropriate to indicate what *attractions* and *advantages* groups *can* offer to potential members. Many of these are implicit in the ways in which the concept of group has been defined. The crucial point to bear in mind is that people become members of groups for *reasons* – that is to say there is some motivation – whether their own, or someone else's. A summary list of these reasons would usefully include the following:

- *Interpersonal attraction.* People join groups because they are attracted to other people in the group. This is particularly true of voluntary groups, but in formal groups the organization's managers should be aware of the potential for personal chemistry in selecting group members and/or of possible techniques likely to generate feelings of interpersonal affiliation.
- *Group activities.* A desire to share in group activities can be a powerful motivation to gain group membership whether in formal or informal groups.

- *Group goals*. A key reason why people form groups, or groups are formed in organizations for particular purposes (whether routine or special), is that in general it is believed that groups can achieve more than any individual or individuals working alone.

  At a voluntary level, individuals may seek membership of a particular group on the basis that it pursues goals that they share or wish to share in achieving.
- *Security and social affiliation*. Group membership can offer participants a sense of belonging and security, the 'safety in numbers' syndrome.
- *Status and self-esteem*. The nature of certain groups is such that it confers a certain cachet upon individual members in their own eyes and those of the wider organization and society. At the same time, the feeling of belonging that can arise from membership of a group may generate self-esteem and self-satisfaction, and members of groups can reinforce such feelings, particularly if group membership is exclusive.
- *Power*. An important motivation to seek group membership is that groups may command power, influence and resources that are necessary and desirable to the achievement of goals or are worth having simply for themselves. The very existence of a group, particularly a formally constituted one with specific aims within an organization, can focus power in a way that individuals in loose alliances cannot.

Stages in group development

However problematic attempts at defining the main characteristics of groups may be, one thing is certain – groups change and develop. They are not static social entities but change in a variety of ways. The most obvious of these is in terms of membership: new members leave and old ones join. More important, however, is the extent to which a new group changes in nature over time. A favoured model among organizational behaviour theorists for understanding this process is that originally devised by Tuckmann (1965), who proposed four stages of group development.

The first of these is the 'forming' stage, during which there is uncertainty about the purpose, structure and leadership of a group; what kinds of behaviour are acceptable within the group; the kind and quality of relationships that will exist between members of the group; and the best means that might be employed to achieve the goals of the group. Second, there is the 'storming' stage, during which conflict arises out of difficulties individuals have in subordinating their individuality to the aims and will of the group. Conflict may also arise over leadership questions and indeed over the goals of the group itself (or at least the methods of achieving these goals). The third stage of group development in Tuckmann's model is 'norming', during which roles are defined, rules for the conduct of the group's behaviour established and a framework, however loose, put in place to facilitate some degree of harmony. Finally, there is the 'performing' stage, during which action is directed towards attainment of goals and objectives, and in which the highest levels of group performance might be expected.

These stages in group development may take place over very short or very long periods of time – or not at all. Some groups may never achieve the 'performing' stage but get 'stuck' at one of the earlier stages. Moreover, a difficulty with the Tuckmann model is that it is purely linear, it does not account for regression. Thus some groups may proceed to one stage but by some turn of events be thrown back to an earlier stage. In order to understand group process, it is thus necessary to have an appreciation of both developmental issues and of the structures that emerge in groups at any given point in time.

Group structure

Structure refers not to the physical form of the group alone but to the system of values, attitudes and procedures that the group creates (or has created for it) and to the group's behaviour. Of most interest are group norms, group cohesion, group conflict and group communications.

Group norms

Norms are standards of behaviour and expression that are shared by members of a group. Many of these are generalized throughout society, but individuals bring to a group their particular interpretation of norms as mediated by their life experiences. Sometimes certain norms are formalized as rules, but the majority of norms are informal and policed by the group such that individuals who breach group norms may have their behaviour questioned.

A norm, then, is a standard of behaviour, a boundary. The concept of norm as boundary is important, because when the boundary is crossed, it threatens danger to the group. Norms encourage conformity and predictability of behaviour, which may be desirable qualities in groups, as they ensure a commonality of standards. However, norms also serve to straitjacket individuals and groups and can encourage narrowness of outlook. Often norms encourage *unthinking* conformity, and, as such, are often subject to controversy and conflict.

A common norm found in work organizations relates to standards of dress, a norm that has particular salience for the hospitality industry. In general terms 'proper' dress (sober clothing, suits and suchlike) is regarded as normal for professional and business persons. Uniforms can mark out workers at other levels of the occupational hierarchy. An unthinking attachment to dress code conventions is a feature of many organizations. There is no evidence to suggest that dressing in one way or another improves work performance (except in certain extreme circumstances, where a job requires protective clothing). At the same time, it cannot be denied that because of normative expectations, there exists a preoccupation with dress that leads in some contexts to certain types of dress being regarded as appropriate/inappropriate. Built on this is an edifice of perception (or prejudice) that associates certain types of dress with the attitudes and values of the wearers relative to the role they are playing.

In the hospitality industry 'uniforms' mark out different work groups and dress standards are expected of staff (chefs' whites, waiting staffs' 'penguin suits', male managers' morning dress) and sometimes of customers. Similarly, certain norms of etiquette are observed when attending a formal dinner (whether in a private residence or hotel/restaurant), e.g. eating food with the 'correct' cutlery, serving people in a particular order (see Mars and Nicod, 1984). Most work groups develop their own norms, and work groups in the hospitality industry are no exception. Several researchers have noted with varying degrees of explicitness that waiting staff have rules against poaching customers on colleagues' stations (cf. Bowey, 1976; Mars and Nicod, 1984). Chefs develop systems of norms that emphasize collective superiority and even hostility to other categories of staff, especially waiting staff (Chivers, 1973; Snow, 1981).

Group cohesion

Norms and their acceptance and application also contribute to the development of group cohesion, the extent to which the bonds between individuals draw them closer together in terms of the sharing of positive relations, amicability and commitment. Benefits of high levels of group cohesion can include high morale and productivity. It would be a mistake, however, to assume that cohesion is singularly *causal* of higher productivity. Other factors must be in place, such as a harnessing of group goals to those of the organization. Similar reservations may be recorded in respect of other benefits supposedly deriving from group cohesion, notably higher levels of individual job satisfaction and better coordination. Higher levels of job satisfaction may arise in group situations for reasons that are less than useful to the organization as a whole, e.g. achievements of a group that are good for the group but not for the organization. Similarly, a group may perform in a highly coordinated way but make little contribution to the success of the organization – indeed they may detract from it. The string section of a large orchestra may give an excellent performance at the expense of other sections, and ultimately the clarity and performance of the entire ensemble (a frequent complaint of music critics and concert-goers!).

Such reservations about the nature of group cohesion lead to consideration of disbenefits that arise from the close intermeshing of interests. One of the most important of these is implied in the previous paragraph, namely the extent to which high group cohesion can produce a level of autonomy of (group) interests that becomes self-serving. In other words, the group acquires such a strong identity that it no longer acts in the interests of the organization as a whole but in the interests of maintaining its own privileges. The interests of the group come to take priority over organizational priorities. Such a phenomenon can be evident in both formal and informal groups and may, in theory, be overcome by organizational strategies to ensure the greatest possible specification of individual and group responsibilities. In practical terms this could mean that, wherever possible, formal groups at least are constituted laterally within the organization, i.e. draw on the range of personnel across the divisions and departments of the organization to avoid the creation of 'power centres'. This can be extended to ensure that, as far as is practical, powerful decision-making groups within the organization are also constituted in this way.

Even so, it is difficult to avoid the growth of powerful groups in an organization entirely, especially if they are informally constituted pressure and interest groups. Related disadvantages arising from high levels of group cohesion include hostility to other groups in the organization (a factor dwelt upon earlier in the context of chefs and cooks) and the difficulties facing new individuals seeking to join a group. If a group is tightly knit, it may make it impossible for new members to be easily incorporated, causing distress to individuals and perhaps to the group (thereby diminishing group effectiveness). Bowey (1976) reports the case of high labour turnover among newly appointed waitresses in a restaurant she studied. Upon investigation by the manager, this was discovered to be attributable to the behaviour of established waiting staff, who in order to protect their own interests were making life difficult for new appointees by a general unpleasantness of demeanour. One aspect of the difficulties highly cohesive groups face in absorbing new members is that the very image of high cohesion has the effect of increasing perceptions of the group as (positively) exclusive and (negatively) cliquish, and in some instances increases the motivation of outsiders to join the group.

A final disbenefit of high group cohesion that should be considered is the extent to which it gives rise to resistance to change. The reactionary tendencies of established groups with high levels of self-interest are a problem that organizational leaders need to confront from time to time. The situation is most complex in the case of informal groups, where it is difficult to reorient the activities of any collective because they are not easily identifiable. Often where formal groups are identified as operating to the detriment of the organization, firm action is required, even to the extent of neutralizing the group. According to Mullins (1992), in a formal group context management can exert the necessary influence on groups during the 'norming' stage of their development with a view to ensuring that a group's development is in accordance with the goals of the organization.

Group conflict

A good deal has already been said about conflict in the hospitality industry. In group theory conflict is generally categorized under two broad headings: *intra-group* and *inter-group* conflict. Causes of intra-group (within group) conflict include differing individual perceptions of group objectives, breakdowns in communications between individual members of the group, external pressures on groups in the form of excessive demands from superiors in the wider organization, and changes in working practices engendered by a change in a group's tasks or the methods by which they are expected to perform those tasks. Conflict in the form of 'creative tension' within a group can be useful. It can 'clear the air' and alleviate stress and hostility within the group. At the most negative extreme, however, unresolved conflict within the group can lead to its effective breakdown. It is thus in the interests of the organization, and formal groups within it, to have mechanisms for the resolution of conflict that cannot be settled at the informal, inter-personal level.

Reasons for inter-group (between group) conflict have already been touched upon. It is worth additionally noting those sources of conflict that arise from within a group as a result of that group's dealings with others. First, formal groups within the organization are generally charged with tasks, whether routine or special, that require resources. This may lead groups to compete with one another for these resources, which may be financial (necessary to the – perceived – efficacy of the group in the performance of their tasks) through to physical resources (such as plant, premises and equipment) and human resources. Second, there may be demarcation disputes between groups, arising when there is a lack of clarity in an organization's intentions in respect of the goals it sets for groups, and the legitimacy or otherwise of a group's area of operations.

Although the analogy is not strictly appropriate, such conflict can be seen to have occurred in the trade-union movement during the 1960s and early 1970s in its approach to the hospitality industry. Despite an earlier agreement (which had seemingly been largely forgotten), the two main unions active in the industry, the GMB (General, Municipal, Boilermakers and Allied Trades Union) and the TGWU (Transport and General Workers' Union), competed for members in hotels and restaurants in a highly destructive way that resulted in industrial disputes and conflict between the unions. This was to a very large extent resolved in 1973, when the two signed a 'spheres of influence' agreement that effectively defined in what sectors and geographical areas each would recruit (see Wood, 1992, for a full account).

A final and related issue here concerns the inter-group conflict that arises when one group seeks to dominate another. In an organizational context this can involve attempts to strategically outmanoeuvre other groups in competition for resources, or in order to attempt neutralization of other groups in terms of their influence within the organization.

Moorhead and Griffin (1989, pp. 301–4) draw on Thomas (1976) and identify five main types of inter-group relations that may lead to conflict. *Avoidance* is where interaction between groups in an organization is unimportant and the groups concerned have incompatible goals. Relations between groups are thus characterized by avoidance, where attempts at interaction (requests for information, views, co-operation) are ignored or given a low priority. *Accommodation* is where certain groups in the organization have compatible goals but group interaction is not considered essential to the achievement of respective group goals. Relations here are usually amicable but do not lead anywhere. This may have potentially negative effects for an organization because the synergy that might be created by group cooperation is not realized. *Competition* is where groups' goals are incompatible but interaction is necessary to the goal attainment of each group. This leads to a competitive state that might be beneficial in motivational terms but may ultimately lead to conflict of the kind described earlier. *Collaboration*, as might be supposed, is where group goals are mutually compatible and interaction is required between groups for achievement of organizational missions. This requires that groups collaborate, but difficulties and potential conflict may arise when efforts are made to determine what programmes of action should be taken and what programmes each group should operate. Finally, *compromise* is where moderate interaction between groups is required but different groups' goals vary in their level of compatibility.

Shamir (1978) notes that in many hotels some departments behave as if other departments did not exist. This may be an instance of avoidance, as the seeming joint goals of waiting staff and chefs (to serve customers in restaurants) may be seen as a less amicable instance of accommodation. Behind this suggestion lies the point that, in theory at least, all organizations are to some extent directed towards the attainment of certain goals, and it is sub-goals or sub-routines that give rise to problems in achieving success at the wider level. This emphasizes the importance for management of *integrating* group functions in order to reduce the potential for conflict by clear specification of mechanisms and procedures for communication and accountability.

Group communications

Everyone communicates. Effective communication between people is important in organizations as in life in general. In its ideal form communication entails the exchange of information and the development of shared meaning. Of course communication or the lack of it is a form of power, and as much disinformation (whether deliberate or in the form of rumour, although neither category is mutually exclusive!) as information is a feature of communications. Similarly, the withholding of information can give individuals, groups and organizations certain competitive or personal advantages over others by virtue of 'doing them down'. Communication then can be viewed as a process of control.

In organizations the principal objectives of effective communication are largely institutional: to direct organizational members, to facilitate competent decision-making, and to articulate organizational goals. This formal communicative process is of course complemented by informal processes – 'grapevines'. Within organizations as a whole the process of communication is to some extent determined in form by organizational structure. In a highly bureaucratic 'pyramid' organization, where power and authority is concentrated at the top, formal communication tends to flow downwards. Organization structures as reflected in organization charts thus to some extent determine the appropriate channels for formal communication. On the assumption that all organizations to some extent comprise a variety of task groups, each contributing to the organizational mission, then communication processes in these groups may be regarded as important because they represent a microcosm of the organization as a whole. Four communicative relationships are important here, namely those between:

- Individuals in groups.
- Individuals and the wider organization.
- Different groups in an organization.
- Groups and the organization.

The second and fourth of these are important, because each individual has relations not only with 'the group' but directly to the organization through

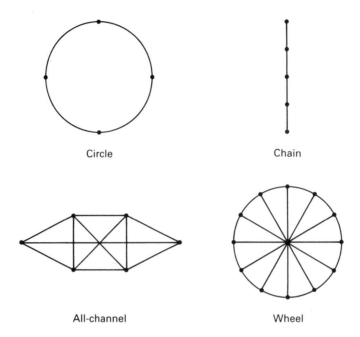

Figure 7.1   Group communication networks: circle, all-channel, chain and wheel

the chain of command. For example, persons may communicate with their supervisors or immediate managers for the performance of routine duties but have certain communications with other sections of the organization that are not always routed through superiors (the salaries office for payment; the personnel or human resource department in respect of contractual arrangements, reviews and appraisal). This process is mirrored in the relation a group has to the organization as a whole through its manager or supervisor. The interests, activities and performance of the group are communicated to those responsible for that group's tasks. In a similar way, communications between individuals in a group are mirrored in those that one group has with others in the organization. Here, differences arise in the latter depending on the formal responsibility/accountability channels. However, *informal* communication between groups may mirror intra-group communication patterns.

This raises an important point, namely that all but a small amount of communication in an organization is to some extent informal. Several different types of communication channel in small groups have been identified and each is illustrative of what may be formal communication (instituted as part of the group's reporting mechanisms) or informal communication (see Figure 7.1). Moreover, it is possible for one or more of these communication patterns to operate at any one time so that patterns of communication within a group vary.

In general it is held that each of these communication networks possesses a different quality of effectiveness. Thus the circle system is best suited to the gathering of a range of different opinions or information, the wheel for routine tasks, the all-channel system for complex tasks, and the chain for rapid communication where time/implementation margins are short. It should be emphasized at this point that each network implies prescribed communication along the channels indicated in Figure 7.1. The provenance of this view of communication networks is attributable among others to Alex Bavelos (Buchanan and Huczynski, 1985, pp. 164–5). In the circle each person communicates with the people on either side. In the wheel network communication flows between the centre and the people at the end of each 'spoke'. The all-channel network allows total freedom of communication and the chain allows communication with the person above and below (except of course at the extremes of the chain). It does not require a huge imaginative leap to work out that each of these networks may mirror a particular group or organizational structure, for example:

- The circle – common to task forces, committees and quality circles.
- The wheel – a typical work group where formal communication is between supervisor and subordinates.
- All-channel – informal groups or formal groups in highly creative organizations (information-dealing organizations; artistic organizations).
- The chain – typical bureaucratic organizations.

Moreover, Bavelas experimented with groups using each network and found that (Buchanan and Huczynski, 1985, p. 165; Moorhead and Griffin, 1989, pp. 576–7):

- Group leaders and committed group workers are generally identified by the centrality of their position in any network.
- The fastest method of communication is the wheel.
- Efficiency of communication reduces as it is decentred, i.e. where there is no central facilitator or communication leader.
- Satisfaction levels of group members were highest in the circle network because everyone took part in the communication process and felt they were being consulted.

Communication, then, is a complex process. Where informality assumes importance in the form of 'grapevine' communication, the process becomes more complex. Robbins (1992, p. 122) suggests that 75 per cent of the information carried on a grapevine in organizations is accurate and that rumours start not as 'titillating gossip' but because issues important and ambiguous in the eyes of organizational members and groups cause anxiety. This serves to re-emphasize the point that the distinction between formal and informal communication is one that is difficult to sustain in reality.

Group performance and effectiveness

As noted earlier, it is generally held that groups are *more* effective as collectivities and can achieve more than any one individual. This generalization invites a certain amount of critical attention. At the basic level of the work–task group, specialization and division of labour in a classic bureaucratic sense is rational for the organization if integration can be achieved. Similarly, if all levels of individual performance are enhanced by group performance, properly controlled, then it should be possible to make the best use of individual talents.

The very idea of 'group' has an ideological bent, however, in that in addition to making the division of tasks within an organization simpler to attain, groups are almost by definition easier to control than a loose connection of individuals. Reality intrudes further in that, because of individual differences and dispositions, there are always likely to be stronger and weaker group members. Groups are to some extent meant to alleviate this by playing to, utilizing and welding together individual strengths, a process of 'magnification', but as anyone who has been a member of a formal (or even informal) organizational group knows, notwithstanding the strength or weakness of the mechanisms of control exerted within the group, it is often the case that weaker individuals are 'carried', and a group's positive drive arises from only part of the group's membership.

The 'groupspeak' of organizational behaviour theory is thus to be treated with some caution. It is quite possible that, in emphasizing groupwork, exceptional *individual* talents are overlooked and that successes attributed to groups are in fact the achievement of one or more of a small number of individuals. Similarly, exceptional talents may be suppressed by groups. Even where emphasis is placed on formal group attainment, and incentives exist to encourage this, groups can tend towards an 'average' performance, as group norms exert a force on acceptable standards of behaviour and performance and drive down the threshold of the latter. Groups allow people to 'hide' from responsibility. Formal or tacit agreement in the shape of normative systems as to what is 'good' or 'bad' can frustrate outstanding performance and outstanding individuals. While this may all sound a little elitist, the main thrust of the argument here is to point out that groups have their downside and even the most effective mechanisms of monitoring and control cannot prevent slips into mediocrity.

It is ironic that in societies like the UK and USA, which promote the concept of individuality and individual abilities, so much emphasis is placed on the importance of groups as an effective means of achieving goals. The strategy in many organizations of setting up 'working parties', 'sub-committees', 'task forces' or similar bodies to probe particular problems is often a means of ensuring that decisions are deferred or change resisted. The world of organizations is an ambiguous one. Lip service at least is paid to the idea of recognizing individual talents, but many of an organization's activities are carried on in groups, often to familiar complaints about the excess of bureaucracy. The old aphorism (and its variants) that a camel is a horse designed by a committee is frequently recirculated in organizations, and reflects the uneasy relation between ideology and reality: in a free enterprise, individualistic culture, organizations cannot live with, nor live without, groups.

One thing is for sure, the necessity of groups to efficient organizational functioning means that group performance factors have received considerable attention. Factors affecting group performance may usefully be classified under three broad headings – membership variables, task variables and environmental variables (Lockwood and Jones, 1984, pp. 108–10).

Membership variables

Membership variables include group size, composition and status. There is no optimum *size* for a group. Over-large groups can increase communication difficulties and discourage some members from participating fully in group activities. Larger groups can, however, often command more resources within the organization, although they may be more bureaucratic, and thus precise control and coordination procedures are required to ensure effectiveness. Group *composition* may be an important issue in ensuring cohesion and effectiveness.

According to Moorhead and Griffin (1989, p. 273) groups are generally classified by whether they are homogeneous (group members are similar in ways essential to the work of the group) or heterogeneous (group members are different in ways essential to group performance). Homogeneous groups are viewed as particularly effective in dealing with simple, linear tasks requiring both speed and cooperation (the latter likely to arise out of the similar backgrounds of group members). Heterogeneous groups are held to be more appropriate to complex, collective tasks requiring creativity, where speed is not essential. *Status* of group members is important because within a group situation it is likely that those perceived as possessing a higher status will be able to exert greater control and influence over group members.

Task variables

Task variables include the nature of tasks (which are likely to influence the composition of the group in organizational leaders' decisions); the time required to perform those tasks (which may influence both the selection by organizational leaders of group members and constrain group development by the imposition of routines geared to rapidity of process); and the importance of the tasks to be performed by the group (which may determine selection of group members, the resources available to the group, and the level of support the group receives from the wider organization).

Environmental variables

Environmental variables include the nature of an organization's systems (which are bound to impinge upon every aspect of the group's activities); and the physical environment in which the group is expected to perform its tasks. It has been observed by Guerrier and Lockwood, 1989, that a major constraint on effective communication between members of a hotel management team is the fact that hotel managers' office accommodation tends to be inadequate.

Teams

One aspect of group performance which has received considerable attention in recent years is the emphasis placed by many organizations on 'teamwork'. Teamwork has become the war cry (or at least something of a mantra) of the 'new management' (Peters and Waterman, 1982).

Empirically, the difference between a group and a team is not easy to establish. There are similar difficulties at a theoretical level. Bennett (1991, p. 154) makes a useful point in this respect when he notes that a team is (i) a special sort of group; and (ii) while all teams are by definition groups, the reverse is not necessarily true.

What sort of group then *is* a team? The organizational behaviour literature is not as useful as it might be in helping to answer this question. In essence, a team is a group that evidences particularly cooperative synergy directed towards goal attainment (Moorhead and Griffin, 1989, p. 746); its defining characteristic is the *voluntary* coordination by group members of their activities to achieve group goals and objectives, while other important characteristics almost always in evidence are a high level of interdependency between members, a high level of group cohesion based on shared perceptions, extensive interaction between members, high levels of mutual support, and a willingness to interchange roles and share workloads (Bennett, 1991, p. 154). To this list, Drummond (1990, p. 237) adds that teams exhibit high levels of morale, mutual trust, respect and warmth, and extensive commitment and group determination. Further, *indicators* that a group is working as a team are high energy levels and high productivity, collectively superior to the efforts of individual team members.

Crudely, then, a team is a group *plus* enhanced interdependence and voluntarism, and a high 'feelgood' factor. The main theme underlying discussions of teams and teamwork in organizations is that organizational leaders can pursue courses of action that will increase the probability of groups becoming teams. For example, Drummond (1990, p. 237–8) writes:

> Three different types of teams can be developed. In a *process team*, each employee applies different skills towards the team's goal. For example, in a dining room, consider the different skills that the host or hostess, server, and cook all use to give the customer a good meal. In a *goal team*, each member works independently on the same task to meet a goal. At a hotel front desk, for instance, the clerks handle similar transactions aimed at satisfactorily checking guests in and out. In a *sequential team*, each employee depends in turn on another member's performing a particular function. For instance, in a fast-food restaurant, the counter worker must wait for the grill cook to prepare the food before filling the customer's order.

While Drummond's description of teams seems to vary little in its possible applications to groups in general, the main point at issue is the extent to which team-building is realistically possible as an organizational *attainment*.

In their study of building a hospitality team, Berger and Vanger (1986, p. 82) write 'In a hotel or restaurant, *teams* of employees will give the consistently superior service that pleases guests and makes the operation a winner, while individual "star" performers will make your service uneven'. Berger and Vanger add that teamwork is not created by physical proximity alone, and it is easy to mistake a group of individuals working *next* to one another for a team, where individuals work *with* each other. One thing is common to the approaches of both Drummond (1990) and Berger and Vanger (1986), namely the point that attempts at team-building often have to be conducted on already existing work (task) groups. Drummond (1990, p. 238) identifies four principal stages to team-building. The first is *diagnosis of team functioning*, which calls for assessment of how a group/team is operating at the present time, and Drummond offers a thirty-three point checklist to assessment with the diagnostic process. These can be happily reduced to seven broad headings:

- *Goals*. Are team goals matched to those of the organization, generally understood and shared by all members; and are methods for achieving goals agreed upon to the extent of giving rise to coordinated action to achieve them?
- *Roles*. Do team members understand one another's roles and do they value their own and others' roles?
- *Leadership*. Are there respected leaders and, if so, are they effective and are their styles of leadership appropriate to the team?
- *Participation*. Is participation in decision-making encouraged, and are all team members encouraged to participate, their views respected and reasons for non-participation explored and rectified?
- *Decisions*. Are decisions assessed and analysed for appropriateness? Are decisions implemented and followed up? Do all team members take responsibility for decisions.
- *Conflict*. Is conflict managed appropriately? What methods are used for preventing and controlling conflict?
- *Team standards*. Is there a team standard, i.e. a standard the whole team subscribes to as opposed to a range of individual standards?

The purpose of the above presentation of Drummond's 'diagnostic kit' as questions is intended to emphasize the point that a negative response to any of the questions is a likely indicator of an absence of 'team spirit'. It is the basis for rectifying an absence of 'teamness', and might be followed by the second stage of team-building – *introduction of the team-building concept*. This entails meeting with a group and exploring the issues summarized above with a view to creating a team context for the group. The voluntary participation of the group is an important ingredient in this stage of the team-building exercise. If a group is unwilling to listen, then a certain amount of cajoling may be necessary. A group cannot, however, be easily pressurized. If a group can be carried, the third stage of team-building is assessment of *current team functioning*, which demands an honest appraisal of current performance relative to team goals and individual concerns. The outcome of this process should be some kind of plan or strategy for creating/enhancing/improving a group's performance as a team. This is followed, finally, by *implementation and monitoring*, which in turn feeds back to diagnostic analysis of team performance.

On the basis of this model the key to successful team building is openness and honesty. Such an approach is not without its problems. As Berger and Vanger (1986) note, team-building may be defined as the process of creating trust and opening communication within a group, but it is necessary to secure the willing participation of all group members (who may feel threatened) and to display an openness that is sometimes regarded as inappropriate, e.g. in discussing individual employee weaknesses in front of peers. Nevertheless, if these problems can be overcome, it is maintained, productivity can be improved, inter-departmental conflict reduced (as a result of better understanding and cooperation between teams) and greater creativity stimulated.

Berger and Vanger place particular emphasis on this last point, suggesting that a cohesive team is likely to be more creative because of the 'risky shift' phenomenon, i.e. the process whereby groups and teams are more likely to take risks in decision-making than individuals would be likely to do alone. Of course increased creativity in decision-making is to be welcomed, but can have its disadvantages in that a tendency to take more risks can lead to teams taking the wrong risks. This needs to be taken into account in efforts at developing teams, and some balance to the creative potential for taking risks should be built into the management process.

In recent years there has been an increase in some sectors of the hospitality industry in the emphasis placed on teamwork, particularly as it relates to food service. This teamwork emphasis has itself often been linked to highly theatrical styles of performance in food service as, for example, with such chains as *TGI Friday's*. Gardner and Wood (1991) studied three such restaurants (all of different ownership) in depth. They found that teamwork was achieved primarily as a result of:

- Substantial training – no food service personnel were allowed to wait on table until they had completed a mixture of off-floor and on-the-job training.
- Careful selection of employees, with emphasis often placed on personality and disposition rather than technical skills (which were taught as part of training as necessary).
- Regular formal meetings of service personnel – at least once a day and sometimes twice a day – to review a performance.
- A small number of explicitly articulated rules of behaviour and procedure.
- Placing emphasis on relations with customers.
- Clear and open systems of performance rewards in addition to formal remuneration (these included bonuses and 'ratings', and in one organization the attainment of a particular rating allowing a staff member to have the pick of the shifts for a week).

It will be seen from the above list that far from the abstract list of issues raised by *theories* of team-building, in the organizations studied by Gardner and Wood (1991), team-building measures took the form of very practical measures to ensure success, most important of which were careful selection of employees (something the hospitality industry is often accused of failing to do properly), proper training and clear demarcation of roles and rules.

Summary

- Groups can be defined in a variety of ways, but all groups have a number of common features – individuals in groups influence each other, and share common interests and objectives, and groups satisfy individual and collective needs.

- The most common type of group found in an organization is the work or task group, where individuals are brought together for the performance of particular tasks.
- The task group is an example of a formal group. Organizations also have informal groups, which may be a powerful influence on the workings of the organization.
- Group development is an observable process, and organizational leaders can and must intervene in this process to ensure that a group's goals match those of the wider organization.
- Groups exhibit structures and systems that are often microcosms of the organization. These include systems of norms, communication structures and patterns of often institutionalized conflict. Managers need to be aware of these systems and how they operate in order to ensure that in groups developing identities of their own, the benefits of group working do not come to be outweighed by disbenefits.
- Teams are groups that exhibit exceptional synergy and cohesion but are directed towards meeting organizational goals in an explicit way. Teams may exhibit a higher level of cohesion and reciprocity among members and a greater informal affiliation between individuals in the team.

Discussion questions

1 What clear-cut differences (if any) exist between groups and teams? How might these differences be illustrated in the context of hospitality organizations?
2 Why might people be motivated to seek membership of a group?
3 Outline the factors that might generate conflict within groups, and suggest means by which such conflict can be ameliorated.
4 Is it reasonable to expect that team-building strategies will be effective in hospitality organizations when so many work tasks are undertaken in isolation and where, in some occupations, competition between workers is a fact of working life?

Part Three
Management and Organizations

8 Management and management careers in organizations

A good deal of effort has been expended on attempts to define both what management is and what managers do. Two 'ideal type' approaches to these questions can be identified. The first of these may be termed the 'prescriptive' model, in which management is defined in terms of extrapolating from personal experience or from some theoretical construct to determine prescriptions for effective management. At the same time as defining management, this approach defines what managers are supposed to do. The prevalent emphasis here is often a highly intuitive one, with little reference to systematic empirical data. There is a substantial market for these 'quick fix' approaches, as is witnessed by the many books published each year by businessmen (and occasionally businesswomen) and academics actively engaged in consultancy.

They are, however, being treated with increasing caution, for reasons that are not hard to discern. Most obvious is the fact that highly personalized 'whizz-bang' approaches to management often give only a partial view of management functions, and even then a very privileged one – that of male, white senior executives, who are able to get into print without too much fear of contradiction. The other most obvious objection to these approaches is that there are no universal prescriptions for good management: any one approach can only have the most limited applications in many organizations. Nevertheless, 'one right way' observations on good management remain popular, not least with managers themselves.

One of the most successful of these management books in recent years, Peters and Waterman's *In Search of Excellence: Lessons from America's Best Run Companies* (1982), written by two consultants with strong academic credentials, suggests that successful companies all have certain distinctive features in common (see Chapter 11). This may well be true, and Peters and Waterman offer a persuasive and valuable account of these features. It could be argued though that what is defined as 'successful' is what is accepted by entrepreneurs and managers as successful. Peters and Waterman base their work on, *inter alia*, interviews with such personnel, and their view is therefore one that reflects the prerogatives and prejudices of their respondents. A further criticism might be that in seeking to identify 'success factors' the authors could naturally be expected to find these factors. In other words, it is always relatively easy to find instances of beliefs that are strongly held – but this does not necessarily yield an effective balance of opinion nor mean that particular beliefs are 'true' or 'right' or hold firm for all circumstances and situations.

The second approach to the study of management may be termed the 'empirical'. The emphasis here is on building up a picture of what managers do by studying their activities. Over the past 30 years or so this approach has generated a huge literature illustrating major themes and issues across a range of organizations, allowing comparisons of the circumstances in which managerial work is undertaken. The fact that this body of literature is based on primary research does not automatically mean that many authors have not drawn prescriptive conclusions from their work as to what makes a 'good' manager. Such prescriptions abound, but have the advantage for the most part of being based on firm evidence.

In point of fact both approaches to management identified here are, as indicated, 'ideal types', i.e. very few single studies or 'guides' to management easily fit the rubric of either model described. The distinction is made in order to emphasize extremities in approaches to the study of management in organizations, and to highlight the danger of generalization. This is particularly true of the study of hospitality managers, whose activities have, in the main, only been closely scrutinized by researchers since the mid-1970s. This leads to consideration of a further important distinction between the two ideal types. It has been noted that it is implicit in the first of these that there are 'principles' of good management that may more or less be applied across the board. The second approach recognizes the essential contingency of management, that general rules, if they exist, must be adapted to the needs of particular industries and organizations. In the context of the hospitality industry this is important, because it is a crucial argument of many industrialists and educators in support of separate business training and education for hospitality managers that the hotel and catering sectors are radically different from other industries to the extent that managers require special skills.

Classical prescriptive approaches to management

It is not possible to consider all the classical prescriptive approaches to management that have been advanced over the years. The intention here is to give a flavour of these by selecting the better known ones for discussion.

Henri Fayol's system

One of the most widely circulated and influential of all prescriptions for effective management was that laid out by Henri Fayol (1841–1925), a French mining engineer, who saw management as comprising five distinct but related skills and areas of activity. These were:

- Forecasting and planning.
- Organizing.

- Commanding.
- Coordinating.
- Controlling.

These five activities were viewed as essential to organizational success. Managers had to *plan* for the future, they had to *organize* resources – human, technical and physical – to achieve this plan, then *'command'* the organization, i.e. put the plan into effect, while *coordinating* the action of the organization and *controlling* all these activities in an effective way.

Fayol spent most of his life as a manager in the engineering industry, and his general theory of management functions, if a little trite by contemporary standards, can be said to derive from first-hand experience of problems encountered by organizational leaders. Further to his five general functions of management, Fayol also proposed thirteen 'principles of management', which, as Pugh and Hickson (1989, p. 87), note 'have become part of managerial know-how'. These principles have indeed been influential and may briefly be summarized as follows.

- *The principle of division of labour and specialization* – to allow creation of individual expertise and higher productivity (see the discussion of Taylorism in Chapter 2).
- *Authority* – the right to command others in the organization and to be accountable (responsible) for issuing such commands and dealing with their consequences.
- *Discipline* – the right to discipline employees but also the requirement for managerial self-discipline in offering positive leadership and making justifiable decisions.
- *Unity of command* – employees should receive directions from only one source in order to avoid conflicting channels of command.
- *Unity of direction* – those engaged in similar work must have common goals and objectives, and these must relate to the goals of the enterprise in general.
- *Priority of the organization* – the organization must be put first and foremost by managers, and managers must lead by example in communicating this to other employees.
- *Remuneration* – payment should satisfy both the requirements of employees and managers.
- *Centralization and decentralization* – managers have to influence the degree of organizational structure in these terms according to the needs of the organization.
- *Order* – both materials and people should be properly ordered (organized), i.e. allocated to a particular physical place in order to improve control and monitoring.
- *Equity* – it is not sufficient to be fair, but fairness must be seen to be practised in managerial decision-making – organizational members must feel that decisions are just, and equitably applied.
- *Stability of tenure* – among management personnel, in particular, stability should be encouraged, as managers are expensive to train.
- *Initiative* – initiative should be encouraged, as it is a source of strength for the organization. Initiative should, however, be contained within a

communicative framework that restrains potential disruption to the organization.

- *Esprit de corps* – the creation of a spirit of teamwork, of harmony and collaboration is essential if divisiveness within the organization is to be avoided and unity of command and objectives is to be ensured.

The power of Fayol's prescriptions lies in the extent to which, though formally articulated in many organizational behaviour and management texts (and, through these, management education), they have been *informally* absorbed into management cultures. While the twentieth century has seen many management gurus (cynics might say they are now two-a-penny), the influence of Fayol's thought, in abstract terms, has probably been matched by only two others – Peter Drucker and Henry Mintzberg.

Peter Drucker

Peter Drucker, academic and consultant, has had a prolific output. Probably his most famous and influential book is *The Practice of Management* (1954). Drucker's emphasis is on the role of the manager in the organization. Management has two principal dimensions – the economic dimension and the time dimension. For managers, the first of these, 'the bottom line', is always the most important, but managers have to try to anticipate the future and make decisions on the basis of their predictions while at the same time assessing the potential consequences of such predictions on future organizational performance. Important in Drucker's analyses are the plurality of objectives of any organization. While there may be overarching mission statements (goals), achieving these objectives depends on making *choices* as to the methods most likely to lead to organizational success. This leads Drucker to be a major proponent of management by objectives (MbO).

Management by objectives remains an influential model or prescription for the conduct of management, and is much misunderstood. The essence of MbO is a kind of 'dictated consensus'. Management decides what is to be done but agrees, rather than dictates, objectives and targets with employees, ensuring that the latter are both responsible and accountable for achieving these. MbO, then, is, superficially at least, a participative middle-way means of managing people, directed towards positive performance through stability and consent. In setting objectives within the organization, management attains clarity of purpose and performance is made measurable. The objectives of the organization can be appraised as decisions are made, in that the part played by organizational members is extensive. Thus whether or not objectives are realistic can be more or less established during the decision-making process. The ultimate test of decisions is of course their outcome. The test of experience allows reflection as to success and failure, and modification of future decision-making processes on the basis of previous outcomes.

Management by objectives is not only intended for application to the 'real world' performance of the organization, but to the performance of individuals, groups and divisions within an organization. Its potential benefits lie in the extent to which it is highly focused upon:

- Major areas of organizational activity.
- Expectations of individual employees in contributing to these areas of activity.
- Supplying targets for attainment.
- Identifying constraints on goal attainment and adjusting expectations accordingly.
- The 'real world' of organizational potential in respect of determining what is or is not possible within a given context or timescale.

Several criticisms can be levelled against MbO. In a general context Drummond (1990, p. 95) notes that in placing emphasis on the attainment of objectives, little is learned (or taken into account) about the nature of individual performance or the strategies employed by individuals to achieve organizational objectives. To a great extent many objectives have a certain unquantifiable, impractical element in the form of external processes and events over which individuals in organizations (or organizations themselves) have little control. Drummond illustrates this in the hospitality context by reference to achieving higher hotel occupancies. Whatever sales activity might be undertaken, a horse can be led to water but it is not always possible to make it drink. However good a sales pitch, it is not possible to force people to stay in a hotel! Mullins (1992, pp. 124–5) notes that MbO has had little impact on the hotel and catering industry, and lists certain criticisms and limitations of MbO. Close scrutiny of these hints at the reasons for lack of application of MbO in hospitality organizations. For MbO to succeed, Mullins suggests, certain conditions must be met. These include:

- Full commitment of top management to MbO.
- Good superior–subordinate relations and genuine staff participation in MbO.
- A commitment to long-term complex objectives over easy short-term objectives.
- Sophisticated performance standards and appraisal systems.

As far as the hospitality industry is concerned, the *ad hoc* nature of management and the unpredictability of demand, when combined with high levels of labour instability (see Chapter 1), can mean that the human and financial cost of introducing MbO is, from managements' point of view, simply not worth it. Further, there is evidence to suggest that management styles in the hospitality industry are in the main disinclined to be participative (see 'Management in hospitality organizations', p. 109, and Chapters 9 and 10). Instead, managers see themselves as the major source of authority. Moreover, the nature of demand for hospitality services means that unit managers tend to focus primarily on short- and medium-term objectives rather than on the long term. Similarly, the absence of a highly developed personnel function and personnel procedures means that implementation of MbO on a systematic basis in hospitality organizations would present administrative problems and costs of dubious benefit to the organization as a whole.

Managerial roles

An important link between legislative approaches to management, such as those offered by Fayol and Drucker, and empirically based studies of what managers actually do is the work of Henry Mintzberg (Mintzberg, 1973), who examined possible and actual managerial roles in organizations. Like Drucker, he was mainly concerned with top managers, though his subsequent analysis has been widely generalized, despite the original model proposed being derived from a limited study of only five chief executives.

According to Mintzberg, managerial roles can be grouped into three broad categories: inter-personal, informational and decisional roles.

Interpersonal roles

According to Mintzberg, there are three principal interpersonal roles: the figurehead role, the leader(ship) role and the liaison role. The *figurehead role* combines formal and symbolic authority: managers represent the organization to the outside world, they perform necessary ritual and legal duties, e.g. the signing of documents, and they have an iconic role within an organization, representing to organizational members the (often distant) embodiment of the organization's mission and values. The *leadership role* is clearly highly significant and comprises responsibility (again, sometimes abstract and indirect) for determining the strategy and direction of the organization and for the motivation of subordinates. The *liaison role* is the one managers fulfil in maintaining lateral relationships within their own organization, e.g. hotel unit general managers meeting their peers, and outside it. Liaison with non-organizational members can be with potential clients, or at very senior levels with people from other institutions such as government or the media. At a local level, unit managers of a hospitality business may belong to employer or professional organizations that bring together people from competing businesses in a social or supportive context, e.g. branches of the British Hospitality Association or the Hotel, Catering and Institutional Management Association, HCIMA.

Informational roles

Informational roles are those in which managers must engage in order to ensure that information or data of benefit to the organization is gathered, disseminated and acted upon. The *monitor role* entails managers keeping their 'ears to the ground' in respect of both internal and external developments that bear on the running of the organization. This is a role that is often delegated internally, through subordinates or special categories of personnel such as executive secretaries. In British government, for example, most ministers have in their parliamentary private secretaries, other MPs who keep them abreast of political feeling as well as performing minor administrative services. The *dissemination role* requires managers to communicate information gathered to others within or outside the organization. This information may not always be factual: often senior managers will wish to pass on views, opinions or less tangible information about how they see the organization, or some aspect of it, developing. In this way culture and values are disseminated from the top down, and the ethos of senior organizational leaders passed on. Finally, the use of the gendered term 'spokesman' reflects the unenlightened era in which Mintzberg's work first appeared. The *spokes(person) role* is similar in quality to that of figurehead in so far as managers formally represent themselves as the embodiment of the organization in communicating information to other (more) senior organizational members or to external agencies with which the organization has relations.

Decisional roles

Managers make decisions. The basis for so doing is their formal status and authority. Mintzberg delineates three principal decisional roles. The *entrepreneurial role* involves analysing the environment for opportunities and changing or encouraging the organization towards exploiting these opportunities. At lower levels of the management structure the entrepreneurial role may be confined to non-strategic operational decisions (such as reducing the number of staff required on a particular shift in a hotel, owing to low occupancy). In the *disturbance handler* role managers deal with unpredictable and usually disruptive events that bear on the functioning and performance of the organization. The *resource allocator* role is perhaps the most important of all the decisional roles. Managers must decide how the organization's resources are to be utilized, or at least how those resources that fall within a manager's purview are to be disposed of. These include financial, human, technical, property and equipment/capital resources. This process of allocation relates closely to the *negotiator role*, in that managers often have to negotiate with, as well as command, others. From within the organization there will be many (often competing) demands for quantities and combinations of resources. Resources are usually finite and managers have to arbitrate between these competing claims as well as negotiate with groups and individuals over their demands.

Management in hospitality organizations

Mintzberg accepts that his typology of managerial roles is relatively mechanistic and that it is impossible, in reality, to pigeonhole separate role functions. Thus all decision role performances are at one and the same time also role performances with informational and interpersonal elements. As a strategy for understanding the range and depth of managerial work, however, Mintzberg's scheme is a valuable tool and one that has been highly influential in studies of management in the hotel and catering field. Some of these studies are examined briefly later in this section. At this point, however, it is appropriate to consider some of the major characteristics of management in hospitality organizations as revealed by contemporary research, a good deal of which has been devoted to identifying similarities and differences between management in hospitality organizations and in other industries. There is little doubt that in many cases the management of hospitality organizations exhibits distinctive and perhaps unusual features compared to other forms of management, though it is important that these are not exaggerated, since the observation that management will differ according to context in at least some respects is a more obvious statement than is generally recognized. The main features of hospitality management can be summarized as follows.

First, hospitality managers come to the industry via a range of career routes (Baum, 1989). Formal educational qualifications (a diploma or degree, for example) are only one such route. It is still possible for managers to rise through the organizational structure without any formal qualifications whether they enter the industry as a management trainee or begin in the industry in some lower-grade occupation. Further, in the small firms sector, proprietor–managers often enter the industry after a career in some other area. This makes for considerable variety and quality of managerial expertise in the hospitality sectors. An important observation is made by Riley and Turam (1988) to the effect that in respect of managerial career paths, time spent obtaining a vocational qualification in the hospitality industry makes little long-term difference to career prospects relative to time spent working in the industry. This may be important to the motivation of managers who have followed the former route. If they cannot see long-term value in their qualifications, they may decide to leave the industry.

Second, there is some evidence to suggest that an early commitment to a career in hospitality management ensures long-term commitment – a variation on the 'catch them young' approach. This view is supported by the research of Baum (1989) and Guerrier (1987). What is unclear is whether 'early commitment' in this context means starting straight into the industry. What is certain is that hospitality managers for the most part obtain their appointments at a relatively early age compared to their counterparts in other industries. This might not be quite the 'triumph' it appears (at least in hotels), since, as Guerrier (1987) implies, via means of a naval metaphor, many hotel industry companies 'rank' their units, however informally, as if they were a fleet of ships, with some units more prestigious than others. A young manager is perhaps likely to achieve unit management status in a smaller, less prestigious unit and graduate after this training to bigger and more prestigious units.

This leads, third, to consideration of the point that for managers to progress within a company, a high degree of mobility is required. A corollary of this is that smaller companies with fewer opportunities for progression to sizeable units with higher levels of responsibility and higher rewards 'force out' junior managers, who seek these opportunities elsewhere. Such mobility can also be encouraged by the fact that in their early careers trainee and junior managers often act as 'dogsbodies', filling gaps as required, and for limited rewards. This can lead either to demotivation or it can increase the motivation of managerial trainees to achieve more senior positions as rapidly as possible.

The fourth and final point concerns the content of hotel managers' jobs and to some extent returns the discussion to Mintzberg's view of managerial roles. In a piece of work predating Mintzberg's study, Nailon (1968) found that, relative to managers in other industries, *hotel* managers (a) undertook a much wider range of activities than their counterparts, (b) saw much less of their peers than managers in other sectors, (c) spent less time alone because of their interaction with customers and work in the supervision of staff, and (d) tended to engage in more or less continuous monitoring of their unit. Other research has confirmed this view of the hotel manager as preoccupied with operational matters and preferring a 'meeting and greeting' role to that of 'flying a desk'. Indeed the 'being there' style of management is confirmed as a normative aspect of hotel culture and may be reasonably extended to include hospitality organizations other than hotels.

For the most part, research into the nature of hospitality management has been of an information gathering kind – finding out what managers actually *do*. The application or 'testing' of management theories in an organizational behaviour context has been fairly limited, but several studies have sought to assess the relevance of Mintzberg's model of managerial roles to hospitality managers. Ley (1980) observed the role activities of seven American managers in a single hotel company and classified these according to Mintzberg's schema. Following this, the company's head office's ratings of each manager were obtained. These revealed that of the seven managers:

- Two were regarded as highly effective.
- Three were regarded as effective.
- Two were regarded as less effective.

These gradings were compared to Ley's own Mintzberg-role classifications and Ley argues that the highly effective managers allocated *less* time to leadership than the two *less* effective managers and *more* time than the less effective managers to entrepreneurial activities. Ley's study is an imperfect one because there is no necessary correlation between his own finding that the entrepreneurial managers scored better and the rating given by the managers' head office. However, given that the hospitality industry is, for economic reasons, one in which margins are often tight, and given the cultural emphasis placed on entrepreneurship in Western industrial life, the results are at least suggestive.

A study of related interest is that by Arnaldo (1981), which secured 194 responses from hospitality managers who self-classified their activities at Arnaldo's request according to Mintzberg's model, and supplied details of both the amount of time spent on each role and the importance they believed should be attached to each role. In terms of the *time* allocated the most important roles were leader, *disseminator* and monitor, while in terms of the *importance* attached to individual roles the most important were leader, *entrepreneur* and monitor. The difference on the time/importance dimensions may be attributable to the difference between the operational realities that faced the managers and the perceived value of each of the roles. Thus, while the leading/monitoring roles were important in both dimensions, managers' desire to be entrepreneurial may to some extent have been thwarted by the day-to-day demands of running their organizations. Self-perception is clearly important here and variation in responses to questions about role performance must be expected. Shortt (1989), in a study of hospitality managers in Northern Ireland, found that, together with leader and entrepreneur, the role of disturbance handler was regarded as most important.

Managers' perceptions of the importance of particular roles are almost bound to vary with context. It might be argued that Mintzberg's framework was, in any case, not intended for unrefined use on anything but the most senior organizational decision-makers.

The differing context of managerial work is an issue very much to the fore in a research report by Ferguson and Berger (1984, p. 30). They observed nine restaurant managers using a modified version of Mintzberg's schema to record activities and come to the important conclusion that:

> Mintzberg described executives' activities as brief, fragmented, and reactive. The restaurant operators' activities in this study seem even further from the textbook description of a planner, organizer, coordinator, and controller than did those in the Mintzberg sample. Planning seems to have been eclipsed by reacting; organizing might be better described as simply carrying on; coordinating appears more like juggling; and controlling seems reduced to full-time watching.

Ferguson and Berger found that restaurant managers spent an enormous amount of time on a variety of contacts – telephone calls, unscheduled and scheduled meetings, and 'tour' meetings (those initiated as a result of touring the unit). For each hour of a normal working day, there were, on average, ten such contacts. The restaurant managers' time was divided as follows:

- Telephone calls – 13 per cent.
- Tours – 6 per cent.
- Unscheduled meetings – 35 per cent.
- Scheduled meetings – 29 per cent.
- Desk sessions – 17 per cent.

While the last two of the categories above suggest a degree of structure to managers' activities, Ferguson and Berger (1984, p. 31) argue that the first three 'suggest reacting, persevering, watching, and in the extreme case, managing by crisis'.

None of this invalidates Mintzberg's analysis but points to the variability of managerial roles in different industrial contexts, a view partially confirmed by Hales and Nightingale (1986) but in the context of differences across sectors of the hospitality industry. The work of Ferguson and Berger (1984) also reinforces the earlier observation about the peripatetic nature of hospitality management work. The mobility and reactiveness of managers in their units is mirrored in the mobility required for career advancement in the industry. Clearly, then, managerial 'activity' – in an almost physical sense – is a cultural norm in the hospitality industry, and responsiveness to operational requirements is deemed a priority. As Ferguson and Berger imply, this represents a considerable deviation from the 'classical' image of the manager as a strategic choice-maker. However, the behaviour of hospitality managers is reinforced by a supportive framework of norms and values that militates against serious questioning of such behaviour, as studies of managerial effectiveness reveal.

Managerial effectiveness

In their study of managerial role sets, Hales and Nightingale (1986, p. 9) found that:

> Senior/head office staff expectations of unit managers seem to be predominantly focused on tasks, rather than activities, upon what the unit manager should achieve rather than what he should actually do...and reflect a concern for broad organisational objectives in the areas of standards, customers, staffing and finance.

To some degree, this observation can be interpreted as meaning that unit managers in hospitality organizations are left to get on with the job in the manner they deem fit, provided they achieve the required results. There is much truth in this statement, and unit managers in the industry do have considerable latitude in the running of their units. As Umbreit (1986, p. 56) puts it:

> Traditionally, the hotel industry has had a strong operational orientation with concern primarily focused on short-term results. Hotel managers have been evaluated on profitability measures and control of expenses. Additional criteria, if any, have included a list of key traits not necessarily related to job performance.

Umbreit argues that such assessments are too limited, because they do not identify the managerial actions and activities that contribute to the attainment of targets (or otherwise), while tending to assume that the targets themselves (profitability, cost control) are all within the influence of the manager when in point of fact external influences may limit the performance of even the most competent manager. By failing to develop behavioural criteria for the assessment of managers, Umbreit argues, companies are in danger of losing competitive edge because they do not ensure the supply of knowledge necessary to effective decision-making. What Umbreit is pointing to, though implicitly, is the extent to which the *ad hoc* management of hospitality industry units is mirrored in the behaviour of head offices towards unit managers. Using a complex research methodology, including the participation of around sixty hotel managers, Umbreit developed seven principal performance dimensions for hotel managers, reflecting, in his view, some of the concerns of those respondents studied by Ley (1980) and Arnaldo (1981), discussed earlier and relating to the over-emphasis placed by senior organizational personnel on financial and cost criteria measures of performance. The seven dimensions Umbreit evolved were:

- The handling of guest complaints and the promotion of guest relations.
- Development of marketing strategy and monitoring of sales programmes.
- Communication with employees.
- The motivation of subordinates and modification of behaviour of staff where appropriate.
- The implementation of policy, the delegation of responsibility and decision-taking.

- The control of operations and the maintenance of product standards.
- The handling of personnel responsibilities within the unit or organization.

In a subsequent report Umbreit and Eder (1987) examine the subjectivity of these behavioural dimensions and discuss the ways in which they may be harnessed to 'objective' outcome measures of performance. Again using an active sample of hotel managers, the authors developed a list of such measures managers themselves felt they ought to be assessed against. The fourteen objective measures identified were:

- Guest comments – on product experience cards.
- Market share attained – the percentage of room nights achieved by a hotel relative to the total available in the market.
- Room nights sold – in a given period.
- Reduction of labour turnover – in a given period compared to a previous period.
- Budget control – the extent to which budgets are achieved and income and expenditure reconciled.
- Food and beverage profit attainment.
- Room profit attainment.
- Employee complaints and grievances – the extent to which these are reduced in a given period relative to a previous period.
- Training attainments of employees – the number of employees achieving completion of training courses in a given period.
- Collection of receivables.
- Number of leadership positions held in the wider community by the manager.
- Hotel ratings – by independent organizations.
- Health and safety record – reduction of accidents in a period relative to earlier periods.
- Adherence to productivity standards by employees.

There can be little doubt that within many hospitality organizations measures of the kind outlined by Umbreit are increasing in importance in the assessment of managers, partly as a result of the development of human resource management philosophies (see Chapter 12). At the same time, however, the culture of the relative independence of unit managers remains strong, as do performance criteria of a more (financially) measurable quality. 'Bottom line' measures of success seem likely to remain dominant in the future. The hospitality industry has a track record of conditioned indifference to personnel administration and excessive bureaucracy, which, particularly in human resource areas, is resisted by hospitality managers at all levels (Aslan and Wood, 1993). Measures almost unavoidably likely to increase pressure and stress on managers cannot be expected to be welcomed with open arms. The individualistic culture of hospitality management is not only a social phenomenon but a social–psychological one, in which much of the attraction of managerial positions lies in the degree of latitude allowed to achieve wider organizational goals and the extent to which managers derive individual – psychological – gratification and pride from devising ways of attaining such goals.

The personality of hospitality managers

Much of what has been discussed in this chapter has a clear bias towards managers in chain organizations. The idea of a hospitality management 'personality' has much wider implications, however. At the anecdotal level, there is good reason to believe that managers in hospitality organizations differ in personality from managers in other organizations. To cope with the wide range of demands, the stress and long hours requires qualities that point to a particular personality being 'attracted' to the hospitality industry. The problems with this view in general have been addressed elsewhere (Wood, 1992a). Of central importance are the problems inherent in separating the social from the psychological, the learned from the apparently innate. In other words, it is to achieve the almost impossible in separating the cultural qualities of organizations that give rise to particular forms of behaviour, attitudes and values, from the values acquired before exposure to hospitality industry employment.

A further difficulty is, as Mullins (1992, p. 127) notes, that research into the personality of managers reveals 'little to explain the nature of leadership or to help in the training of future leaders'. It is possible to go further than this in stating that most management-personality studies in a hospitality industry context have placed too great an emphasis on self-reporting in assessing personality. Thus Worsfold (1989) found that, compared to other managers, hotel managers exhibited greater assertiveness and imagination and placed much emphasis on social skills. What remains unclear is (*a*) how exactly these dimensions are being measured; (*b*) whether, in personality terms, such traits convert into action; (*c*) whether the factors mentioned are the product of exposure to the culture of the industry or resultant from earlier influences on personality formation; and (*d*) whether in themselves the personality traits observed are in some way more worthy than those observed elsewhere. A similar problem is reflected in a study by Stone (1988), who, *inter alia*, found hotel managers to be more assertive, competitive, stubborn, spontaneous, cynical and practical. These are all qualities that, from the earlier discussion, can be seen to be prized in the hospitality industry, i.e. they are very much a feature of the industry's management culture, and legitimate surprise might be expressed at *not* finding hospitality managers possessing such 'qualities'.

One of the most interesting studies of the personality aspects of hospitality managers (specifically, hotel managers) was undertaken by Shaner (1978), using a scale of values that differentiated between terminal values (goals that a person seeks to attain) and instrumental values (forms of behaviour designed to achieve terminal values). Using earlier national data derived from administering the test to a large sample, Shaner invited respondents to complete the same exercise, thus facilitating comparisons between the national survey data and that derived from the hotel sample. For each set of values, terminal and instrumental, eighteen items were listed, and respondents invited to rank these. Only the top five in each category need concern the present discussion.

In respect of instrumental values there were relatively few differences. The hotel managers rated honesty, ambition, responsibility, capability and broad-mindedness as the most important instrumental values: the earlier national sample reversed the second and third of these in order and maintained the rank of the first and fifth. The only significant difference was with the 'capability' variable, which the national sample ranked ninth – its fourth value being forgivingness. Here, then, the action-oriented, activity-centred values of the hospitality manager once again becomes apparent. The largest differences occurred on the terminal-values ranking. Here, the hotel managers ranked, one to five, a sense of accomplishment, family security, self-respect, wisdom, and happiness as the most important terminal conditions. The national sample, in contrast, ranked, one to five, 'a world at peace', family security, freedom, equality, and self-respect, exhibiting a quite substantial difference.

The real interest of Shaner's study lies in the extent to which, while not directly concerned with personality, his data do seek to address a range of general phenomena, of general values, and compare the performance of different groups accordingly. This does not necessarily make the data more reliable but it does highlight the need to avoid narrowing the variables measured to those that apply only in a managerial context. It is also a highly suggestive study, indicating that there is considerable scope and potential for further studies of personality and personality-related factors in the study of hospitality managers.

Summary

The nature of hospitality management is a fascinating topic. What is clear from the review in this chapter is that hospitality management appears, in the broadest sense, to be less systematic, more creative, more reactive and less predictable than other forms of management. The reasons for this lie mainly in the culture of the industry, and particularly in management culture. The key issues appear to be as follows:

- Approaches to the study of management can be broadly grouped into those that unilaterally legislate for broad principles of 'good' management and those that approach the nature of management from the perspective of studies of managerial activity.
- So-called classical pronouncements on principles of management have been very influential on managerial behaviour, often being incorporated into management cultures through education.
- One of the most influential of prescriptive theories is Mintzberg's conception of managerial roles, which has been quite thoroughly applied in several studies of management in the hospitality industry.
- Hotel and catering management differs from other forms of management in that hotel and catering managers tend to be more active, concern themselves more with operational matters, and require a high degree of mobility to ensure career advancement.
- Research is generally agreed that hospitality managers spend much of their time interacting with others, particularly staff and guests. This is regarded as normal for the industry, and a form of behaviour that is generally rewarded. Several commentators have suggested, however,

that the 'hands on' style is not necessarily positive and may be detrimental to both effective strategic management and the engagement of effective operational control (through assuming too great a responsibility for such operation and failing to delegate).

Discussion questions

1 Consider how 'management by objectives' might be applied to the operative workforce in a hospitality organization. What changes would it be necessary to implement to current industry practices for MbO to be a success?
2 Identify the main elements present in the training and early career development of hotel managers, and outline the advantages and disadvantages of such development in the light of the relatively early age at which hotel managers gain senior positions.
3 Outline a policy for assessment of the effectiveness of managers in at least three different types of hospitality organization. Why might criteria of managerial effectiveness vary between sectors of the hospitality industry?
4 How different is the work of hospitality managers from that of managers in other industries?

9 Leadership

In many ways leadership (or at least the quest to define, study and teach it) can be described as the Holy Grail of organizational behaviour theory. As with motivation (see Chapter 10), much effort has been directed towards discovering what it is, without any outstanding success. The benefits to be derived from identifying the magic ingredients of successful leadership are clear in so far as they could, in theory, be encouraged and inculcated through training. Unfortunately, the question 'What makes a good leader?' has resisted simple answers. Leadership is a complex phenomenon made more complex by the fact that any judgement as to what makes a 'good' leader is necessarily subjective and can therefore be only arrived at consensually.

This is closely reflected in attempts to define leadership. Definitions are necessary for proper study, yet how can proper study be made if definition of the phenomenon under scrutiny is problematic or even impossible? The question mirrors a basic philosophical and methodological problem, in that a phenomenon must be defined by adducing its qualities and yet its qualities (in this case, those of leadership) can only be identified through its definition. To a large extent therefore it has been necessary in the study of leadership to operationalize definitions of the phenomenon and proceed accordingly. Common in contemporary approaches is the definition adopted by Moorhead and Griffin (1989, p. 322), who argue that leadership is both a *process* and a *property*. Thus, as a process, it is generally accepted that leadership involves the use of non-coercive influence to direct and coordinate people. As a property, leadership is a quality attributed to those who appear able to exert such influence successfully.

The limitations, and indeed the circularity, of such definitions are clear to see. The key to unravelling them lies in two observations: first, that leadership is non-coercive (the qualities of leadership, whatever they may be, are articulated without force); and, second, that leadership is not simply management. Managers can direct subordinates through the use of formal power and authority but this is not necessarily leadership. A manager is not always a leader. It is with this point in mind that one of the main problems with all leadership theories is thrown into relief, namely the implicit (sometimes explicit) view that leaders necessarily possess some extraordinary qualities that create a degree of voluntariness among followers, i.e. if leadership as a concept is to be rendered meaningful, then to be adjudged a 'good' leader (and there are no others), there must be willing followers.

In arguing this way attention must be directed towards the 'measurement' of leadership. If leadership *is* a process *and* a property, as described above, then logical identification or definition of a person as a leader must be simultaneous with the definition of the qualities of leadership (the components of 'influence') and with the measurement of leadership (that acts of leadership have been performed). A difficulty lies in adopting too low level a definition of leadership, for if organizational leadership is not necessarily the same as managerial power and authority (and most commentators are at least agreed that it is not), then it must be inherently distinctive. The problem then becomes one of differentiating between these two, which is a question ultimately of measurement. In this context measurement is not necessarily some unit of account, some numeric value. Rather, measurement is a problem primarily of comparison, of degree (and imprecise degree at that), of comparing leaders to non-leaders.

The issue is confused further by the widely accepted view that leadership may be formal or informal. Formal leadership is normally equated with managers as leaders, i.e. individuals who are both, and informal leadership with leaders who have little or no managerial power but who nevertheless are able to successfully influence others. With this and the other issues raised above in mind, the remainder of this chapter examines some key approaches to the study of leadership. In so doing a sceptical view is adopted. Organizational behaviour texts tend to recite the litany of leadership theories and conclude by saying that no single approach is adequate to the definition or characterization of leadership. They also give the impression that no combination of these theories is adequate to the task. Students of organizational behaviour are thus entitled to enquire as to the purpose of studying leadership. Indeed Robbins (1992, pp. 151–2) makes a similar point:

> Leadership may not always be important. Data from numerous studies collectively demonstrate that, in many situations, whatever behaviors leaders exhibit are irrelevant. Certain individual, job, and organizational variables can act as substitutes for leadership, negating the formal leader's ability to exert either positive or negative influence over subordinate attitudes and effectiveness.

The response to this is to point to the fact that in most industrial (and increasingly non-industrial) organizations, however limited real understanding may be, leadership qualities are believed to exist, and to reside in an individual's personality. Paradoxically it is also believed that leadership qualities may be acquired. Questions about leadership often figure in selection interviews, too. So, apart from the intrinsic intellectual enjoyment to be derived from academics performing intellectual cartwheels, the value in studying and understanding leadership lies in the extent of people's beliefs about the abstract and physical existence of 'leadership' as a phenomenon.

Trait theories

The earliest theories of leadership were so-called trait theories. The rationale for these relied on identifying 'leaders' and then seeking to identify the *intrinsic* qualities of leadership. Crudely, but largely accurately, the implication of trait theories was that leaders are born, not made. Accordingly, in identifying and measuring leadership traits, other leaders could be identified. The overtones of eugenics in this approach still has popular appeal. The idea that leaders are born rather than made accords with the sentiments of many in the community at large. It is also an approach that discourages judgemental or critical approaches to leadership. It is not necessary, following trait theories, to like or approve of leaders, leaders 'just are'.

The dangers inherent in such an approach are evident. At a theoretical level, it is necessary in accepting a trait approach to acknowledge leaders as leaders, warts and all. At a practical level, it means classifying the likes of Churchill, Gandhi, Hitler, Mussolini, Stalin, Napoleon, Margaret Thatcher and Idi Amin – and any number of other people broadly accepted as 'leaders' – under the same heading. In short, it is an acceptance of definitions of leadership qualities that takes no cognizance of how those qualities are put to use. At a more fundamental level, the results of trait research often led to long lists of traits, meaningless in any practical sense and often riddled with contradictions. As Moorhead and Griffin (1989, p. 325) somewhat amusingly put it:

> ...the results of many studies were inconsistent...some found that effective leaders tended to be taller than ineffective leaders, while others came to the opposite conclusion. Some writers even suggested leadership traits based on body shape, astrological sign or handwriting characteristics!

Behavioural approaches

Trait theories have not entirely withered on the vine. The successors to trait conceptions of leadership in purely historical terms are a range of theories normally grouped under the 'behavioural' heading. As might be imagined, the direction of this research was to examine what types of behaviour were most commonly associated with leaders. If trait theories were concerned primarily with leadership as a property, then behavioural theories were concerned with leadership as process. Both types of theory, however, were concerned with isolating what were believed to be universal characteristics of leadership, i.e. characteristics that would apply to all leaders.

The Ohio and Michigan studies

During the 1940s and 1950s studies into leader behaviours were undertaken at the Universities of Ohio and Michigan, USA. At Ohio, researchers administered questionnaires to subordinate personnel in military and industrial organizations with the aim of assessing their perceptions of leaders. Management–leadership behaviour, it was claimed, could be accounted for along two dimensions – *initiating structure* and *consideration*. Initiating structure is where leaders closely define their own role and that of subordinates in order to achieve goals through precise task allocation and the setting of performance standards. Consideration embraces such factors as the trust and respect leaders show for subordinates' status, satisfaction and general well-being.

A major conclusion of these studies was that individuals who rated 'high' on both dimensions tended to achieve higher levels of subordinate performance and contentment than did individuals who exhibited other combinations of high/low ratings. However, this was not always the case, and 'leaders' with high/high ratings were often found to direct groups that exhibited on occasions high absenteeism and low job satisfaction. In other words, the variability of outcomes suggested that a high rating in initiating structure and consideration was not a sufficient basis to identify universally effective leadership.

These findings were to some extent confirmed by the Michigan studies (Bryman, 1992). Here also, two main dimensions of leadership behaviour were constructed as a result of interviews with all levels of personnel in both high- and low-productivity work groups. The two categories devised here were seen as polar extremities of a single scale. They were *employee-oriented* and *task-* (or production-) *oriented* approaches to leadership. Leaders who were employee-oriented demonstrated concern for interpersonal relations and employee welfare, whereas task-oriented leaders emphasized technical and organizational dimensions of group behaviour. Unsurprisingly, the Michigan researchers claimed that employee-centred leaders were more effective, and associated with groups that exhibited high productivity and job satisfaction.

The managerial grid

For such a limited instrument, the managerial (later leadership) grid developed originally by Blake and Mouton (1964) has been done to death as a means of describing styles of leadership in the tradition of behavioural research. It is not the intention to repeat the process here. Essentially, the grid is a square divided into eighty-one smaller squares by means of a nine-point scale on each of the vertical and horizontal axes. The vertical axis runs from 1 at origin to 9 and represents 'concern for people', whereas the horizontal axis represents 'concern for production'. According to the authors, each square in the grid represents a particular management/leadership position represented by coordinates (1,1 being the lowest and 9,9 the highest). The antecedents of the model can be clearly seen in the Ohio and Michigan studies. It is a relatively limited model, exhibiting the same problems as those studies, namely the idealization of leadership behaviour (emphasizing what might be rather than what is) and a tendency to reduce leadership to a set of factors of supposedly universal application articulated in statements about the types of management that might be found at various points of the grid.

Contingency theories of leadership

Trait and behavioural models of leadership lack a concern with situational factors. Like the Hawthorne studies undertaken by Mayo and his colleagues (see Chapter 2 above), little attention was paid in behavioural studies to the contexts in which leadership roles were performed or to the contingent factors that influenced leadership behaviour. Following from behavioural theories, a concern with the contingencies of leadership actively began to exercise researchers from the 1960s onwards. The underlying theme of most of these approaches was that leadership is not necessarily or simply a matter of personal qualities, or of the style of the leader, but of the circumstances in which leadership is performed. This not only means that a given situation (physical and social environment, organizational culture) can determine leadership styles and strategies but admits of the possibility that leaders may be good and effective in one context but not another. The two best known contingency theories of leadership are the Fiedler and path–goal models.

The Fiedler model of leadership

Fiedler (1967) began from the premise that it was necessary to identify the dimensions to leadership style. To achieve this, he designed the least preferred co-worker (LPC) test, which required respondents to describe the one person that they had least enjoyed working with in their career. This test was in fact a simple list of sixteen pairs of bi-polar adjectives, e.g. good–bad, nice–nasty, clean–dirty (not the terms used by Fiedler, these are just for illustration here). Each pair of adjectives was separated by an eight-point scale, sometimes running one way, sometimes another (a common feature of such tests – called semantic differential tests – the methodology of which is unimportant to the general themes here). For each pair of adjectives, respondents indicated a rating of between one and eight. From these, Fiedler asserted that the more generous the total rating of the LPC, the more a respondent was interested in good inter-personal relations, and the lower the rating of the LPC, the more the respondent was task-oriented.

Here, then, the behavioural tradition of leadership becomes evident. More important, however, are two methodological objections. The first is whether the LPC questionnaire is adequate to the task of measuring the factors claimed for it – inter-personal relations and concern with task and productivity. Semantic differential tests have been a feature of psychological testing for many years, and they do have their uses. As single instruments, however, they have limitations and are normally best applied along with other measures if some validity is to be assured. Reliance upon this instrument has subsequently proved highly controversial, as Robbins (1992) notes. The latter also argues that in respect of determining the leadership 'style' of individuals Fiedler sees leadership style as fixed, thus reflecting elements of a trait approach to leadership. In many ways such a position is to be admired if only for the attempt to integrate different research traditions. In general Fiedler sees leadership behaviour and style as varying according to task/inter-personal relationships, but, as represented in any one individual, he argues that leadership style is unlikely to change.

What then precisely is 'contingent' about Fiedler's theory? Simply put, Fiedler argues that leadership types must be matched to situations, and there are three possible situational or contingent dimensions. *Leader–member relations* are those that exist between leaders and their subordinates and embrace such elements as mutual trust, respect and confidence. The state of these relations is either 'good' or 'poor'. The second contingency is that of *task structure*, the organization of work and the clarity and purpose of that organization, which may be essentially structured (high) or unstructured (low). Finally, there is *position power*, which is the degree of formal power a leader has to make decisions in respect of recruitment and selection, discipline, promotion and dismissal. Such power is generally either strong or weak.

The mixing of good–poor, high–low and strong–weak on each of these contingency variables in a manner that accounts for all possible combinations yields eight contexts in which leadership might function, e.g. *good* leader–member relations, *high* task structure and *strong* position power is the most favourable of these eight. In contrast, poor leader–member relations, low task structure and weak position power is the least favourable context. Both of these represent extremes of the eight-point scale. Fiedler found in research applications that if inter-personal and task leadership were compared, then task–oriented leaders performed best at the extremes of the scale, whereas relationship–oriented leaders performed better in the middle range of the scale.

The central difficulty with the Fiedler model is that, because Fiedler believes management style to be fixed, leaders have to be matched to an appropriate situation. This matching is undertaken via analysis of LPC questionnaires, the limitations of which have already been commented upon. Any matching of leaders to situations is necessarily a subjective judgement, and therefore a fairly imprecise one. Furthermore, the ideal type task- and relationship-centred groups are not necessarily a rational basis for building leadership models. Flexibility is also a problem, for even if an individual's leadership style does not change (a contentious enough view), then situations might, necessitating in the theory's logic the replacement of leaders from time to time. Undoubtedly, one of the attractions of the Fiedler model is that it has some of the trappings of 'science', but while some commentators see it as a step forward, as offering a reasonable means of analysing leadership, e.g. Robbins, 1992, others regard it as erratic and flawed (Bryman, 1992).

Path–goal theory

One of the most influential contingency theories of motivation is path–goal theory principally developed by Evans (1970) and House (1971: see also House and Mitchell, 1974). The basis of this view of leadership is the expectancy theory of motivation (see Chapter 10), which has, at its heart, the view that the attitudes and behaviour of an individual have their roots in:

- Expectancy – the extent to which job performance leads to outcomes perceived as positive and favourable to the individual.
- Valence – whether or not the value of these outcomes is positive or negative to the individual.

The path–goal approach to leadership takes this view and develops it in terms of arguing that leaders' behaviour influences the expectancies of subordinates by clarifying the 'paths' to successful goal achievement. It is important to note here the assumption that goal achievement (or attendant values such as success and rewards) is a sufficient value in its own right for subordinates to want to aspire to achieve, a rather narrow view, which might be regarded as a little too rosy in that it plays down instrumentalism among workers.

In path–goal theory, then, leadership is closely linked to motivation, the latter being both a principal characteristic *and* measurement of leadership. Path–goal theory links leader behaviour to situational factors (contingencies) in much the same way as Fiedler's model. The principal types of leadership behaviours are:

- Directive or instrumental leadership – where leadership entails clarification of expectations of subordinates and the procedures for attaining goals.
- Supportive leadership – a variant on the 'concern for people' style of leadership, this is where the needs of subordinates for status, support and affection are a prominent part of the leader's style.
- Participative leadership – where leaders consult subordinates and take their views and feelings into account in making decisions about a group's activities and direction.
- Achievement-oriented leadership – where the leader sets very high standards and places confidence in subordinates to achieve these standards.

A central tenet of path–goal theory is that (unlike with Fiedler's model) leadership styles may vary between audiences and over time. The success or failure of various types of leadership style will, however, be influenced by situational factors, of which there are two principal types. The first is the *personal characteristics of subordinates*, which include the locus of control (self-perceptions of whether what happens to individuals is largely a result of their own actions and behaviour or attributable to external factors over which they have limited control) and perceived ability (the extent to which individuals, in effect, view themselves as 'up to a job'). The second set of situational factors are *environmental characteristics*, which include task structure (the degree of complexity of tasks), the authority system of the organization (whether flexible or rigid, authoritative or participative), and the constitution of the work group (whether the group is conducive to effective performance, and whether indeed it functions as a group).

As with other theories of leadership considered so far in this chapter, path–goal theory has had its ups and downs in terms of results. Some studies have claimed that 'employee performance and satisfaction are likely to be positively influenced when the leader compensates for things lacking in either the employee or the work setting' (Robbins, 1992, p. 147). Again, however, key problems have been evident in conflicting results from different studies and problems over the issue of causality, e.g. in respect of whether situational factors are the primary influence on the style of leadership adopted or whether the latter is the primary influence on the creation of particular situational circumstances.

A note on leadership styles

Leadership 'style' has been a major preoccupation of research in the field, although many authors are at pains to avoid using the term 'style', one reason seemingly being that it could court accusations of over-simplification. Yet there can be little doubt that, given the highly uncertain nature and conclusions of leadership research, 'style' remains an attractive short-hand way for talking about leadership and not only among academics: for practising managers 'leadership style' is a readily tangible concept, and one that permits the possibility of flexibility of *attitude*, i.e. leadership style *can be changed*, and managers with inappropriate styles directed towards alternatives. Provided it does not act as a substitute for rigorous analysis of the framework of employee relations, it does not need a cynic to suggest that such a philosophy or ideology is, in some respects, as good as many of the theories discussed so far in this chapter.

In point of fact, in addition to the implicit acceptance of 'style' as an issue in the work of the theorists reported above, there has been a fair amount of explicit consideration of leadership styles. Much of what has resulted *does* appear simplistic. Terms used to describe styles of leadership include the following, none of which require explication:

- Autocratic.
- Permissive.
- Consultative.
- Democratic.
- Laissez-faire.
- Dictatorial.
- Paternalistic.

Of course these terms describe particular patterns of behaviour, but like most of the labels employed by leadership researchers they are to some extent idealized: few people employ only one style, and styles vary according to the audiences to which they are directed. A hotel general manager may employ an autocratic style of leadership in dealing with restaurant staff but a more emollient style with, say, chefs. This is not necessarily a conscious process but derives more from a 'What can I get away with?' attitude. Leaders might adopt different styles, dependent on their perceptions of the power held by audiences for those styles. Hence, those with considerable power and potential for disrupting the organization, e.g. senior chefs, might be perceived by leaders as requiring different handling from operative workers, who have relatively little power.

It needs to be emphasized here that no moral judgement is being made as to these dispositions. Management theorists in general disapprove of autocratic and dictatorial styles of leadership and management, and there is some measure of agreement among organizational behaviour theorists that participative and consultative leadership in many contexts gives rise to greater commitment, motivation and productivity on the part of employees. Realities vary, however, and the various 'styles' of leadership noted above are probably adequate in their description of behaviour that exists in all organizations to a greater or lesser degree.

Leadership in the hospitality industry

As noted in Chapter 8, a major characteristic of management in the hospitality industry is a 'being there' style that stresses 'hands on' operational control of units and frequent interaction with organizational members at all levels as well as intervention in the running of units. It is perhaps surprising that, given the emphasis placed on leadership by hospitality organizations (Guerrier, 1987; Worsfold, 1989), more research has not been undertaken into the subject in hotel and catering contexts. Certainly the reputation of managerial leadership in hotel and catering organizations is easy to pin down. Perhaps unhappily, the general view from the range of research sources available is that hospitality managers are authoritarian, dictatorial, and heavy-handed, and hold a unitary view of managerial and leadership relationships, i.e. they see themselves as the principal source of authority, and resent and do not accept alternative 'power centres', e.g. organized labour in the form of trade unions, staff associations and so on. If we bear in mind that the studies reviewed in Chapter 8 revealed that hospitality managers' ratings of different roles reveals them to regard leadership as a prime function, the image of leadership to emerge from research might be regarded as unfortunate.

Certainly managers sometimes object to being depicted in such negative terms. However, the existing evidence is clear in showing that 'being there' styles of management engender informality of communication and a directive style of leadership and control tinged by authoritarian and paternalistic attitudes. Guerrier and Lockwood (1989) discovered that many hotel managers saw the development of staff and their care and nurturing as part of their role, but did little to convert this belief into action. In the same study the authors found that staff perceived managers as being highly critical, controlling and autocratic. Similarly, Worsfold (1989) interviewed managers and found a high level of awareness of participative styles of managerial leadership, though none of his sample had adopted such styles. This bears out the work of Croney (1988), who analysed management and leadership style in four hotel groups.

Croney found a commitment at corporate level to a management/leadership style that employed communication, consultation and involvement on the part of employees, but participation was generally seen as being management-led, i.e. 'top down', with managers taking any initiative and setting the boundaries of tolerance. This picture coincides to some degree with Hales' observation that bodies like consultative committees are used more as a means of allowing employees to air their grievances, and for directing the attention of employees towards peripheral and relatively unimportant issues (see Hales, 1987).

One of the most interesting studies of leadership in the hospitality industry was undertaken (in the USA) by Nebel and Stearns (1977), who applied Fiedler's techniques, including an LPC questionnaire, to a sample of hospitality industry employees. Nebel and Stearns report that over a range of measured contingencies (group relations, task structure, position power, employee need for independence, employee personal characteristics and educational attainment) the most effective management style indicated for the hospitality organization (task-centred/inter-personal–participative) would seem likely to be a task-oriented one. The problem with this finding is that Fiedler's model may be as prone to diagnosing the leadership situations that *actually* exist within an organization as much as those that *may* be appropriate to the situation. In any case the Nebel and Stearns study offers useful confirmation of the tendency towards mechanistic, authority-centred leadership in hospitality organizations in general, and a comparative insight into the situation in the USA.

Also of interest from the perspective of the hospitality industry is Fiedler's later application of his 'leader match' theory to hotels (Sepic, Mahar and Fiedler, 1980). This investigation studied a sample of sixty-four people holding managerial positions in three chain-owned hotels in northwest America, who were put through a 'leader match' training programme based on Fiedler's theory. The valid sample (those finally selected to participate in the training) numbered twenty-seven persons in all, who were exposed to a programme that encouraged managers-as-leaders to use strategies to modify the work situation in order to improve goal attainment. Participants were rated 'before' and 'after' training on a number of dimensions (ratings awarded by their unit's executive assistant managers), and these results compared to those of a control group. Unsurprisingly, the study found that performance ratings among the hotel managers improved as a result of the 'leader match' training, findings which conform to Fiedler's development of his theory (see Fiedler, Chemers and Mahor, 1976, for methodological details).

However, the study of the hospitality industry is notably lacking in methodological detail and the authors go to some trouble to discuss the possible influence of experimenter effect, i.e. the idea that taking part in the study increased performance effects on the basis of the participants being made to feel self-conscious (see the earlier discussion of the Hawthorne experiments in Chapter 2). Whatever the potential shortcomings of Fiedler's theory, however, it must be noted that its influence has been profound, and perhaps personal judgements based on a reading of his research output are the most satisfactory method of deciding the relevance of this work.

The culture of leadership in the hospitality industry

So far, attention has focused on leadership research and applications to the hospitality industry. Consideration should also be directed towards understanding why the leadership styles found in hospitality organizations have come about and persist. Some of these have already been touched upon, e.g. the relative autonomy hospitality managers have in the running of their units; the culture of hands-on management. To these may be added, in the case of the small-firm sector at least, the highly personal nature of the hospitality business. For many small business owners, the management of a hotel or restaurant allows them freedom to be their own boss and to express themselves through the business. It is not altogether surprising therefore (and indeed, to a degree, understandable) that they should wish to exert direct control over the operation of their businesses, as control is a major reason for entering the hospitality industry in the first place (Seymour, 1985).

One of the main reasons why the hospitality industry has a reputation for autocratic management centres on the 'standard view' (already articulated several times in this text) of the unpredictability of demand for hospitality services, which requires off-the-cuff and *ad hoc* responses by management. Because demand is erratic, the argument goes, in order to manage labour effectively and achieve budgetary and revenue targets, managers have to *react*, and, in reacting, adjust inputs to outputs as best they can. Labour is the easiest input to adjust, and what might be regarded as sloppy personnel management in other industrial sectors is regarded as the norm in hotels and catering – sending staff home due to lack of business, hiring casual workers at short notice, and so on. The main question is whether or not it is possible, given the supposedly *ad hoc* nature of hospitality management, for managers to be anything other than autocratic in their style.

If labour is the only resource that can be effectively adjusted to meet demand, then there is little room for participative styles of leadership. Of course, in arguing thus, one of the major difficulties facing hospitality organizations becomes apparent, namely the treatment of labour as primarily a resource, not in the 'value added' sense as the backbone of the organization (see Chapter 12) but in the sense of being highly disposable. Encouraged for many years to believe that manipulation of the labour supply is the most effective means of inducing flexibility into the management of the organization in order to achieve financial goals, the hospitality industry has difficulties coming to terms with anything approaching participative styles of leadership.

This is not to say that autocratic leadership is a desirable feature of hospitality managers' own behaviour, but it might well be a necessary one. Not all (autocratic) managers are 'nasty' people. Given the importance of labour supply adjustment to the day-to-day efficiency of the organization however, authoritarian styles of leadership and management are the most effective and organizationally necessary. This is not to excuse or condemn the approach, but to point out that autocratic leadership styles in the hotel and catering industry are deep rooted and not readily amenable to change.

If this seems a somewhat pessimistic view, it is one that finds resonance not only in published research findings but in the experiences of many employees in the industry. The problem of leadership theory is, though, that however much it seeks to avoid explicit labelling of some leadership approaches as superior to others, then certain leadership styles *are* regarded as better than others, even within contingency theories. Unfortunately, this tends to over-simplify the situation, since dominant leadership styles in organizations may well be best suited to achieving organizational goals – in the hospitality case a view borne out by the work of Nebel and Stearns (1977) referred to earlier.

Summary

- Leadership is generally defined in terms of a process (what leaders do) and a property (the qualities of leadership that people possess).

main theories of leadership are those that emphasize it as a *trait* ... leads to the view that leadership qualities are innate and leaders ... not made); *behavioural perspectives* (which seek to identify the behaviour associated with successful leaders); and *contingency* ... ...ich build on the first two but see leadership behaviour as ... and modified by the circumstances – contingencies – in which ... function).

... various theoretical perspectives have been limited in their ... ...tory success in advancing hard and fast characteristics of leader-... ...ugh many possibilities have been opened up as to cause and ... ... should be noted, however, that the complexity of leadership ...eory may be responsible in part for the popularity of more simplistic conceptions of leadership in terms of various 'styles' that may be adopted in the motivation of organizational members.

- Few studies of leadership in the hospitality industry have been undertaken and there must be some doubt as to whether the structure of labour relations in the sector is conducive to the kind of claims for effective leadership arising from theoretical study of the subject. The need to control closely the supply and activities of labour by operational regulation in the hospitality industry leaves little scope for the participative styles of management that are lauded by researchers as one means of increasing productivity and contentment at work.

Discussion questions

1   Are leaders born or made?
2   Outline the characteristics of, respectively, an effective manager and an effective leader. What strategies might hospitality organizations pursue in order to increase the probability that their managers will also be effective leaders?
3   Consider the advantages and disadvantages to hospitality organizations of various leadership behaviours and styles. Must effective leadership in hospitality organizations always be directed and autocratic?
4   Why do hospitality managers tend to be operationally rather than strategically biased in the performance of their work? What consequences might this behaviour have for organizational performance?

10 The management of motivation

No text on organizational behaviour would be complete without some discussion of motivation, yet the study of motivation often seems pointless. This is because other than describing a number of theories, discussion of motivation rarely seems to lead anywhere. The main difficulty with motivation as a concept is that it is most often presented as explaining human behaviour when more usually it merely describes an idealized view of such behaviour. This can be confirmed by looking at the many varieties of motivation theory that have grown up since the 1950s.

Concepts of motivation

From Part One of this book it will be recalled that early discussion of the nature of work tended to polarize between those that saw, with varying degrees of explicitness, motivation as being primarily a matter of money, and those who took a contrary view and saw motivation and experience of work being related primarily (but not exclusively) to non-economic needs. The human relations 'school' was largely responsible for promulgating the latter view and their heirs, members of the so-called neo-human relations group of writers, have become most widely known through their writings on motivation. This is particularly true of those authors of content theories of motivation, which place emphasis on *what* motivates, seeking to identify and account for the specific influences that motivate people. In contrast, process theories of motivation view the phenomenon as a complex of dynamic variables that, taken together, both enable and delimit motivation.

Content theories

Many so-called theories of motivation are, as previously indicated, a product of the neo-human relations group of writers. The most widely known of these theories is Maslow's hierarchy of needs, though it is a little unfair to lump Maslow in with the neo-human relations writers. Though he influenced their work and was in turn influenced by the human relations movement, as a psychologist he to a large extent stood outside attempts to popularize his work in a management context.

A.H. Maslow (1943) postulated a now famous hierarchy of needs (Figure 10.1), comprising five levels, the model as a whole underpinned by two

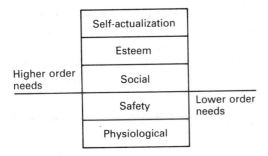

Figure 10.1 Maslow's hierarchy of needs

other sets of needs rarely referred to in the organizational behaviour context – cognitive needs and aesthetic needs (the need to be free to express one's views and to know and understand, and the need for beauty and form), both of which were deemed to be prerequisites to the satisfaction of the other five needs (Buchanan and Huczynki, 1985). According to Maslow, each person has five principal sets of needs and, as each is satisfied, the desire to achieve the next need higher in the hierarchy becomes dominant.

At the bottom of the hierarchy, there are two 'lower order' needs, so-called because they are usually met externally. They are:

- *Level 1: Physiological needs* – for food, drink and shelter, clothing, heat, sex and the satisfaction of other bodily functions.
- *Level 2: Safety needs* – for security and protection from physical and emotional disruption and harm.

Above these come the 'higher order' needs, so-called because for Maslow these were needs that if satisfied at all were satisfied internally, within the self. These were:

- *Level 3: Social needs* – for affection, friendship, acceptance and general 'belongingness', the need to feel wanted, valued and worthwhile.
- *Level 4: Esteem needs* – for respect, attention, recognition of achievement as well as internal needs for self-respect, what might be termed the 'feelgood' needs.
- *Level 5: Self-actualization needs* – for Maslow, the most important needs of all, self-actualization represents the need for creative personal fulfilment, to achieve the best possible in all aspects of life.

It is common in organizational behaviour texts to criticize Maslow's hierarchy for its lack of empirical grounding, i.e. there is no evidence to suggest such a hierarchy exists in reality. This is to a degree unkind, as a similar criticism can be extended to at least most other content theories of motivation. Although Maslow used the metaphor of a hierarchy, he was aware that some fluidity could exist, and indeed a major criticism of the hierarchy is that lower order needs may not be met and yet individuals may still have a longing for the fulfilment of higher order needs. By the same token, not all needs may exist, if at all, in the psyche of all individuals. It is possible to accept in the abstract that there are any number of exceptions to the hierarchy. A specific if extreme example might be the hermit living in his or her cave, who has, at a basic level at least, satisfied lower order needs but for whom the higher order needs of sociability and esteem of others are irrelevant.

A further criticism of Maslow's hierarchy is that individuals may aspire to and attain a particular 'level' but be frustrated at that level and regress to the one below (it will be recalled that a similar criticism was made of the linear-stage model of group development – see Chapter 7). This view is indeed a central tenet of Alderfer's ERG theory, which is usually presented as a refinement of Maslow's hierarchy.

Alderfer (1972) proposes three principal needs – existence (E), relatedness (R) and growth (G). Existence needs more or less correspond to Maslow's physiological and safety needs, relatedness to his social and esteem needs, and growth to self-actualization (although a close reading of Alderfer reveals, as several commentators have noted, that there is some overlap between relatedness and growth relative to Maslow's equivalent esteem needs, i.e. social esteem needs form part of both Alderfer's relatedness and growth, one desire for growth being the esteem of others).

Alderfer concurs with Maslow that different types of needs may motivate individuals at the same time, and that in general people move logically in a linear fashion from one need stage to another. However, Alderfer conceives of these stages as part of a continuum rather than a hierarchy, and he allows, as already noted, for the frustration of needs, and possible regression from stages in the continuum.

Models that rely on hierarchies and stages are all very well, but there are few explanations of what happens in conditions of regression when individuals reach the bottom or minimal stage. Presumably they drop off! A less programmatic content theory of motivation is provided by Frederick Herzberg, whose two-factor or motivation-hygiene theory is not only widely known but has the added interest of deriving from empirical research conducted by Herzberg and colleagues (see, for example, Herzberg, Mausner and Snyderman, 1959; also Herzberg, 1968).

Herzberg and his associates interviewed professional workers in accountancy and engineering and asked them to relate events in the workplace that had increased and decreased satisfaction and motivation. Analysis of interviews revealed that different factors were associated with the two kinds of feelings, not a remarkable find in itself but one to which Herzberg lent an interesting logical twist. The main factors generating dissatisfaction (the so-called hygiene or maintenance factors, hygiene because hygiene helps prevent illness but does not improve health, and because hygiene is to some extent a function of environment) were:

- Inadequate pay and remuneration.
- Poor interpersonal relations.
- Poor supervision in the workplace.
- Company policy and administration.

The main factors generating satisfaction (the motivation or motivating/growth factors) were:

- A sense of achievement in performance and completion of work.
- Recognition from superiors and peers of work performed.
- The responsibility assumed as part of the work process.
- Varied and interesting work.
- The prospect of promotion.

The logical twist in Herzberg's analysis comes from the observation that the dissatisfiers and satisfiers are not in any operational sense opposites. Thus the lessening of any of the hygiene factors or their absence from the organizational career of an individual, i.e. the amelioration of such conditions, for example, by the improvement of pay and working conditions, does not necessarily lead to satisfaction. The removal or alleviation of dissatisfiers may bring peace and stasis but is not likely to motivate. Rather, the alleviation of dissatisfiers placates rather than motivates (Robbins, 1992, p. 49). The opposite of dissatisfaction is therefore *no dissatisfaction* rather than satisfaction. Similarly, as far as motivating factors are concerned, these are regarded as intrinsically important. Weaknesses in these areas leads, as it were, to a state of *no satisfaction* rather than dissatisfaction.

There have of course been many criticisms of Herzberg's theory. An obvious point of contention is the original sample(s) Herzberg used as a basis for constructing his theory. The terms and conditions of employment of professional workers are generally better than those of the average operative employee. It is therefore not really sensible to construct a theory of motivation on this basis. A further criticism of the two-factor theory is the obvious influence of the human relations perspective, emphasizing as it does the social–psychological dimensions to work over the instrumental (money, earning a living). Despite these (and other) criticisms, Riley (1991, p. 46) makes a telling point when he writes, 'The unique contribution of Herzberg is in breaking the mould of one continuous dimension and at least introducing the idea of neutrality which also opens up the possibility that we may be indifferent to certain aspects of work'.

This is useful in focusing attention on Herzberg's abandonment of linear theories, with *their* emphasis on movement up and down (or along) some scale of motivational sophistication. Herzberg recognizes that motivation is a complex phenomenon but, despite this, the accusation of over-simplification has justifiably been levelled against him, as it has against Douglas McGregor.

McGregor's Theory X and Theory Y are concerned with leadership as well as motivation. The labels 'Theory X' and 'Theory Y' refer not to some systematic theory of these, but are methods of describing managerial viewpoints on the subjects. McGregor (1960, 1966) argues that managers' attitudes to their workforce are to a large extent determined as a result of the way in which they group assumptions about human behaviour. Theory X assumptions articulate a view of human nature that, like Thomas Hobbes, sees life as 'solitary, poor, nasty, brutish and short'. A little exaggeration perhaps, but Theory X assumptions are pessimistic and include the views that:

- People dislike working, it is alien to their nature and they will do everything possible to avoid it.

- Since people dislike working, they must be coerced, cajoled, threatened and otherwise pushed to achieve organizational goals.
- Most employees seek to avoid responsibility and will look for formal guidance, direction and authority at every opportunity.
- Security is regarded by most employees as more important than ambition and advancement.

By way of contrast, managers who hold Theory Y views believe that:

- Most people view work as important in itself and as natural as play or leisure; dissatisfaction arises from the circumstances in which work is performed.
- Given the opportunity, employees will, if committed to organizational or personal objectives, give of their best and seek to exercise self-direction and self-control in their work.
- Given the commitment outlined immediately above, most employees will learn to accept and actively seek responsibility in the workplace.
- Creativity is not the prerogative of management, nor is creativity a quality to be found only in management; rather, it is distributed throughout the organization and much creativity remains unutilized.

These encapsulations of social attitudes to work bear striking resemblances to the Taylorist (Theory X) and human relations school (Theory Y) view of human nature, and the associations with Herzberg's theory are also clear. In addition, if both Theory X and Theory Y are regarded as ideal types, then Theory X can be seen as primarily directed towards the satisfaction of lower order needs in the sense defined by Maslow, whereas Theory Y views higher order need satisfaction as the primary motivator.

Of course both theories *must* be regarded as ideal types. McGregor, whose work has received little empirical support, clearly believes that, for the majority, a Theory Y view of work is dominant or at least desired, and that an environment satisfying or encouraging these values in connection with employment is most likely to maximize individual motivation. The job of the manager is therefore to harness resources to create such an environment. It is here that ideal types yield to idealism, and a rather simplistic idealism at that, for, as with so many other theories of motivation (and leadership for that matter), it could be argued that McGregor's arguments amount to little more than the old, old story that happy workers will be productive and motivated workers.

Yet, despite the interconnections between the theories of motivation so far discussed, interconnections that would be expected in a field of research where each new contribution built on previous work, it is possible to discern from Maslow to McGregor a gentle shift away from the preeminence of the psychological in motivation to the importance of the social. In all the theories there is a belief, articulated with varying degrees of explicitness, that motivation is a matter of psychology, of the satisfaction of individual needs. However, the means by which individual needs are satisfied (or not) are inherently social, arising from the social structure of, in this case, the organization and workplace. McClelland (1961) recognized this in his needs theory of motivation, placing considerable emphasis on the culture of motivational needs. At the heart of his view is a belief that individuals' aspirations can be classified under three broad headings, and each of these sets of needs can exist at one and the same time. The three principal needs are:

- nAff – the need for affiliation, for successful and enjoyable personal relationships.
- nPow – the need for power, to control and exert influence over others.
- nAch – the need for achievement.

Within any single individual the strength of these needs may vary. Thus some people may feel a strong need for all three – power, affiliation and achievement – whereas others only have a strength of desire for one or two. It is the need for achievement that has exercised most debate in motivational theory, and the logic of McClelland's argument here is that some people have a high need for achievement, whereas others have less or little of such a need. The extent to which achievement motivation develops in the workplace is dependent on cultural influences (the set of characteristics and advantages or disadvantages that persons bring with them to the organization); occupational experiences (the extent to which persons' jobs and affiliations with others in similar positions encourages motivation); and the type of organization (including the extent to which organizational structure encourages motivated individuals). McClelland suggests that for high achievers, money is important but primarily as a symbol of success in the attainment of goals. People with high achievement needs can also be identified as exhibiting certain characteristics, namely:

- A preference for seeking and accepting personal responsibility in the performance of work, including a degree of autonomy.
- The setting of goals that are realistically attainable (a corollary of which is the tendency to avoid taking extravagant risks).
- A desire for specific feedback on performance.
- Preoccupation with task performance.

For high achievers, the nature and quality of achievement is extremely personal, and it is this, rather than the rewards of success, that is crucial to understanding motivation; for if motivation is to be increased, then an environment that stimulates the need for achievement has to be created in an organization. Having said this, McClelland and various critics of his work have entered several *caveats*. One such is the extent to which the social forces that create those with high needs for achievement come about – little is known about this subject, and it appears suspiciously like a 'black box' theory of motivation in which extraneous and unspecified conditions must be present for the theoretical scheme to work. In practical terms also, whereas high need achievers tend to be successful, they may rarely reach the top, because top management posts require the ability to delegate, to take, on occasions, high risk decisions, and to act with often little feedback. At the risk of doing a disservice to McClelland's view of motivation, the needs-achievement perspective perhaps best applies to the organizational specialists, without whom the organization would function less well but who are regarded as too iconoclastic (even, occasionally, eccentric) and too much as individualists to be team players entrusted with senior management roles.

Process theories

In many ways McClelland's needs-achievement theory of motivation is both a content theory (in that it seeks to identify *what* motivates) and a process theory (in that it recognizes motivation to be a phenomenon that is enabled or constrained by a variety of complex influences). The major process theories, however, are the so-called expectancy theories, associated with the work of Vroom and Porter and Lawler.

Vroom (1964) is generally accredited with the application of expectancy theory to work organizations. The basis of expectancy theory in general terms is the *rationality* of individuals' decision-making processes. People in general are seen as motivated by their expectations that an action, A, will have an outcome, B. The strength of motivation at work depends on individuals' perceptions of whether the effort expended on a particular task or tasks (or on general work behaviour) will lead to successful performance and, hence, outcomes, particularly reward outcomes. In other words, people calculate the probability of certain outcomes to particular actions, and the level of motivation is accordingly set by the degree to which outcomes are positive for the individual. Vroom identifies three key variables in the expectancy process. They are:

- The expectancy relationship of effort to performance, i.e. the perceived probability that effort leads to satisfactory performance – or the belief individuals have that they can do a job at least competently.
- The expectancy relationship of performance to outcome(s) – the calculation that performance will generate certain outcomes.
- Outcomes – in essence, anything that results from performance.

Vroom uses the term 'valence' to describe the quality and nature of outcomes. Outcomes can have a positive or negative valence for the individual. For example, outcomes with a positive valence would include recognition for work done, promotions and pay rises. Outcomes with a negative valence would be those that led to increased stress or fatigue, or which detracted from the credibility and self-esteem of the individual.

Two points should be made here. The first is that, in Vroom's terms, the extent to which an individual calculates the probability of certain outcomes must logically vary in accuracy – thus any work performance can generate a number of outcomes, some positive, some negative, or perhaps all negative/positive. In other words, all expectancies (expectations) carry an element of risk as to outcomes. Second, the logic of this model suggests that for motivation to occur, the environment must be such that an individual can reasonably expect, on a regular basis, to exert effort that will lead to satisfactory (or better) performance and that performance will in turn result in outcomes that are valued by the individual and by others. A conclusion to be drawn from this variety of expectancy theory is that the motivational environment should make provision for clear and unambiguous specification of the relation between effort and performance, on the one hand, and rewards and recognition, on the other.

The relation between effort and performance is one considered in Porter and Lawler's model of expectancy theory (Porter and Lawler, 1968). Porter and Lawler make the very reasonable observation that the relation between effort and performance is mediated by a variety of socio-cultural factors and psychological dispositions. Predominant among these is individual ability (certain expectancies are reasonable only if the individual has the ability to perform the work likely to give rise to such expectancies); role perceptions (the disposition to work brought from outside the organization and developed within it, for workers with a highly instrumental attitude or who are concerned only to 'get by' in their employment are likely to perceive the effort–performance–outcome relation differently); and the quality of rewards and the value placed upon them. This last point is interesting, because Porter and Lawler effectively differentiate between intrinsic and extrinsic rewards. For some people, intrinsic rewards may be more important than extrinsic, i.e. the satisfaction gained from doing a good job may outweigh financial or other tangible rewards. Rewards may be viewed pragmatically, some tasks soliciting effort from employees for what intrinsic needs they satisfy, others for what financial or career rewards they bring.

Expectancy theories like those described above are, then, not only process-oriented in the sense that they give weight to the behavioural rather than attitudinal or need aspects of individuals, but they are also highly contingent. The nature of motivation, like the nature of leadership, is viewed as highly complex and, like leadership, hard and fast conclusions about motivation are difficult to draw (whether from content or process theories). Thus motivational theorists urge caution in the application of their theories, a judicious strategy but also an extremely frustrating one, made all the more frustrating by the extent to which much of what passes for theory has the all too obvious appearance of dressed-up commonsense.

Earlier, the extent to which many (in particular content) theories of motivation are rooted in the neo-human relations school of organizational theory was noted. In Chapter 2 Watson's comment about the reductionist nature of the neo-human relations school was recorded (Watson, 1980) and it is difficult not to be sympathetic to this point of view. While admitting the complexity of the phenomenon, most motivation theorists assert the possibility of uncovering the essence of motivation without actually considering the extent to which such an enterprise is either possible or reasonable. The academic arguments aside, however, from the sophisticated pretensions of motivation theorists it is difficult to conclude anything other than the fact that their work opens up a number of possibilities about stimulating motivation but few hard and fast conclusions. Perhaps, then, motivation is the ultimate in contingencies – anything may happen and probably will!

The love of money

One criticism often levelled against all theories of motivation is that they do not take account of how difficult it is to motivate those workers in the most uninspiring and routinized jobs. The rise of the instrumental worker would suggest that many people fall into the category of working primarily for money, or, more precisely, the things that money can buy. Money seems to have a bad name in motivation theory, perhaps unsurprisingly, as the majority of such theories are predicated on the view that to regard money as the prime or only motivation to work is inadequate and naive. There is a lurking suspicion that the invisibility of discussions of money as a motivator in the literature on the subject has much to do with the vested interests of motivation theorists. After all, if in the *majority* of cases the *majority* of people could be demonstrated to regard (more) money as an incentive to work (harder), then a substantial academic industry would be in danger of folding completely! Even eminently practical theorists like Riley (1991) in the hotel and catering context will not wear such a view. Riley (1991, p. 46) writes:

> It could be argued that all this human potential stuff fades when put against the moral simplicity of having to earn a living. This imperative argument underpins the 'pay as the only real motivator' school of thought...however one might feel about human potential, much work simply cannot be organized to meet human potential needs. Dishwashing and room cleaning cannot be constructed other than for what they are – mundane work. However...these broad arguments don't add up...True, many people must be abstracted out and feel like robots but the very lack of dissent suggests most people have endlessly subtle adaption systems which can turn moronic work into something, at least worth possessing, if not even cherishing.

Riley is undoubtedly correct in suggesting that people can invest much even in the most demeaning tasks – the history of social scientific investigation into work demonstrates the fact. In relating this to the absence of dissent, however, there is scope for contention. The point about many low grade jobs is that people who need work and can get nothing better are stuck with these posts if they want to work at all. Further, the fact that in the hotel and catering industry labour turnover is generally quite high may be interpreted as a form of dissent. Still, it is indeed the case that this does not mean that money is the only motivator in such contexts. However, there is a case for regarding money motivation as deserving of greater attention than has hitherto been the case. Robbins (1992, pp. 60–1) implores his readers, 'Don't ignore money!', and cites a study by Locke *et al.* (1980), which produced some interesting findings:

> Maybe the best case for 'money as a motivator' is a recent review of eighty studies evaluating motivational methods and their impacts on employee productivity. Goal setting alone produced, on average, a 16 percent increase in productivity; efforts to redesign jobs in order to make them more interesting and challenging yielded 8 to 16 percent increases; employee participation in decision making produced a median increase of less than one percent; while monetary incentives led to an average increase of 30 percent.

Quod erat demonstrandum? Certainly one swallow does not make a summer (or eighty swallows for that matter, though with this number it might be expected that the sun would at least shine a little!), but the study by Locke *et al.* does at least invite a more guarded approach to the role of money as a motivator.

Hostility to acceptance of money as a key work incentive might perhaps have something to do with the ruthlessness with which early management theorists pressed their case and later researchers reacted against them. F.W. Taylor's slogan, 'A fair day's pay for a fair day's work' encapsulated, in the words of Rose (1988, p. 33) the view that 'The worker was primarily instrumental in his approach to work. Social rewards in work were of no account beside the wage packet'. The response of researchers in the human relations school set a trend against this view, a trend that has been developed and maintained through most subsequent schools of organization theory to the extent that money as a motivator has virtually been written out of accounts of workplace motivation. Yet, as was shown above, the inconclusive nature of much motivation theory suggests that dismissiveness of 'money motivation' is a little impertinent and has little justification on merit – in any contingency, money should be treated as just as valid a potential motivator as other factors.

One motivational theory in which money (or at least rewards in general) figures is that associated with Adams (1965) – equity theory. This theory proceeds from the assumption that motivation is related to how individuals perceive their treatment *vis-à-vis* others in the organization. Equity is perceived if individuals feel that they are being comparably or favourably treated relative to others in a similar situation within the organization *for the amount of effort that is being channelled into work*. Inequity occurs if these perceptions are oppositional.

There are a number of possible responses to perceptions of inequity. First, employees may seek to reduce inequity by direct action, by demanding more of what is perceived as absent in the reward package (usually money). Second, they may sit and suffer or, third, increase or decrease their inputs into work (in respect of the latter, become demotivated, in the case of the former become more highly motivated in order to seek correction of the perceived inequity). Clearly a major derived measure of equity/inequity is formal reward – money – and it is this aspect of equity theory that has excited most interest, although social rewards (esteem, recognition and so on) are clearly important. It is not financial reward in absolute terms that is important, though, but the extent to which that reward is perceived relative to the rewards of others and the efforts they put into their work. The consequences of this observation for management are clear: payment and reward systems must be seen to be closely related to effort, must be visible and easily understood, and in themselves must be perceived as based on fair differentials.

Motivating hospitality workers

There are few studies of motivational theory applied to the hospitality industry. As with leadership, there is much talk among industry leaders of the need for highly motivated workers but little evidence of anything approaching sophisticated motivation strategies except in some large corporations. Adopting the most cynical view, there is little reason why industry leaders *should* turn to motivational theory for guidance if its theoretical knowledge base is so weak and inconclusive. But a number of interesting observations about motivation in hospitality contexts can be made, and at the outset it is best to consider the 'commonsense' wisdom of the industry in this respect.

Paramount in this commonsense wisdom is a view often articulated by industry operators that tipping is a major motivator, together with such other 'perks' as subsidized food and accommodation. The thing to note about tipping is that only a proportion of industry workers are in a position to receive tips. Tipping is, as Brown and Winyard (1975, p. 12) put it, 'one of the great unknowns of the hotel and catering industry', and also, from employees' perspectives, one of the most unwelcome because it is degrading. Dronfield and Soto (1980) argue that in any case only around 50 per cent of the hotel and catering workforce (mainly food service workers) are in a position to receive tips, and tips cannot thus be considered a general motivator.

Against this, many employers and managers (and a not insubstantial number of workers) persist with the view that tipping can be a motivator, encouraging workers to give a higher standard of service. However, Nailon (1978), in a classically definitive study, dismisses this point of view. Tips are not an incentive in the normal sense, he suggests, because the effort a person puts into serving a customer may not be met with a commensurate reward. In the language of expectancy theory, the effort-to-performance to (successful) outcome relationship must be assigned a conservative probability.

It is this latter area – financial security – that provides one of the most interesting areas for research into motivation in hospitality organizations. In the UK payment was, for many years, regulated by wages councils, which set minimum rates below which employers could not legally sink. The effect of this system was that, in addition to acting as a protection, the wages council rates, revised annually, acted as a benchmark, and actual rates paid by employers did not greatly exceed the wages council minima. In 1986 the then government abolished differentials in wages councils industries by allowing councils to set only one rate for all occupations (previously, different rates for certain specified occupations had been permitted).

Low pay (relative to other industries) was – and is – defended by employers on the grounds of the possibilities for earning tips plus other payments in kind – subsidized food and accommodation and also knock-offs, a term referring to items that employees usually steal (or are allowed to take) with managements' connivance, a process institutionalized in the hospitality industry and regarded as a legitimate aspect of rewards (see Wood, 1992, for a comprehensive review). If these observations are considered in the context of equity theory and the other evidence discussed earlier, then the picture of the industry that emerges is one of a sector with large numbers of low-grade jobs, relatively undifferentiated either in terms of payment or content. It is unsurprising therefore that many workers consider themselves to be poorly paid and that lack of motivation is reflected in high labour turnover, a major cause of which is workers moving in order to secure increases in their rewards.

To this view it may be objected that many organizations in the hospitality industry operate a system of differentials, and indeed this is true. Such increments are, however, rarely based, at least at the operative level, on job analysis, but rather reflect minor 'career' adjustments and are designed to suppress the wages of newcomers for a period of 'training' or probation rather than reward skill or enterprise. Furthermore, in certain sections of the industry what passes for 'motivational rewards' is often obscure and negotiated individually between the worker and his or her manager – the so-called individual contract. Here, workers who possess some special skill or other value to a manager or employer are rewarded with (usually non-financial) benefits. The essence of the individual contract is secrecy, although in many hospitality units it is difficult to keep these things secret for long and, as anybody with even minimal experience of employment at an operative level will report, there are many instances of what is normally construed as 'favouritism' in rewards in evidence, and this can often demotivate other workers.

Similarly, the oft-argued motivational force of gratuities (one, it must in fairness be noted, admitted to by operative workers, or some at least) needs to be considered in the light of low basic pay. In such a context the possibility of securing tips may be regarded as a negative motivational force in the sense that it represents something that must be accepted as a counter to low pay. Nailon (1978) is undoubtedly correct in pointing out that tipping cannot be regarded as a normal form of incentive.

It seems fair to suggest that in an industry such as hotels and catering, which is characterized by low wage strategies on the part of employers and considerable instability in the labour force (compounded by hiring policies that utilize increasing numbers of casual workers), a motivational strategy would be difficult to implement. The content theories of motivation considered in the first part of this chapter may be 'applied' with as much or as little legitimacy to hospitality organizations as any others. It is, however, to the environmental and contextual factors that attention must be addressed in appreciating the relevance of motivation to the hospitality sector.

Many people give as a reason for entering the industry the desire to work with people, but this in itself is not a sufficient 'satisfier'. For those people for whom hotel and catering employment is the only option, then other satisfiers must be sought. With the exception of a number of enlightened employers (the number of which in chain organizations at least appears to be increasing) who employ leadership and motivational strategies designed to deliver a better product and adequately reward workers in all dimensions, there seems little prospect of motivation achieving any significance in management strategy for as long as a substantial pool of cheap labour remains available for employment in hospitality services. Furthermore, if contingency theories are to be believed, then essential to a positive motivational climate is a *balance* between environmental and intrinsic satisfiers at work, and the rewards for that work. In other words, it is difficult to motivate people who are in the most general terms poorly rewarded in financial terms. This is an issue that has to be addressed, together with the social variables, if the effort–reward relationship is to be given tangible potentiality among workers.

A last word on money

In the hospitality context the issue of money motivation has been addressed directly by Weaver (1988), and it is worth considering his work if only because he abandons much of the pretence associated with motivation theory. The strength of Weaver's work lies in his consideration of the hourly paid worker, who, he suggests, benefits little from conventional motivational strategies or indeed sees them as having any meaning. Hourly paid workers feel little attachment to their jobs; this is one of the reasons for high labour turnover in the industry, and is also instrumental in explaining the lack of success of managerial strategies for motivation based on appeals to company loyalty or promises of career advancement. In short, Weaver argues, all the conventional theories of motivation are pretty limited in their application to hourly paid workers, since these (Maslow's hierarchy of needs, Herzberg's motivation-hygiene theory, McGregor's Theory X and Y) address issues such as self-development, personal challenge and growth, and intrinsic satisfaction, which simply have no relevance. Weaver (1988, p. 42) writes:

> Hotel employees are often more cynical then employees in most other industries, perhaps because they work in an environment where they see how people really behave when they're away from home. Hourly employees in the industry are fully aware of what their interests are and are not easily motivated by programs that they perceive as being nothing but hot air.

This hard-hitting view of motivation of hourly workers has obvious applications to the hospitality industry in the UK, where most operative workers fall into such a category. At the risk of putting words into Weaver's mouth, he appears to be saying something along the lines of 'let's ditch the sham' about motivational theory and concentrate on the basics. What Weaver in fact argues for is 'Theory M' (one of the charming things about McGregor's Theory X and Theory Y is the range of other alphabetically titled theories it has led to – see Chapter 11 for consideration of Ouchi's Theory Z!).

Theory M – where M stands for money – is based on the premise that motivation should be achieved via higher wages paid for higher than average productivity levels. Workers who achieve productivity levels (perhaps measured in increased sales) would, in Weaver's scheme of things, be rewarded with a percentage of any increase in sales or savings to the company generated by their productivity achievements. This would mean that calculating a performance base from the average performance of staff over a given time period would be required. In food and beverage (and in particular food service), where Weaver sees his strategy as having the easiest and most obvious application, workers would be paid a percentage of sales for the first value over this base (say 5 per cent of the first £100 of sales over the base). Further scales would be built on this for higher amounts.

In the food and beverage department, Weaver argues, the added advantage of this approach is that employees are motivated to make more sales and thus familiarize themselves with the product range more as well as giving a higher quality of service to customers. Labour turnover should also be reduced as a clear link between the effort–reward relation is established. Other departments in a hotel can be incorporated within such a scheme – the room sales division would receive a bonus on the basis of rooms sold, and in room-cleaning and other departments similar bonuses could be paid for finishing tasks more quickly to the required standard (yielding possible staff reductions as greater efficiency is achieved).

No doubt there are those who would argue that Weaver's view is too simplistic, and it is indeed necessary for observers to weigh the evidence for themselves. The appeal of views like those of Weaver is that they have a certain simple logic as opposed to the often obtuse and ultimately inconclusive theories of the content/process variety. An interesting attempt to apply Herzberg's motivation-hygiene theory to the hospitality industry is reported by Chitiris (1988). Chitiris set out to test the generalizations of Herzberg's theory in the context of the Greek hotel industry, in which employment is looked upon by workers as a last resort and where turnover is high. Some 287 employees were given a questionnaire–interview and asked to rate levels of job satisfaction and the importance of certain job factors. Included in the questionnaire were the following 'motivators' and 'hygiene' factors:

MOTIVATORS
- Merit bonuses
- Advancement
- Use of initiative
- Job content
- Opportunities for personal development

HYGIENE FACTORS
- Salary
- Overtime payment arrangements
- Physical job demands
- Physical working conditions
- Supervisory systems
- Job security
- Leadership styles

Chitiris found that workers in the Greek hotel industry were by and large more interested in hygiene factors than motivators, lending some support to the view that in low-grade jobs where basic expectations (hygiene factors) are not met no amount of motivational instruments can make significant impact on improving employee performance.

In the end it is worthwhile in assessing motivational theories to bear in mind that different things motivate different people – but all people usually work at least for financial reward.

Summary

Motivation, like leadership, is a complex topic about which there are few certainties. The main points of the discussion contained in this chapter are as follows.

- Motivation is defined as the non-coercive influencing of others to behave in a particular way.
- Theories of motivation have developed through (i) models of need hierarchies and scales that are centrally concerned with how individuals achieve psychological gratification; (ii) models based on the perceptual aspects of individuals' attitudes to motivation; and (iii) essentially contingent theories of motivation that emphasize social need gratification.
- Following immediately from this, (i) and (ii) are generally classified under the heading of content theories of motivation (focusing on what motivates), while contingency explanations of motivation are normally labelled as 'process theories' – which are based on the premise that motivation is enabled and constrained by the interaction of various factors that arise in a given social situation.
- Few theories of motivation give much weight to the role of money in motivating individuals in the workplace, though growing instrumentalism among the workforces of advanced industrial societies would suggest that money is important and underrated as a motivational influence by theorists.
- Theories of motivation have had little application to the hospitality industry through research. Hotel and catering workers constitute one of those groups of workers – the low and hourly paid – who are accepted as being among the most difficult to motivate. This has led Weaver to propose a Theory M, a simple bonus scheme based on sales–finance ratios as the best means of motivating such workers.

Discussion questions

1 Which of the many theories of motivation is most convincing in its applications to hospitality organizations?
2 Why is it difficult to motivate operative workers in hospitality organizations?
3 Consider the relevance of motivation-hygiene theory to the motivation of management employees in the hospitality industry.
4 What truth is there in the assertion that Maslow's hierarchy of needs provides a useful theory for understanding the motivation of both hospitality industry employees and consumers?

Part Four
Issues in Organizational Behaviour

11 Organizational culture

The final section of this book examines in brief some key issues in organizational behaviour, beginning with organizational culture, which was a 'buzz' phrase of the 1980s. Yet, as Moorhead and Griffin (1989, p. 493) note, there is no broadly accepted or agreed definition of organizational culture. Organizational theorists have therefore adopted various definitions and indeed, Moorhead and Griffin (1989, p. 494) list nine of these, including that of Deal and Kennedy (1982, p. 4), who define any organizational culture as 'the way we do things round here'.

In point of fact close inspection of discussions of organizational culture reveals what can only be construed as either a remarkable lack of self-awareness on the part of commentators or a surprising degree of disingenuousness. This is because there is an almost universal failure to admit that most interest in organizational culture arises from attempts by investigators to identify 'success' factors in industrial organizations or, to put it another way, what makes some organizations (more) successful and some less, or not, successful. In short, debates about organizational culture tend to derive their impetus from analysis of successful companies, and these success factors are extrapolated into an analytic framework that is intended, whether implicitly or explicitly, to define at the same time the reasons for lack of success. This extrapolation from the particular to the general is highly questionable, though of course it does not necessarily invalidate the findings of research into the nature of 'success' factors in business organizations.

In search of the blindingly obvious?

In order to explore the foregoing points in more detail, it is necessary only to examine the work of one of the most frequently cited sources of inspiration for discussions of organizational culture – Peters and Waterman's *In Search of Excellence: Lessons from America's Best-Run Companies*.

Reference has already been made to the work of Peters and Waterman (see Chapter 8), whose book is possibly the most influential work on management of the last 20 years in so far as its impact goes well beyond the ivory towers of academia. Peters and Waterman (1982) sought to identify the factors that made successful US companies successful. As Moorhead and Griffin (1989, p. 506) put it, 'Their analysis rapidly turned to the cultural values that led to successful management practices'. Peters and Waterman identified nine major characteristics of successful companies. Each is considered in turn.

Bias for action

Successful companies are, according to Peters and Waterman, those where managers have a 'can do' approach and are prepared to take risks. Even if information-gathering and dissemination systems are of the highest order, and even if companies are highly analytic in their business strategies, decisions should be taken without the 'full facts', on the grounds, argue the authors, that it is always impossible to *have* the full facts on any situation. Delaying taking a decision is the same as not making a decision. Furthermore, a bias for action includes a willingness to experiment with new ideas and products.

Staying close to the customer

Valuing customers is essential to business success, and Peters and Waterman argue that successful companies are those that utilize customers as sources of information about the standard of existing products and services as well as the potential for new ones. Closely linked to this is the fact that successful companies put enormous emphasis on product and service quality and reliability.

Autonomy and entrepreneurship

Peters and Waterman argue that successful and innovative companies are those that foster many leaders and creative individuals – even at the risk of making mistakes. Rather than use bureaucratic 'stranglehold' styles of control, such companies are likely to decentralize their operations, perhaps even breaking the company up into semi-independent units.

A corollary of this is that excellent companies develop clear communication strategies characterized by (i) informality in the communication process; (ii) intensity of the communications process, including brainstorming by all levels of the management and workforce; (iii) physical support for communications strategies (Peters and Waterman cite the case of the ex-IBM employee who complained to his new boss that there were no blackboards available to aid communication and the exchange of ideas); and (iv) the existence of forcing devices, i.e. 'programs that virtually institutionalize innovation' (Peters and Waterman, 1982, p. 222) including, for example, the hiring (or internal development) of 'mavericks', who are allowed resources and a free hand to develop new ideas and innovations. The intense informal communication system itself acts as an effective mechanism of control, since the granting of latitude and the growth of competition within the company when combined with access to resources, stimulates others to take a positive interest in what is being done and what is achieved.

Productivity through people

Successful companies not only subscribe 'in words' to the view that people are the most important of the business' assets but do so in deeds. There is a genuine commitment to people. Peters and Waterman (1982, p. 239) concede that most employers say people are vital to the enterprise but all too often the reality is the 'lip service disaster' or the 'gimmicks disaster' – the former is self-explanatory, the latter refers to the latest management novelties. The authors cite quality circles and managerial grids as examples, all perfectly legitimate in their own right but limited in use if not forming part of an integrated package that has the support of top management. A company orientation towards people has a tough aspect to it. According to Peters and Waterman (1982, p. 239), successful companies are measurement- and performance-oriented. Furthermore, the authors note that a genuine orientation to people often goes back a long way in the history of successful companies:

> The orientation toward people in these companies often started decades ago – full employment policies in times of recession, extraordinary amounts of training when no training was the norm, everybody on a first-name basis in times much more formal than ours, and so on. Caring runs in the veins of the managers of these institutions.

Hands-on management

One problem faced by business organizations is that, as they are promoted, senior managers often lose touch with the basics of the business and adopt more specialized roles. The companies studied by Peters and Waterman were characteristically different in this respect: senior managers were required to stay in touch with the nature of the business they were in. Furthermore, managers were expected to monitor their environments regularly, and to employ 'management by walking around', observing, questioning and responding to the situations they found.

Values and beliefs

Excellent companies in the Peters and Waterman study had a clearly articulated philosophy, a set of beliefs that usually centred on:

- Being the best.
- Being concerned with both broad creative issues *and* mechanical detail, the minutiae of operationalizing the company's philosophy.
- The importance of individuality, of people as individuals.
- The need to give quality and service to customers that outstripped that of rivals.
- Providing encouragement to everyone to innovate while supporting occasional failures.
- Informality in order to encourage communication.
- The importance of profit and company growth.

Sticking to the knitting

Successful companies concentrate on the business they know and rarely wander outside their field(s) of expertise. Diversification into other industries unrelated to the main business is rare, although some diversification into related areas is not unusual.

Simple form, lean staff

Peters and Waterman argue that successful firms tend to have 'flat' rather than 'tall' organizational structures, and relatively small corporate 'head office' type units. The status emphasis is thus shifted, in that managers' status is not determined (as in some organizations) by the number of subordinates that work to them, but by their effectiveness and impact on the organization. Interestingly, Peters and Waterman criticise matrix structures of organization (see Chapter 3 above) on the grounds that, while perhaps 'flattening' the organizational structure, their effect is, in many instances, more cosmetic than real. This is because matrix structures, like their more traditional forebears, tend to dilute business priorities, placing emphasis on organizational maintenance rather than business maintenance. Implicit to the matrix structure is an attempt to advance on many fronts, which, Peters and Waterman imply, more often than not means that there is little advancement on any front.

Loose–tight organization

The proposal that successful companies are simultaneously loose and tight in their organization is not a paradox. What Peters and Waterman argue is in fact two different things. Tight organization is a reference to the intensity with which values are shared by individuals in the organization and encouraged by organizational leaders. Loose organization is a reference to the formal organization of the business, to the absence of bureaucratic procedures, rules and regulations, and excessive numbers of staff.

More alphabet soup

In the area of organizational culture the work of William Ouchi (1981) is now, perhaps a little unfairly, conventionally grouped with that of Peters and Waterman. Ouchi contends with a problem that has preoccupied western politicians and industrialists for many years, namely how it is that Japanese industry appears to outperform western industry. Ouchi identifies a number of dimensions to organizational culture in Japanese firms that he then compares to typical American firms and American firms that have sought to adopt the Japanese model. The term 'Theory Z' is used to describe the latter model of management, with the clear allusion being to McGregor's theories 'X' and 'Y'.

The central issue is that Japanese industry has higher levels of sociality among employers, and between employers and employees. That is, there is greater trust, subtlety and intimacy in workplace relations than in the West (see Moorhead and Griffin, 1989; Pugh and Hickson, 1989). Workers trust their bosses more, partly because of the authority structure of Japanese society, but also because of the culture created through the subtlety of inter-personal relations, which is based on employers and employees developing a considerable knowledge of one another's personal circumstances, and the intimacy engendered by such relations, which emphasizes caring and supportiveness. To a large degree, these are all underpinned by the structural characteristics of Japanese industry, with its tradition of lifelong employment. Many employees and managers are recruited to companies and serve with them until retirement, although this privilege is one confined to males, women usually being required to retire on marriage. Retirement age for men is often at 55, so as to allow younger workers to be recruited, and it is traditionally the case that one company does not employ those who have spent time with another.

This approach to recruitment and careers emphasizes a form of paternalistic collectivism that encourages loyalty to the company. The company acquires a status not dissimilar to that of the family. One aspect of this collectivist attitude is that there is less competition between individuals, and this is underpinned by a system of payment graduated for up to 10 years on the basis of advances related to the year of entry to the company.

According to Ouchi, typical US firms exhibit the following characteristics relative to their Japanese counterparts.

- They are less committed to employees at all levels and hold the expectation that employment is short-term in nature and that people will move on.
- Short-termism in promotional decisions is evident, and is based on readily understandable quantitative dimensions to performance, as opposed to the deferred progress of Japanese employees and managers, in which promotion is an altogether slower process.
- Careers in US firms tend to be validated against performance in specialized, single-function managerial roles, e.g. marketing manager, human resources manager, whereas in Japanese companies careers most valued are multi-functional, with managers acquiring experience of many different functions.
- Control in US firms is directive and bureaucratic, whereas in Japanese companies it is 'more cultural', being encoded in the mores and practices of the organization. Control is perhaps more imprecise, but employees have longer to learn and 'absorb' the culture and practices of the organization by virtue of the long apprenticeships they serve.
- Decision-making in US companies is normally centred on designated managers, who accept responsibility for such decisions, often taking them in isolation from the majority of the workforce. In contrast, decision-making in Japanese firms tends to call for wide workgroup consensus.

The conditions prevailing in many Japanese firms, then, offer a different form of capitalist enterprise to that found in the West. Competitiveness almost appears to be a concept reserved for the general performance of the company relative to other companies. Within the organization, employees are encouraged to be more collectivist and cooperative.

Theory Z type American companies are those that have sought to adopt Japanese methods of management but differ to some degree from Japanese companies in the way they apply these methods. For example, Ouchi claims that although in Type Z US firms career paths are broad, they are not as broad as those in Japanese firms. Perhaps most important, however, is his observation on responsibility. Even in Type Z US firms, Ouchi suggests, decision-making is inextricably linked to individual responsibility (as with typical US companies), as opposed to being viewed as a collective process linked to collective responsibility for decisions taken. One reason for this is the highly individualistic nature of American society, but power is also important. The role of manager has, in Western society, conventionally been viewed as one that has certain prerogatives attached to it, key prerogatives being decision-making and the direction of others.

Organizational culture and the hospitality industry

The organizational culture 'industry' has had some impact on hospitality industry research. Reyes and Kleiner (1990) seek to develop an abstract model suited to establishing an organizational culture. The first stage of this process is creation of a 'vision' for the organization, encompassing its basic purpose. It calls for consultation with customers and employees. The latter should be polled as to their views, the writers suggest, though, interestingly, Reyes and Kleiner see it as the task of senior management to 'hammer out' these views to produce a coherent vision. 'Including workers in the process of establishing organizational purpose increases employee self-efficacy, the belief in one's abilities', they write (1990, p. 27), and consultation seems to be the limit to employee participation in the hospitality context, if Reyes and Kleiner are to be believed, lending some credence to the assertion of mainstream writers on organization theory, like Thompson and McHugh (1990), that while organizational culture approaches present themselves as participative and an alternative to overtly controlling organizational discipline strategies, they may in reality pay little more than lip service to the ideal of participation. Reyes and Kleiner do little to assuage the fears represented by Thompson and McHugh's observation and sometimes verge on the surreal in making such remarks as (1990, p. 28):

> Guided by the mission statement they helped develop, the employees will adopt the organisational purpose. The employees will work with management when the vision is real to them.

No evidence is advanced to support these claims. The emphasis on 'vision' is illustrated by reference to Disneyland and McDonald's. The Disney vision is one of 'theatre', whereas McDonald's vision is clean restaurants and consistent quality of food. These may well be accurate descriptions, but in not elaborating their arguments empirically Reyes and Kleiner ignore the extent to which the success of these organizations is also built on highly controlled human resource strategies, the use of technology and cost-efficiency in labour utilization (Ritzer, 1992).

A more considered but ultimately no more satisfying analysis of organizational culture in the hospitality industry is offered by Woods (1989, p. 82), who begins promisingly by noting that:

> A commonly held misconception about culture is that top management can somehow drive or build a company's culture. While management can greatly influence many elements of a company's culture, all members of your organization exert influence over your culture.

Woods argues that organizational cultures have at least three main levels (see also Dyer, 1986; Schein, 1985): the manifest or visible level (rituals, ceremonies, slogans, legends, myths and sagas); the strategic level (beliefs about strategic vision, capital and product market expectations, and internal approaches to management); and the level of deep meaning (embracing the values and assumptions with which the organization operates). Woods studied five restaurant companies, interviewing 300 persons drawn from managerial and operative levels and applied the above framework to the study of actions, behaviour and documentation within the organizations. Woods reports that a comparison of the levels of culture across all five organizations yields few points of similarity. He does suggest that all the organizations studied had some things in common, namely a predominantly young workforce and a body of hourly paid staff who were predominantly women (whereas most managers were men), but the implications of these points for organizational culture are not made clear, and it is doubtful whether the extensive study of the five restaurant organizations Woods reports upon was necessary to establishing these facts, as they are highly generalized throughout the hospitality industry (see Wood, 1992b), and a feature of the culture of hospitality organizations only in the sense of being a widespread feature of the *structure* of industry product and labour markets.

In a further advocacy of the concept of organizational culture Lundberg and Woods (1990, p. 5) again begin from some interesting premises, writing that 'culture has become an almost faddish part of organizational and corporate language'. They go on to pursue the 'levels of culture' line of argument, suggesting that managers can modify culture by understanding the manifest, strategic and deep meanings of organizational culture and thereafter (i) ensuring the 'fit' between different levels of culture, i.e. ensuring that strategic, manifest and deep meanings – or core – levels of culture are more closely integrated; (ii) acting to increase or decrease the strength of organizational culture in whole or in part in order to effect change; (iii) adjusting the fit between organizational culture as a whole and the culture of various sub-units of the organization where these differ; and (iv) replacing aspects of organizational culture with new values and meanings.

The choice of which strategy to pursue in modifying organizational culture may be restricted by the circumstances in which the organization operates, and specifically the extent to which management of the organization's internal affairs is executed relative to responses and adaptation to the external environment and likely future events. These needs, which all organizations experience, must, according to the authors, be integrated with the activities of managers in seeking to create an organizational culture. Lundberg and Woods identify three major managerial roles in this respect. The first is the manager as cultural spokesperson, i.e. as a person who aids other organizational members to appreciate the symbolic dimensions to organizational events, people and actions. This role may be formal or informal, but in culture-oriented organizations arrangements are usually formalized to the extent of the provision of modes of training designed to inculcate employees with the essential cultural values of the organization. The second managerial role of importance is that of the manager as cultural assessor, whereby managers monitor organizational culture through assessment of organizational units and individuals (particularly other managers) and advise on the maintenance of cultural values. The third role here is that of manager as facilitator of cultural modification, which entails the manager encouraging organizational members in the initiation and management of cultural change.

Lundberg and Woods (1990) base their arguments on the research of Woods (1989), whose study of relatively small restaurant companies with readily identifiable cultures and cultural consciousness allowed for some flexibility in interpretation of managerial roles. That is to say, the companies studied were characterized by sufficient diversity and personal influence and involvement of senior staff to allow for considerable variations in organizational 'style'. This is a clear limitation, in that culture is likely to vary at the small business and large chain ends of the industrial spectrum. Further, it is clear that senior executives in Woods' research took 'culture' fairly seriously, at least in an abstract sense, and this may well give rise to different strategies from those that might be adopted by, say, chain organizations, where personal involvement of organizational leaders in day-to-day management of the firm may not be so great.

In other words, cultures vary. The work of the authors considered in this discussion cannot therefore be accepted uncritically, though at the same time it is important to recognize that organizational leaders' belief in 'culture' is an important influence on organizational management. In this respect the studies so far undertaken in the hospitality field offer a useful if limited insight into some of the problems that do exist in understanding hotel and catering organizational culture. These limitations arise from the imprecise (and occasionally plain faulty) reasoning that underpins many so-called 'culture' approaches to management and organizations. For the sake of clarity, only some of the principal reservations about the work of what Thompson and McHugh call the 'corporate culture merchants' are considered here (see Thompson and McHugh, 1990, Chapter 6, whose summary of the issues is one of the best presently available).

The limitations of culture

One difficulty with the culture approach to organizations is very specific. It is the perceived inadequacies of the work of Peters and Waterman (1982) whose *In Search of Excellence* is the most visible (if not the *initiator*) of contributions to the genre. Certain reservations about their study have already been mentioned (see the opening remarks of this chapter, also Chapter 8). The main criticism of Peters and Waterman is that the methodology they employ in their study does not bear close scrutiny. Thompson and McHugh (1990, p. 233) write that companies 'were selected and treated in a cavalier and uncontrolled manner, some being dropped from the original list and evidence from others not in the sample at all being used'. The methodological weaknesses in Peters and Waterman's research need not be detailed, as they are fairly widely agreed among academic commentators. Suffice it to say that their work might not pass muster in terms of specification of necessary definitions (e.g. of 'success') in sample selection, or in the general treatment of results. It may be a little unfair to single out one work in particular for such criticism but given the impact of *In Search of Excellence* on studies of organizational culture, the exercise is a legitimate one.

A second weakness in the work of Peters and Waterman (1982, p. 26) is their own admission (and one picked up on in subsequent research only selectively) that 'Unfortunately, what we found was that associated with almost every excellent company was a strong leader (or two) who seemed to have a lot to do with making the company excellent in the first place'. The use of the negative 'Unfortunately' is important here, as this observation does indeed detract from offering any systematic account of *sociocultural* dimensions to organizational success. On the one hand, it could be argued that influential leaders form the culture of the organization (much as in the Woods, 1989, restaurant study, the companies selected for study all varied in terms of 'cultural' elements), in which case successful organizational culture is to some degree arbitrary. Alternatively, if, as Peters and Waterman (and others) maintain, 'success' factors in organizational management can be discerned as regular patterns and structures, then there must be an array of social mechanisms responsible for these factors that transcend the influence of any one individual.

How these two potentially contradictory views can be reconciled is unclear: if organizational culture is, in essence, the product of arbitrary or at least contingent individual-leader influences, then it is difficult to see how exactly these are institutionalized in a manner that permits them to persist over time. At one and the same time the authors appear to be saying that organizational culture is both the product of (*a*) strong individualistic forces that can be traced to one or a handful of leaders, and (*b*) strong and systematic social influences within the organization.

The problem with meaning in Peters and Waterman's study is compounded, thirdly, by the manner in which successful companies are defined *as* successful. Peters and Waterman used financial criteria as the mainspring to selecting their sample of successful companies, and then proceeded to seek information as to the reasons for this success by focusing on internal organizational processes. They largely ignored the position of the organizations studied within the markets and industries in which they operated. Little attention was paid to external and social and economic factors that influenced the performance of the firms studied.

Peters and Waterman have been fair game for all kinds of critics and much of what has been said could, in reality, be applied to many other authors of the 'culture' movement. The general conclusion to be drawn is that organizational culture approaches have profound limitations. In the hospitality context some of these can be seen in the Woods (1989) study. It has already been noted that many of the features identified by Woods as constituting aspects of the hospitality industry's 'culture' are in fact structural in nature, relating to the manner in which organizations interface with labour markets. Through the actions of their leaders, organizations make *choices* about how to staff their firms, and to this end it is found that hospitality industry companies rely heavily on young, female, and part-time labour.

As indicated earlier, it is unclear as to why all the intellectual paraphernalia of the 'culture' approach employed by Woods in his study is necessary to establishing this, but, interestingly, in arriving at the conclusions he does, Woods points to a much broader approach to organizational culture, one that is excluded from the Peters and Waterman style of commentary. Peters and Waterman are, like many other writers in this field, concerned almost exclusively with the managerial contribution to organizational culture. Yet culture is not simply a matter of management decision or behaviour but the product of all an organization's members. While it is proper to be sceptical about organizational culture approaches advanced by the likes of Peters and Waterman, the phenomenon of organizational culture itself remains, as Thompson and McHugh (1990, pp. 234–5) note, a genuinely interesting field, but only if 'notions of culture which mistake style as substance' are abandoned.

The substance of an organization's culture is formed through the actions of both employers and employees, and is contingent on the social and economic circumstances in which an organization operates and the kinds of decision it makes about staffing, and about objectives and goals, and the methods by which it is intended these will be achieved. In the hospitality industry much of an organization's culture is composed of practices, values and behaviours that derive from the nature of the workforce, which is largely part-time and low paid. For example, practices such as tipping and methods used by staff to increase the likelihood of a tip being received are in part a response to the need to enhance income to compensate for poor pay. The 'culture' of labour turnover is likewise a part-response to poor conditions of employment and the desire of employees to seek ever marginal increments to pay by taking slightly better remunerated jobs as and when they become available. On a final note here, 'management by walking around', so important a feature of Peters and Waterman's observations of successful firms, has arguably always been a feature of hospitality managers' work patterns without any discernible effect on the creation of high-powered cultures à la Peters and Waterman.

It may be objected that the other factors identified by Peters and Waterman need to be present for companies to be successful, a fair point if it were not for the fact that those aspects of organizational culture which writers like Peters and Waterman see as lending themselves to creating a positive culture all have another side, a constraining or controlling side as well as an enabling aspect. Indeed, it has been the main achievement of the organizational culture school of writers to present their arguments as alternatives to control in the workplace, as a means whereby organizational members can be enlisted voluntarily in the pursuit of organizational goals.

In this somewhat unreal world conflict has all but been eradicated, and organizational members united in pursuit of organizational goals.

In this respect organizational culture approaches have been frequently compared with the human relations school approach to industrial relations. Organizational culture approaches are in fact human relations writ large. The central claim is to have achieved harmony and purpose by the use of non-controlling and participative styles of organizational management. These in turn have been facilitated to some extent (so the argument goes) by new approaches to employee relations, the most important of which is the development of 'human resource management', which is examined in Chapter 12, which follows.

Summary

- Organizational culture is the system of values, attitudes and symbols that grows up within an organization as a result of the activities of its members and the interaction of an organization with the external environment.
- Modern discussions of organizational culture have tended to centre on the 'In search of excellence' thesis, which is concerned with the effect of the 'correct' organizational culture on organizational success (particularly in the business context) and the effectiveness of management in creating cultures conducive to this success.
- These approaches to culture place great emphasis on the talents and abilities of organizational leaders in creating the necessary 'vision' for organizational success and in following this vision through in implementing practices that are intended to encourage involvement and participation by all organizational members while removing mechanistic controls over employees in order to generate a climate of trust.
- Studies of the organizational culture phenomenon in the hospitality industry tend to emphasize the importance of organizational leaders in the creation of an appropriate cultural environment, suggesting a tension between individualistic and organizational influences in developing and sustaining culture. It is unclear as to the extent to which organizational culture can be maintained without the influence of charismatic organizational leaders. Studies in the restaurant industry suggest that 'positive' culture is dependent on senior organizational members keeping close control of procedures and practices within the organization in accordance with a personal rather than systematic vision of an organization's mission. In addition, the practices of hospitality managers tend not to be participative and can be excessively controlling, suggesting little match between industry practices and current debates about culture in organizations at the abstract level.

Discussion questions

1   Assess one or more sectors of the hospitality industry against the criteria for organizational and business success outlined by Peters and Waterman.

2   Compare and contrast the organizational cultures of different types of hospitality operation.
3   Outline a specimen policy for the creation of an 'organizational culture' in a new three-star hotel.
4   Can 'culture' ever overcome conflict in hospitality organizations?

12 Human resource management

Like organizational culture, 'human resource management' enjoyed much popularity during the 1980s, although it seems to have transcended organizational culture approaches and had a more profound effect on employees. The objective of this chapter is to outline some of the key issues bearing on 'human resource management' in work organizations, and consider implications for the hospitality industry.

What is human resource management?

The first thing to note is that human resource management is not a simple synonym for personnel management. Many people do use these terms interchangeably, but human resource management is generally conceived as having a much wider scope than personnel management alone. Personnel management is only one element of HRM. Notwithstanding some disputes among academics (and variations in business practice that lead to different emphases), Singh (1992) identifies three component elements to HRM:

- The activities of traditional personnel management, e.g. recruitment, remuneration.
- A specific managerial and organizational 'philosophy' that regards labour as (*a*) the *major* organizational asset, and (*b*) instinctively willing and able to be developed.
- Integration of the personnel management function into the strategic management of the organization.

HRM has its origins in the United States and, in particular, the innovating practices of a small number of large companies, among the most frequently cited being International Business Machines (IBM) and Hewlett-Packard (Towers, 1992). However, as Singh (1992) notes, there is little evidence that human resource management is at all widespread in United States industries. In short, there is a difficulty in establishing the relative degree of hype and reality when examining the claims of organizations to have HRM strategies and policies.

These problems notwithstanding, two issues in the current literature on HRM concerning the *motives* for introducing human resource management policies are worth considering. The first centres on HRM as anti- or non-union. There is some consensus that in the UK at least, the evolving pattern of employee relations and the move towards HRM-type approaches in industry are in part due to the declining significance of trade unions, whose powers have been considerably circumscribed since 1979 as a result of legislative measures by government. HRM fills this gap, so one argument goes, by providing more authoritarian–paternalistic styles of management, which are highly individualistic (and embrace strategies to increase individual commitment to the organization) while at the same time undermining trade unionism or providing a bulwark against unions securing a foothold in organizations.

There are two problems with this view. One is, as Guest (1992) notes, the extent of union derecognition (which might be one indicator of the extent to which HRM policies are anti-union) which was not exceptional during the 1980s. The second is that in industries with little experience of trade unionism, such as hotels and catering, the failure of trade unions has had less to do with enlightened personnel or human resource management strategies than with covert hostility on the part of employees to unions entering the industry, and the failure of unions themselves to devote the necessary resources to organization of the hospitality trades (Wood, 1992; Macaulay and Wood, 1992; Aslan and Wood, 1993).

A second issue bearing on the motives to introduce HRM relates to the evolution of the 'mission statement' approach to organizational strategy. While by no means entirely novel, the widespread development or refinement of organizational mission statements was very much a feature of 1980s approaches to employee relations, and to some extent has grown out of concern with organizational culture (see Chapter 11). As suggested earlier, such statements frequently contain pronouncements about the key role of human resources in defining how organizational missions are to be realized. Yet, as Guest (1992) argues, evidence is suggestive of the fact that more often than not this is little more than lip service to the concept – or put another way, in Hamlet's terms, 'more honoured in the breach than the observance'.

There are therefore some grounds for being sceptical of the very concept of human resource management as a universal, in that by its very nature, extending beyond formalized personnel policies and procedures to link labour management to strategy and culture, HRM can admit a wide range of variants. This is an important point. In places like the UK, where 'traditional' personnel management has developed under the auspices of a strong professional association (the Institute of Personnel Management, IPM) and where there is broad acceptance of the personnel function as specialist in nature and requiring people of appropriately attained standards of knowledge and training, then there has been an evolution of standard practices with wide acceptance across many different types of organization. A broad consensus exists as to both the scope of personnel management and relevant personnel techniques, and the methods of their administration and delivery.

In this sense human resource management can be seen as a source of potential *instability* as far as the process of labour relations is concerned, since the linking of personnel issues to organizational philosophy and strategy allows for much greater flexibility in employee relations policies and may, ironically, undermine such policies or their execution by allowing greater interference by (or, more neutrally, use of) non-specialists in the human resource/personnel/labour function.

There are two basic counters to this view. The first is somewhat unfortunate in that it concerns the status of the personnel function in organizations. This has always been open to question, and even where developed and sophisticated systems have existed, they have sometimes been at best tolerated as a necessary evil. The possibility that a human resource management approach to labour may undermine the personnel function seems, in these circumstances, to be at least, in *prima facie* terms, suspect. A second and more positive view is that the growth of HRM brings the personnel function 'centre stage', enhancing its importance in the organization. Objections to this view have already been noted, in that there is reason to believe that many organizations make little more than a 'nod and a wink' to HRM. Perhaps a more important issue here relates less to this third characteristic of HRM identified by Singh (1992), namely the extent to which HRM personnel techniques management are *integrated* into the strategic management function of the organization, than to the effect such integration has on the nature and quality of personnel techniques and activities.

One key feature of *some* HRM approaches is the creation of highly individualized relationships between employees and the employer in which collective representation and action (among the workforce) is discouraged, particularly as it relates to trade unionism, and individual employees are instead encouraged to enter into more 'personal' relationships with their employer. In this, and the general HRM context/philosophy, specific emphasis is placed on 'quality' in the belief that the quality of the organization and its products/services is closely related to the quality of staff. The pursuit of quality in this respect places great stress on particular personnel techniques, functions and policies, namely (Guest, 1992):

- Recruitment and selection.
- Training.
- The encouragement of flexibility.

In the discussion that follows some of the key elements in each of the above areas are highlighted.

Recruitment and selection

Traditional personnel management has always placed a great deal of emphasis on recruitment and selection. HRM strategies have perhaps enhanced this aspect of the personnel specialist's role. Anderson (1992) identifies six principal elements of employee selection: application forms, selection interviews, selection tests, references, group selection methods, and assessment centres, none of which are mutually exclusive. Anderson notes that, traditionally, personnel management 'technique' has concentrated on matching people to jobs and, though he does not cite specific examples, it may be observed that this has previously been reflected in the emphasis on the practices of job analysis, description and design. Anderson (1992, p. 183) suggests that there is a belief in some quarters that such an approach is too mechanistic, and 'in practice, greater recognition is being given to adopting recruitment and selection practices to permit the assessment of candidates in terms of their suitability for the corporate culture as opposed to a specific job'.

This is clearly consonant with an HRM approach to organizations, though it does not mean that mechanistic methods of employee selection are any less widely used. Indeed there has in some areas perhaps been a greater interest on the part of corporate human resource departments in these techniques (especially psychometric testing), which at the same time is balanced by equal stress on more 'organic' techniques, such as group selection and assessment centre methods. Interviewing remains as important as ever in most organizations, and has assumed a new significance in the light of developing interest in regular performance appraisal.

Psychometric tests

Psychometric tests fall into one of two broad categories – those that seek to measure cognitive abilities and aptitudes, and those that measure more abstract phenomena, such as personality. Intelligence tests could, in theory, fall into either category, except in so far as they infer a concrete value (intelligence quotient – IQ) from a person's performance on a series of problems in which the only options are usually right/wrong. This is almost always certainly true of general ability/aptitude tests also. However, the latter may be stand-alone in the sense that they are not designed to infer IQ, only establish particular competencies (or lack of them).

Psychometric tests are most frequently used in the selection of management, which raises some doubts about the value-added emphasis placed on recruitment and selection in HRM ideologies, as many candidates for operative or non-managerial roles within an organization are excluded. This said, there is some evidence that, while regularly used for management selection in the USA, tests are less widely employed in the UK. Robertson and Makin (1986) found that 64 per cent of British organizations in their survey did not use personality tests and 74 per cent used no cognitive tests. Despite this, there are an increasing number of business-oriented selection and personality manuals available to the general public and these are designed to familiarize individuals with the kinds of test they may encounter (Barrett and Williams, 1990; Bryon and Modha, 1991); and it is not unlikely that at some point in their employment careers people will encounter such tests as part of the recruitment and selection process.

Of current interest in some quarters, including the hospitality industry, is the use of 'biodata' techniques in recruitment and selection (see Mitchell, 1989; Ineson and Brown, 1992). The biodata approach may be used as an adjunct or alternative to other kinds of tests and selection methods. It is based on assigning values to selected groups of items relating to an individual's life history. 'Hard' data are normally collected on a special form (a weighted application blank or WAB) and 'soft' data (attitudinal data, for example) through a questionnaire administered at some point in the selection process. The data collected are compared to control data, which are constituted according to the prime interests of the recruiter. For example, Ineson and Brown (1992) were interested in the possible use of biodata screening to assess interpersonal skills and job flexibility, while Mitchell (1989) focused on the propensity to labour stability among new hires selected by means of a biodata database of previous employees. The success of biodata screening, then, relies on the creation of a suitable database, normally drawing on personnel data collected over time by the organization that is employing the system.

The maintenance of this control data can be expensive and needs to be constantly monitored in order to ensure validity of the biodata instrument. This goes some way to explaining why its use is still somewhat limited in industry. Ineson and Brown (1992) report that a biodata-like system for certain operative positions with Holiday Inn was likely to incur development costs running into hundreds of thousands of pounds. Further, while both Ineson and Brown and Mitchell (1989) make large claims for the predictive accuracy of biodata, the criteria examined by biodata methods are arguably as mechanistic as psychometric tests, as well as restricting the potential for qualitative judgements.

Like psychometric tests, the biodata approach may also to some extent be seen as part of the 'Taylorization' of work, reducing individuals and individual talents, abilities and dispositions to mere ciphers, values on a scale. While this undoubtedly has a positive appeal for many employers, it also creates the potential for contradictions within HRM strategies dedicated to building organizational culture, at one and the same time encouraging the hiring of a uniform cadre of employees (those that 'fit' the organizational culture) while reducing the potential for creative difference and independence deemed appropriate to the values of experimentation and entrepreneurship that are a part of 'culture' approaches to organization and management.

Group assessment and assessment centres

Qualitative judgements in selection remain part of group assessment and assessment centre methods of selection, and may be directed towards seeking to appraise candidates' social and communication skills in addition to personality, aptitude and leadership potential. There are a variety of group selection techniques, classified by Plumbley (1985) into three general types:

- Leaderless groups, where a group is asked to discuss a topic for a period of time observed by selectors: no formal group leader is appointed.
- Command exercises, where individuals are briefed on a particular hypothetical problem and asked to prepare recommendations within a given time for the problem's resolution, subsequently debating these and defending them against competitor applicants.
- Problem-solving exercises, in which the group as a whole has to work together to solve a particular problem within a given time.

Assessment centres refer not necessarily to a physical place but to a battery of assessment techniques – tests, interviews, group problem-solving – administered in order to obtain a rounded assessment of candidates over a range of measures.

Interviews – the case of appraisal

Interviews remain important in recruitment and selection, and have gained in significance within HRM, where increased emphasis on performance appraisal has been a feature of many HRM strategies. The objectives of appraisal normally include the assessment of past, current and likely future performance (including obstacles to the enhancement of performance within the organization), and determination of what assistance can be rendered by the organization in career planning, both within and outside the organization. Most importantly, appraisal is also often linked to decisions about remuneration, though this should normally constitute only one aspect of the process.

Appraisals should be open and committed, and need to be undertaken by someone who is acceptable to both the appraisee and the organization. This need not necessarily be an employee's line manager but must be clearly someone who has knowledge of an employee's work. To some extent this can be facilitated by ensuring proper documentation is completed before the appraisal of employees.

At the centre of the appraisal process lies the appraisal interview, which is not intended to be a meeting at which grievances are aired or serious criticisms made of the appraisee or organization/employer but rather a constructive dialogue between appraiser and appraisee. Riley (1991, p. 108) makes the very important point that the key to successful appraisal is a thorough understanding on the part of both parties of organizational expectations of specific jobs (i.e. appraisees' jobs) and a similar clarity in respect of accepted organizational performance indicators. The four key elements to be established in the appraisal interview are assessment of performance, assessment of priorities, assessment of barriers to performance, and agreement as to plans for future personal development. Riley also points out that appraisal interviews are time-consuming and should not be sidelined on grounds of time-saving or because the parties to the appraisal assume a cosy relationship of the 'You and I know each other, let's just get this sorted out quickly' type. For appraisal to be successful it also goes without saying that appraisers must not use the appraisal situation as an opportunity to settle old scores with appraisees, or to defend particular organizational practices or decisions.

Training

In recent years training of the workforce has received increased attention from UK industry and government. For the latter in particular, training has been seen as a necessity because of the belief that the UK is competitively disadvantaged *vis-à-vis* other nations in this area. So important has the emphasis on training become that since the early 1980s the government has set in place many schemes in conjunction with industrial and other organizations to complement existing public and private sector provision. Most importantly, from the point of view of this discussion, HRM theory treats training as of crucial importance yet, as Hyman (1992, p. 259) perceptively puts it: 'As employers are consistently failing to train their staff and managers, it is difficult to see how they can be realistically pursuing an HRM approach which is dependent upon learning as the vital route to effective work and organizational performance'.

As noted in Chapter 4, Riley (1991) has argued that the work of most hospitality industry employees comprises a bundle of usually low-level tasks requiring a certain amount of discretionary self-organization. Historically, the hospitality industry (or at least some sectors of it) has not been known for the high standard of training it offers. Nor has the problem seemingly been unique to the UK. Of the USA, Tanke (1990, p. 165) writes:

> In recent years service – or the seeming lack of it – in American society has been making headlines. The hospitality industry has, along with other industries that provide service, had its share of negative publicity. When you think about it, it is really amazing that individuals that are willing to spend thousands and even millions of dollars building a new restaurant or renovating an old landmark hotel fail to allocate enough dollars for training.

In some sectors there is evidence that this situation is changing, that an increasingly systematized attitude towards training is emerging. The question is 'What kind of training?' There are few hospitality industry jobs (that of chef remaining, still, an exception) that require employees to exercise sophisticated technical or task-related skills in the same sense, say, as a computer programmer or a production designer. Yet there is some scope for arguing that the skill content of certain jobs is higher than has traditionally been assumed, e.g. the skills required in room-cleaning and maintenance, work traditionally performed by women but given a low status by (usually male) managers. That employers do not, for the most part, regard training as particularly significant or sophisticated is reflected in the *laissez-faire* attitude adopted to labour turnover and the hiring of part-time and casual workers in large numbers. Of course this is a generalization, but, like all generalizations, is broadly true of many hospitality organizations.

Where employers have perceived the need for more and better training in recent years is in the area of social and communications skills. The problems alluded to in the quotation from Tanke above concern the need to improve and maintain good standards of service. In the UK and USA a good deal of interest in social and communication skills has arisen in the context of concerns over total quality management (TQM). The cynic might argue that this is in fact an instance of enlightened *self-interest*, as TQM and social and communication skills training are not without benefits to the industry (in terms of reducing customer perceptions of poor service). The boom in the communication and social skills industry, which is closely related to sentiments derived from HRM and TQM systems of values, may not be without its pitfalls. Approaches to skills training in these areas fall into two broad categories within the hospitality industry – what will be termed here the 'systematic' and the 'arbitrary'. The systematic approach is associated with a very strong corporate TQM culture – as with, for example, the Disney Corporation and McDonald's – where employee behaviour towards customers may be firmly regulated in order to ensure consistent attitudes and dispositions towards clients. In some cases this might even call for close regulation of the range of employees' verbal utterances (Kottak, 1978).

The arbitary approach, which is much more widespread, requires employers to subscribe to some broad and usually abstract notion of appropriate social and communication skills. In her study of the phenomenon Clark (1993) found that hotel managers usually understood such skills in terms of standards of behaviour that they perceived themselves as embodying! In contrast to 'systematic' approaches to social and communication skills training, these managers believe that appropriate behaviours were largely commonsense in nature and staff learnt or acquired social and communication skills by following managerial role examples. There was little that was systematic about managers' attempts to inculcate staff with these skills, and formal training was non-existent.

Formal training

Whether in respect of social, communication or *technical* skills, there is a belief in some quarters that better training will bring organizational benefits. In the hospitality industry this equation, crudely expressed, runs something like this: better training equals better service equals more satisfied customers equals better 'bottom line' performance (the latter is, itself, often crudely articulated in terms of the view that satisfied guests will return again or act as informal advertising conduits to other potential clients). The proposition is an interesting one but lacks empirical support – indeed it is an ideological assertion in the sense that though there is no evidence to support the veracity of the causal chain of reasoning, the belief that the 'equation' is true is nevertheless very strong.

It may be that in this context the industry is in some ways ahead of academic commentators and the 'training junkies'. The relative neglect of training in the hospitality industry does not seem to have had any measurable effect on the industry's long-term growth or business success. The motivation to train employees in an industry with high labour turnover is bound to be tempered by assessment of the associated financial benefits and disbenefits, and consideration of the relatively limited skills required in most occupations. Indeed it is axiomatic in the work of hospitality industry labour market analysts that employers have actively sought to deskill work in order to gain control of (and reduce) labour costs – not only labour costs in payroll terms but in terms of associated costs such as training (see Riley, 1991; Wood, 1992). Despite this, there is evidence that, in the corporate sector at least, formal qualifications and formal training of employees at all levels has gained in importance. An interesting feature of these developments is the extent to which many are related to *institutional arrangements* for training, i.e. the formal training mechanisms put in place by government and government-related bodies.

Higher education and training

By the end of the 1980s there were over forty first degree courses in hospitality management available in the UK, many higher national diploma courses and an increasing number of postgraduate 1-year conversion courses in the field, designed for students with degree qualifications in other subjects who desired to enter the hospitality sector. In 1965 there were only two degree courses. Historically, hospitality management education has developed and been maintained separately from general management and business studies education, making the field of hospitality studies one of the largest specialist areas of management education available in institutions of higher education. Few, if any, industries have the basic training of their prospective management cadre so heavily subsidized by government.

All institutions offering education in hospitality management naturally claim to base their programmes of study on the requirements of industry, but industrialists' complaints about the lack of adequacy of graduates and diplomates to their needs are perennial. Furthermore, the hospitality industry is reputed to have a high wastage rate, with many of those graduates/diplomates entering the industry upon completion of their studies leaving after a relatively short period. Empirical evidence in support of this latter proposition is slight, but the situation is being gradually clarified by new research (Barron and Maxwell, 1993). If wastage rates are as high as is popularly believed, then, given the cost to the taxpayer of maintaining extensive higher education provision when combined with employers' doubts over the quality of output, there appears to be a major mismatch of individuals to organizational needs, which, if not corrected, may raise serious doubts about both educational strategies and employers' human resource policies.

Youth and employment training

During the 1980s a number of schemes to encourage the training of young workers were set in place. Youth Training (YT) Schemes today have places for 16- and 17-year-olds who have not secured a job nor are in full-time education. Employment Training (ET) Schemes are for workers aged 18–59 who have been unemployed for 6 months or longer. For each scheme there are other qualifying characteristics that may permit access to training (Hayter, 1993). Training schemes pay an allowance or wage (sometimes both) and may comprise a mixture of on-the-job and college training. A variety of organizations run the schemes, from individual employers to government-sponsored local Training and Enterprise Councils (Local Enterprise Companies in Scotland).

National Vocational Qualifications

National Vocational Qualifications (NVQs, Scottish Vocational Qualifications, or SVQs, in Scotland) came into being in 1992 after several years of preparation, and reflect the belief of government and many employers that industry-oriented education and training are not vocational enough, placing too much emphasis on theoretical knowledge at the expense of performance-related applications of that knowledge. The central philosophy of NVQs is that performance is the key to workplace competence, and NVQs are accordingly competence-based, their attainment and award being related to achievements in work performance. NVQs are offered by a variety of organizations, including employers, and are independently audited to ensure quality standards. They may include college study as well as on-the-job training. NVQs are ordered into five levels, the fifth level being the highest. In the hospitality industry, development of NVQs is well advanced and some large hotel companies are operating the lower level qualifications (see Teare, Adams and Messenger, 1992). The potential of NVQs for standardizing training across the industry and raising quality is considerable, though the NVQ system is immensely bureaucratic, and the ever-present difficulty of 'selling' training in this form to the dominant small-firm sector has not been tackled in any systematic fashion.

What is perhaps most interesting about the institutional arrangements for training that arose during the 1980s is the extent to which they harness the power of government to industrial and other organizations in various partnerships. In many ways the subsidy to industry paid by government in terms of the financing and development of training in these forms runs counter to the free-market spirit of that period. It is thus sometimes difficult to see where partnership ends and the holding of industry's hands begins. What is clear is the extent to which the initiatives of the state in respect of training have to some extent coincided with the spirit of human resource management philosophies that grew up in the UK during the same period. The danger is that, in putting so much emphasis on training, it will come to be viewed as a universal panacea for industrial ills, obscuring the tendency towards short-termism in British industry that exists particularly in respect of investment in technology and manufacturing (Randlesome, 1990).

Flexibility

Workforce flexibility has been a key aspect of human resource management philosophies. The flexible working debate is, at one level, concerned with the attempt to create workforces that are capable of performing a variety of often unified tasks according to organizational demands. The term unified is important here because it signals a return to the 'rounded' worker, who is allowed a degree of discretionary intellectual and manual freedom in the performance of work. This contrasts with the highly specialized worker, who functions in a very narrow way as part of a rigorous division of labour and who is closely controlled.

In the UK at least flexible working has been seen less as a theoretical exercise or training challenge than as a means of managing industrial cost structures. In a study conducted by the Advisory, Conciliation and Arbitration Service (ACAS) (1988) it was found that most employers were seeking to introduce flexible working in order to increase productivity and reduce labour costs. Far from heralding the resurrection of an old philosophy of work therefore, it appears that flexibility is not used as a means of reconstituting labour as a more highly trained, multi-skilled resource, but instead as a device for controlling labour inputs (and therefore labour costs) to the organization.

The two principal types of work flexibility are numerical flexibility and functional flexibility. Numerical flexibility consists of adjusting the number of workers employed, or the length of time worked, to meet demand by the use of temporary, part-time and casual employers; increased overtime working; changes in shift patterns; variable working times; and devices such as job-sharing. Functional flexibility consists of increasing the flexibility of employees in terms of the skills they are able to employ in their work. Often referred to as multi-skilling, functional flexibility entails costs to the firm, as money needs to be spent on (re)training workers to meet these demands. In this respect functional flexibility may be seen as a less attractive option than numerical flexibility to firms with relatively low skill requirements where labour can be hired relatively cheaply.

The flexibility debate has attracted a good deal of interest from researchers in the hotel and catering field (see Wood, 1992, for a review). The main findings of investigations to date can be summarized as follows. First, numerical flexibility has been found to be fairly extensively employed at operative level in the hospitality industry, particularly in respect of the use of female part-time labour. Women are likely to be 'numerically flexible' and male workers 'functionally flexible', i.e. women's skills are rarely developed across a range of tasks. Rather, women are employed for specific tasks at particular times of the day, and consequently have much less opportunity to develop those skills that would make them functionally flexible. A *caveat* to these general trends is that hospitality organizations staff their units in many different ways, and units (hotels, restaurants) that experience little fluctuation in business levels often rely on a core of full-time staff, with only a small periphery of part-time casual workers.

Second, little evidence has been found of the use of functional flexibility in the hospitality industry. Lockwood and Guerrier (1989) found little evidence from their study of hotels that functional flexibility was an issue, and indeed cross-departmental working was not actively encouraged. This might be attributable to the phenomenon of departmentalization in hotels. The department is the basis of budgeting standards as a cost-centre, and the traditional approach to hotel management that supports this concept of separate departments oriented towards particular financial and service targets is well entrenched. The sceptic would also note that functional flexibility requires money (for training) and a relatively stable demand environment. The latter is especially important, as it is far easier in conditions of relatively uncertain demand for employers to vary total labour input than skill mix. Perhaps of greater significance is the way in which much of the hospitality sector operates on a 24-hour a day basis, making it difficult to schedule a small, core, multi-skilled workforce to 'cover all the angles'. Yet, as Lockwood and Guerrier (1989) show, there are circumstances in which this does occur, and it is therefore achievable (see also Mars, Bryant and Mitchell, 1979).

The real problem with functional flexibility is, as Riley (1992) notes, that management in the hospitality industry needs a good argument to support more widespread adoption, especially when current practices dependent on numerical flexibility have proven successful in both matching labour supply to customer demand and controlling labour costs. One barrier to the adoption of functional flexibility is managers' perception of the costs associated with functional flexibility in the light of *high labour turnover*, and their acceptance of high labour instability as a fact of life and something to be accepted rather than ameliorated. Riley (1992, p. 367) rightly implies that labour stability is necessary to the implementation of functional flexibility schemes, and remarks that 'functional flexibility will evolve only when there is a constant qualitative demand from consumers which forces management to retain their staff'.

Human resource management in the hospitality industry

From the foregoing discussion it appears that in the hotel and catering context there is real and potential tension between certain aspects of human resource management policies. The emphasis on recruitment and training with a view to the maintenance of stability within the workforce does not rest easily with the contrary practice of encouraging a numerically flexible workforce. In any human resource strategy there are, however, bound to be tensions, and as the purpose of this and other chapters in Part Four is to outline some potential issues and controversies in organizational behaviour, it would serve to consider the point that the degree of variability of practices within the hospitality industry means that while it is possible to make broad generalizations about labour strategies, there will always be some exceptions to the general trend. In concluding the present discussion it is important to put the hospitality industry's practices into some context.

To say that hotels and catering have, in the past, somewhat neglected the personnel and human resource functions is to articulate a near truism. In the UK the Commission on Industrial Relations (1971) found few hotel companies had industrial relations or personnel policies and strategies. Johnson (1978) argues that hospitality organizations tend to marginalize the personnel function, the responsibility for which often lies with unit managers who have little or no training in the area. Kelliher and Johnson (1987) reported that the presence of a personnel specialist in a hotel unit was closely related to the size of the unit, larger hotels being more likely to have specialist personnel managers. In smaller establishments responsibility for personnel was delegated to a wide variety of people, all of whom held other functional responsibilities, from the managing director to the general manager's secretary! In medium-sized hotels personnel responsibilities tended to fall to assistant managers, many of whom had no formal training *or* previous experience of personnel matters, but whose confidence in performing their duties was unaffected because of their ability to rely on standard company personnel manuals. Croney (1988) found that executive level company support for personnel and human resource management policies bore little relation to what happened at unit level. Across a range of variables, including pay, recruitment, selection and employee participation, Croney found considerable variation between statements of company philosophy and the beliefs and practices of unit managers.

One of the most compelling commentaries on hospitality organizations' attitudes towards the personnel function is offered by Umbreit (1987), who reports, *inter alia*, that a study of hotel managers in three different companies requiring respondents to weight the importance of seven hotel manager performance measures yielded a lowest weighting in the case of all three firms for the handling of personnel issues. As Umbreit's review shows, the majority of all studies of what goes in hospitality (and particularly hotel) organizations demonstrate that, despite paying lip service to the concept of effective human resource management policies and their value to organizational success, most hotel executives and managers operate in an environment where such policies are notable by their absence.

Umbreit is optimistic that in order to maintain operational quality, the conventional short-termism that characterizes hospitality management practices will eventually give way to systematic human resource policies. Certainly there is some intimation in the trade press that in large companies at least, there is a more positive move in this direction, but it remains too early to make any hard and fast judgements of the commitment of the corporate sectors of the industry in this respect. The hospitality industry has a considerable track record of both contriteness and personnel initiatives in response to criticism. The development of high quality human resource strategies is perhaps antithetical to the pursuit of the low wage policies that typify the industry, and is reflected in the hiring of large numbers of part-time and casual workers.

In one of the few direct studies of HRM policies in hospitality organizations so far undertaken, Ishak and Murrmann (1990) found that out of five human resource management practices deemed central to integrated business strategy, only four (human resource planning, staffing, appraisal, and training and development) exhibited anything approaching significant levels of integration into the strategies of the restaurant firms studied, and one, compensation, was not deemed by respondents to be integral to business strategy at all. The implications of Ishak and Murrmann's analysis appear to be that (*a*) there is a possibility that human resource management strategies in hospitality organizations exclude remuneration from their scope, and (*b*) that this might be attributable to the highly localized nature of wages bargaining – even in chain organizations – and the discretion allowed managers in setting remuneration levels. Whatever the case, it must certainly be true that even if the majority of chains adopted the kind of human resource strategies held up as 'ideal', the necessary improvements to total quality and employee relations that might be engendered would be unlikely to be felt in the small-firms sector which dominates the hospitality industry and in which both product and service quality and working conditions are generally held to be much more variable.

On a more contentious note, it might be argued that until hospitality organizations are prepared to address the role of competitive payment for employees seriously, then any attempts at developing integrated human resource management strategies are unlikely to resolve the fundamental problems of motivation and retention that are beloved of theoreticians but are perhaps largely inappropriate in a sector where skill levels and requirements are low, and labour plentiful and cheap.

Summary

- Human resource management is a term that describes the integration of personnel practices into the strategic missions of organizations that, in turn, recognize that people are the major organizational asset.
- The extent to which business organizations pay more than lip service to the concept of human resource management is, on the balance of evidence, in doubt.
- Human resource strategies place particular emphasis on recruitment and selection, training, and flexibility in the employment relationship.
- In recent years there has been a growth in emphasis on training in most sectors of the economy, heavily motivated by government. This is certainly the case in the field of hospitality, where training has received enormous emphasis.
- Hospitality organizations have always had a poor reputation for effective personnel management practices, though it appears that many hospitality organizations, particularly in the corporate sector, now seek to adopt a human resource management approach to employee relations. This is tempered by the knowledge that pay and rewards remain generally low in the industry, with little evidence of training being linked to greater rewards. Low wage strategies may well be inimical to the effective development of human resource management strategies. Limited research evidence suggests that this view is supported by the failure of many operators in the industry to regard remuneration as an integral element of organizational human resource strategy.

Discussion questions

1 How is human resource management supposed to differ from traditional personnel management and administration?
2 Outline factors that might be considered appropriate for inclusion in an appraisal strategy for managerial workers in hospitality organizations.
3 What reasons (if any) can be advanced in support of the view that conditions of employment in hospitality organizations would be improved, and labour turnover reduced, if employers invested more in training?
4 Discuss the proposition that effective human resource management in the hospitality industry must link performance to pay.

13 Power and empowerment

The nature of power in organizations is an important issue if only because of its relative neglect in mainstream organizational behaviour texts (Thompson and McHugh, 1990, p. 140). At the outset, three observations can be made about the treatment of power in organizational behaviour theory. These are that:

- Power is generally dealt with in the context of organizations' internal relations, i.e. discussion focuses on internal power relations and does not take particular account of the ways in which these relations can extend beyond the organization.
- Power is often conceived of as primarily an individual and inter-personal 'property', as something that is exercised by individuals, or channelled between individuals; this sometimes leads power as a property of groups within the organization to be underrated.
- Power is often related to concerns about how those in positions of leadership and authority should exercise power rather than the quality or legitimacy of that power.

These themes will be detectable to a greater or lesser degree throughout the chapter in the review of key concepts that follows.

Definitions of power

Power is a notoriously slippery concept to define. At one level, it is easy to slip into cosy definitions that see power as akin to leadership, i.e. power is the ability to influence others (Moorhead and Griffin, 1989, p. 356). There is a difference between power and leadership, however: the quality of power rests not so much on its relative features (abilities to influence) but on its absolute qualities in respect of how power is exercised. Power may well be exercised through the influencing of others but it may also be coercive, whereas the very woolliness of the concept of leadership implies a charismatic non-coercive quality (see Chapter 9). Coercive power can itself take several forms. At one extreme, power is the ability of individuals or groups to *impose* their will on others by threat of violence or other sanctions. Power may also descend from the position held by an individual, i.e. the power to obtain others' compliance rests on the legitimacy of that individual's position.

In reality, then, power is a complex phenomenon, and definitions in terms of influence alone are certainly inadequate to any comprehensive understanding of the many facets of power. Influence – particularly informal influence – is an important aspect of power, indeed may in some settings even *be* power, but in most organizational contexts power is much more than this. The most important features of power may be said to be:

- The ability to secure the compliance of others in particular courses of action by virtue of force, threat of sanctions (for a failure to comply), or legitimate authority that has broadly accepted cultural significance.
- The ability to secure the compliance of others in particular courses of action by virtue of *personal* influence sometimes unrelated to formal sources of authority but always resting on the willingness of those at whom power is directed to subordinate themselves to the will of those who seek to influence.

Bases of power

In order to elaborate the definitional problems associated with the concept of power, it is necessary to examine in greater detail the various sources of power available to individuals within the organization. The most persistently influential model of sources or bases of power in organizations is that offered by French and Raven (1959), who identified five major forms of power deriving from the structure and distribution of organizational resources. These were:

- Reward power.
- Coercive power.
- Referent power.
- Legitimate power.
- Expert power.

Reward power

Reward power is where one person commands the resources necessary to reward others. Rewards may not always take the form of financial remuneration but may include promotions, increased social status and enhanced opportunities for job satisfaction through people being allocated more rewarding tasks.

Reward power has important implications for the hospitality industry. In addition to basic pay and other formalized and semi-formalized rewards, such as subsidized food (meals on duty) and accommodation, some occupations in the industry are, as previously noted, characterized by access to informal rewards. In respect of tipped occupations, a supervisor or manager in a restaurant may, for example, be able to control the allocation of both waiting stations and customers to those stations, and can therefore influence which employees get the 'best' stations (the physical geography of many restaurants can influence the level of tip receipts by virtue of the fact that 'badly' located stations, e.g. those with tables near kitchen doors, are rarely allocated to 'better' clients) and to which stations the 'best' customers (visibly wealthy or regular clients) are allocated (see Bowey, 1976, and Mars and Nicod, 1984, for an elaboration of these points).

Coercive power

Coercive power rests for its potency on the relation between fear and harm. A person that seeks to exercise coercive power within an organization may physically or psychologically be able to harm others through the application of sanctions or discipline. If reward power has potentially positive associations for behaviour, then coercive power relies for its force on the possible negative outcomes for those who are subjected to that power. Of course, coercive power in most organizations often takes more subtle forms than the threat of physical harm; the real potential for coercive power lies in psychological harm (humiliation of individuals in the eyes of others) or in terms of material deprivation, e.g. depriving a person of some aspect of status or remuneration.

Referent power

Referent power is a concept that returns to the formal/informal dichotomy existing in many social settings and manifesting itself in organizations in formal and informal groups and leaders. Referent power is that associated intrinsically with an individual's personality. The individual garners the cooperation and acquiescence of others by virtue of his or her quasi-charismatic qualities. Referent power may coincide with formal organizational authority or it may not (see the discussion on leadership in Chapter 9), but the essence of this form of power lies in the positive emotional response it engenders in others.

Legitimate power

Legitimate power is that which derives from an individual's position within the organization. It is legitimate because the organization vests power and authority in that position. Each position in an organization is closely related to every other, and the limits or boundaries of legitimate power associated with any single position are usually established by these relationships. Thus the head of department A has legitimate power over subordinates in department A but probably likely as not over subordinates in department B.

Expert power

Expert power, as the term suggests, derives from some technical or other expert quality an individual possesses and which others feel obliged to accept as being in some way exceptional. Often expert power is related to knowledge and/or information. Expert power may accrue to individuals who have a specialist formal training or skill in some area, skill and training which *within the organization* is relatively scarce. Another form of expert power is that deriving from experience in a particular organizational role over a period of time. It is not uncommon to find organizations where long-serving individuals in some posts have acquired so much information about the qualities of that post and the way it impacts on the running of the organization that they are widely regarded within the organization as 'expert'. The same applies also to those who have served with the organization for a long time and have acquired a reputation as 'fixers'.

Power and its uses

The foregoing typology says quite a lot about the types and sources of power within the organization. As with all ideal types, however, it is important to remember that in reality, individuals who wield power may utilize different combinations of sources and types of power. This was hinted at in the two main characteristics of power suggested earlier, and it is a theme taken up by several other writers. Moorhead and Griffin (1989, pp. 360–2), for example, highlight the simple distinction between *position* and *personal* power. Position power (that associated with a particular job or role in the organization) encompasses legitimate, reward and some aspects of coercive and expert power. Personal power 'belongs' to individuals irrespective of their positions in the organization and embraces referent power, and often elements of expert, coercive and reward power as well.

Arguments about sources and types of power are of academic interest and can ultimately tend towards sterility. One reason for this is the aforementioned tendency in some organizational behaviour contexts to view power as *primarily* an individual or inter-personal phenomenon. The typology of French and Raven (1959) can in each individual respect be applied to groups in some degree (a fact these authors at least implicitly recognize). It is undoubtedly true that there are many organizations in which the power and authority of individuals are important features of organizational life. However, power is also exercised by groups or sub-units within organizations, by *coalitions* of interest groups or individuals. These coalitions will, usually, be based on occupational groups or sub-units and divisions of the organization.

In the case of both individual and collective/group models of power the main issue is the reason why power is sought and the uses to which it is put. In considering these points, it is necessary to make a distinction between the power exercised by the organization, and by individuals/groups within the organization, while at the same time avoiding the trap of treating organizations as if they have in some way a life of their own. The power exercised by the organization is exercised through its office-holders and is in theory directed towards achieving organizational goals and controlling the resources – including human resources – necessary to such goal attainment. In this context power is the means by which control over the direction of the organization is achieved.

Depending on the organizational structure, power is distributed among office-holders by senior decision-makers and organizational controllers. In highly bureaucratic and mechanistic organizations the power of office-holders will be fairly clearly defined. In more cooperative 'organic' organizations the distribution of power will be more blurred. In arguing thus, it is important to avoid treating power as if it were some tangible artefact. Sometimes it is possible to observe power being exercised but in many instances power derives its strength, so to speak, from *not* being used. Rather, the possibility that power *may* be used is sufficient to ensure compliance of an organization's members with the organization's rules and mission. A corollary of this position is that, while 'the organization's power' cannot be divorced from the individuals within the organization that exercise power, for many individuals working in organizations there is an abstract concept of organizational power, which may be manifest in a 'them and us' attitude or in an equation of the power of office-holders with the power of the organization.

At the same time, it is too simplistic to view power as something wholly abstract. Organizational members are often aware of (indeed are sometimes active in) power games. Power does not simply flow in one direction within an organization, e.g. flowing downwards from the top to other organizational members. Rather it can flow in several directions as individuals within the organization seek to acquire some element of power for themselves or for the groups of which they are members. Thus the power of office-holders within the organization (managers and the like) may be used as a basis for securing more resources for themselves or their departments or for seizing more power within an organization in order to influence the organization's mission. In extreme circumstances, an attempt may be made to change the nature of the *total* power structure of the organization itself, e.g. boardroom coups.

The activities of those who already possess some power may be complemented by the activities of those who are relatively powerless. For example, 'ordinary' members of the organization, the non-managerial workforce, may seek to acquire power through a variety of means – formal means such as trade unions perhaps being the most common. There are, however, informal means of attaining power and control over aspects of organizational processes and procedures. The tendency to slow production in order to seize some power and control over the work process is a feature of many industrial settings (Roy, 1952, is a classic study, though in the catering context Paterson, 1981, is instructive).

Within an organization therefore, power may be sought and exercised for a variety of reasons. It is important to note in arguing thus that power within organizations is not distributed equally, nor are power relationships static. In respect of the latter, particular alliances between individuals or groups for a specific purpose that exist today may not exist tomorrow. Alliances and loyalties shift according to mutual interests. In addition, power that exists in one centre within an organization may vary in strength from time to time. For example, a department within an organization that has a strong leader commanding considerable power may well have its status affected by that person leaving.

It is necessary to recognize, however, that the unequal distribution of power within organizations manifests itself not only in relations between the relatively powerful. One of the principal uses to which organizational power is put is control, especially the control by organizational office-holders (the relatively powerful) over its 'ordinary' members (the relatively powerless). The importance of the concept of relativity has already been laboured somewhat, but the main point is that, however power is distributed, however much or little power individuals and groups have, there are competing structures of power within an organization – and sometimes the competition is very weak. Put another way, one purpose of the vesting of powers in organizational office-holders is to give them control over the relatively powerless, control to direct, discipline, punish and reward but also control over the balance of power itself, to maintain the inequalities in the distribution of power between organizational controllers and leaders and other organizational members. The distribution of power is therefore nearly always unequal and biased in favour of 'the organization'.

Power in hospitality organizations

Power in large hospitality organizations tends to be heavily devolved to units and to the managers of these units. Certain organizational office-holders tend to enjoy – all other things being equal – a great deal of power. Because of the responsibilities they bear, general managers have considerable scope for exercising power. In certain circumstances (and ensuring that analysis is not clouded by the industry's often apocryphal folklore) head chefs also enjoy a deal of latitude and power. A general manager's power may be described variously as position power, or reward, coercive or legitimate power. Within the domain of the kitchen this may also be true of the head chef, though, in the organization of a unit as a whole the head chef's power may derive more from his or her particular expertise as a highly skilled worker. In respect of the wider management team, power and authority is drawn from a variety of sources. Food and beverage managers tend to enjoy considerable leverage, not simply because of the intrinsic importance of the food and beverage function but because, within the hospitality industry more generally, the food and beverage management route is regarded as especially significant in securing more senior positions.

An important observation is the extent to which in most organizations power is gendered. Hospitality organizations are no exception. Low status departments within a hotel, for example, are usually those headed and extensively staffed by women. Women's management careers in the industry also tend to follow routes that lead them into positions of limited status and power – so-called staff positions, such as sales and marketing, and personnel – despite the fact that the hospitality sector has one of the highest proportions of women managers of any industry (see Wood, 1992, for a review of this issue). In a 1992 article by Mel Jones in the trade magazine

Caterer and Hotelkeeper (reported in Hayter, 1993) it was revealed that, for seven hotel groups on which explicit information was available, only 9.7 per cent of general managers were women (35 out of 358).

In many hospitality organizations power (or managerial power at any rate) tends to be exercised directly. The culture of management 'by walking about', whereby members of the management team adopt a 'hands-on', direct supervisory role, means that subordinate members of the organization are fairly tightly policed. Furthermore, management guards its prerogatives jealously, which explains how (rightly or wrongly) hospitality managers have acquired the reputation for autocratic, heavy-handed styles of administration (Dronfield and Soto, 1980). In these contexts power is directed explicitly towards control and monitoring of employees in order that managers retain a tight rein on operational standards and their responsibility for product and service quality.

Empowerment in hospitality organizations

Very much part of the organizational culture and human resource management movements of the 1980s onwards, employee empowerment has also attracted the attention of hospitality organizations and academic analysts in the field. The essence of empowerment in a hospitality context is enshrined in the remarks of E.G. Sullivan, a former regional vice-president of Hyatt Hotels in the USA (quoted in Brymer, 1991, p. 58):

> Managers in the hotel business must train employees and empower them to handle most guest incidents on the spot and with good judgement – promptly, professionally, and courteously. This will improve guest service and satisfaction, create a better working environment for the employees, and free up more time for managers to focus on the tasks of being a manager.

Brymer notes that, for many, these suggestions had the appearance of radicalism, and he implies that strategies like these are likely to be greeted with some resistance, as decision-making authority in hospitality organizations is something that managers have often worked hard to secure.

Employee empowerment 'is the process of decentralizing decision-making in an organization, whereby managers give more discretion and autonomy to the front-line employees' (Brymer, 1991, p. 59). In hospitality organizations empowerment can take at least two forms – devolution of decision-making powers to staff in respect of customer care, and the devolution of power to enable wider decisions about organizational procedures and processes to be taken by front-line workers. Brymer and other commentators on empowerment in hospitality organizations, e.g. Jones and Davies (1991) and Sternberg (1992), have identified a number of features of empowerment and empowerment programmes (many of which will be common to other kinds of organization). These include the following:

- Employee empowerment is a philosophy of leadership requiring the support of senior organizational executives.

- Empowerment requires a reorientation of traditional approaches to hierarchical, managerial authority-centred organizational practices through the devolution of power to operative 'front-line' workers.
- The surrender of certain control and decision-making capacities to front-line workers by managers requires both an individual and collective emotional commitment (in terms of trusting employees to make decisions) and a systematic commitment to ensure that empowerment strategies are clearly defined in terms of the latitude allowed front-line workers.
- A corollary of the preceding point is that empowerment strategies require that front-line workers be properly *trained* in the necessary skills (social skills, communication skills, and decision-making skills).

A number of observations can be made about the characteristics of empowerment. First, those research reports that have examined the implementation of empowerment strategies in hospitality organizations have highlighted the fact that a major barrier to successful empowerment is the *lack of trust* that managers and other organizational office-holders have in the capacity of ordinary front-line employees to make decisions that are usually the province of management. For example, Sternberg (1992, p. 72) writes that resistance to empowerment schemes arises among executives and managers because of lack of trust of the workforce and urges that 'In responding to our work force, we must move from an attitude of distrust and control to one of trust and respect'.

The sources of mistrust include of course the reluctance of managers to give up the hard-earned power that is so integral to their position. However, another source of mistrust is managements' concern that employees might 'give away too much, without regard to costs and the bottom line' (Brymer, 1991, p. 58). In other words, managers are concerned that empowered employees will make decisions that are not in accordance with organizational interests.

This leads, secondly, to another general point about empowerment that has more specific implications for hospitality organizations. This is that recognition of problems of trust and control of operative employees by managers in organizations generates the regularization of empowerment policies. This may be represented by the dichotomy between *structured* and *flexible* empowerment (Brymer, 1991).

Structured empowerment lays down precisely those specific courses of action front-line employees may take in certain specified circumstances, e.g. if a guest complains about noise from the ventilation system in their room there will be a specific instruction as to what course of action an employee should take. The problem with structured empowerment systems is that it is, in reality, virtually impossible to legislate for all possible guest complaints and problems. The main advantage of structured systems is that they provide for standardized responses to problems (equity in the treatment of guests), set parameters – where appropriate – for financial compensation allowed to guests (thereby acting as a means of cost control) and ensure that employee empowerment is an explicit articulation of the wishes of management.

As presented by Brymer (1991), flexible empowerment does not differ extensively from the structured variety. Here again general recommendations are laid down about financial compensation that may be made to guests under certain conditions. The major difference between structured and flexible empowerment systems is that, in general, very few *specific* instances of employee behaviour are legislated for. Thus employees are not provided with a blow-by-blow list of potential customer problems with instructions on how to respond. The advantage of this approach is that financial constraints are maintained in respect of compensation. The major disadvantage is that the level of standardization of employee responses to clients is of a lower order, and may generate inconsistencies in the application of these standards.

The third and final comment that follows from this is that despite the potential for different types of employee empowerment in hospitality organizations – empowerment to make decisions concerning internal organizational processes and procedures as well as empowerment to serve customers better – it is the latter that has proved to be most attractive to organizational leaders in the sector if existing research evidence is to be believed. This suggests that trust in the decision-making capacities of employees extends only so far, and there is caution in the approach of hotel and catering managers to the empowerment of workers in respect of internal organizational processes. This may of course change, as might the seeming preference for 'structured' empowerment. In fact there is little in the way of extensive hard evidence to say whether 'structured' empowerment schemes are, in reality, more popular than the flexible variety within the hospitality industry. This does not matter, however, in that it seems that, as currently practiced, empowerment in hotel and catering organizations amounts to little more than a convenient label for describing enhanced customer care schemes.

This view is to an extent supported by Wynne (1993) in her study of empowerment and customer service in a five-star hotel. She argues that employee empowerment is frequently a means whereby management expands the role of front-line workers – a form of job enlargement – without providing additional rewards. Since empowerment in a customer-care context often requires extra training, and implies skill enhancement, the empowered employee is therefore one who performs extra, skilled, work duties for no extra rewards (see also Hales, 1987, whose analysis of quality of working life measures in hospitality organizations partially supports Wynne's research findings). Wynne is emphatic in stating that extra work for no extra money is *not* empowerment. Increased responsibility without additional reward is, she suggests, a form of additional organizational–managerial control, as mistakes made by empowered employees rest with them. In situations of 'structured empowerment' as described by Brymer (1991), the increased pressure of responsibility on employees might be considerable, as formalized and bureaucratic documentation on how, and to what degree, employees should respond to clients' problems and complaints reduces scope for initiative but allows sufficient flexibility for managerial interpretations of erroneous responses.

Perhaps what much of this discussion demonstrates is how reluctant those who hold power are to relinquish it. Further, as Wynne (1993) observes, the idea that power can in some way be isolated and 'parcelled out' to individuals and groups in organizations is a somewhat fanciful notion. Power, as was suggested in the earlier discussion, is a highly complex phenomenon not easily amenable to precise identification, quantification or evaluation of its effects in use.

Summary

- Power is difficult to define, having many facets. In organizations power is distinguished from leadership in that leadership is largely non-coercive, whereas even in organizations power may, theoretically, be used coercively.
- Power may derive from formal (organizational) sources or informal (organizational and personal–charismatic) sources. Power is the ability to secure the willing subordination of others.
- While power has many personal or individualistic associations, much power in organizations is centred in groups or coalitions of individuals. Power tends to be unequally distributed in organizations, but there may, nevertheless, be competing power structures in an organization.
- Power in hospitality organizations is often exercised direct by virtue of the close physical proximity of organizational officers (managers, supervisors) to employees.
- Recent interest in the nature of power in organizations has focused on empowerment – the devolution of power to ordinary organizational members by organizational office-holders.
- In hospitality organizations, empowerment has tended to be directed towards customer care, allowing employees some scope for dealing with client grievances and problems without reference to management. This empowerment, however, is usually a highly structured phenomenon that legislates for particular courses of action rather than allowing for the exercise of too much employee discretion.
- The fashion for empowerment in hospitality organizations is perhaps attributable to the greater control empowerment gives managers over employees in terms of increasing the latters' responsibility without increasing their rewards.

Discussion questions

1 In hospitality organizations how far is power the personal 'property' of individuals and how much does it derive from organizational imperatives?
2 Consider how far different types of power may be identified as being present in hospitality organizations.
3 How is managerial power exercised in hospitality organizations and with what general consequences?
4 Is use of the term empowerment a convenient way of disguising managerial strategies to get more out of employees for no extra reward?

14 Conclusion: organizational behaviour and the hospitality industry

The objective of this book has been to offer an overview of the main concerns of organizational behaviour and indicate possible relations and applications to the hospitality industry. Throughout, it has been assumed that a sceptical approach to these issues is proper: not sceptical in a destructive sense, but in pointing to strengths and weaknesses in organizational behaviour approaches. No subject discipline or subject area has a monopoly on truth, and may be strengthened if practitioners, producers and consumers of the knowledge created adopt a sceptical stance to research findings and wider theoretical claims. The objective of this last chapter is to place organizational behaviour in some sort of context by arguing that the history of the way in which its role as a subject has been conceptualized is seriously limiting to its potential. The argument presented is simple – even simplistic – and short. It will be, for some people at least, controversial. If the following discussion has a single aim, it is to encourage an appreciation of both the strengths *and* weaknesses of organizational behaviour.

Theoretical issues

As indicated in Chapter 1, organizational behaviour is less a discrete discipline than a field of study. It draws on a variety of social science disciplines – principally sociology and psychology but also economics and politics – to study topics relevant in an organizational setting. Organizations are the *focus* of study and any knowledge from whatever source that can help in increasing understanding and creating further knowledge is fair game to the organizational behaviour specialist.

This is an acceptable intellectual ambition and one that has received considerable commendation from teachers and researchers in the hospitality field. Slattery (1983), for example, sees the proper duty of the researcher as being to focus on hospitality 'problems' and utilize whatever resources are available in analysing and solving these. Wood (1988) has criticized this view, pointing out that from the stance of the researcher, teacher and student, subjects like organizational behaviour can fragment knowledge so much as to render the field of study meaningless and lacking in integrity. Wood in turn has been taken to task by Mullins (1992, p. 30) for urging a form of social science teaching on hospitality management courses that is firmly grounded in systematic knowledge and is therefore, in the first instance, generalized, i.e. knowledge must hold as knowledge before the question of its vocational relevance or applications is considered. Mullins writes that 'such an approach...would seem unlikely to gain favour with either students or practitioners' and goes on to argue that 'The use of the social sciences should be seen as part of the toolkit of management, to be drawn upon and used as particular circumstances demand'.

On the first point Mullins may be right but on the second he is surely wrong. The idea that the social sciences should be seen as a toolkit is an unfortunate analogy, for it assumes that management (or managers) have access to the body of systematic knowledge that *is* social science – and few if anybody has this, even social scientists! Students and managers rarely make use of social scientific knowledge in a direct sense in the business context but rather employ models and concepts, theories, conclusions and prescriptions that arise, in this case, from organizational behaviour, and it is these for the most part that embody the application of social science to organizational 'problems' by researchers. It is thus of some importance that the conclusions to be drawn from the application of these concepts to organizational behaviour are laid bare in terms of the assumptions and methods employed to arrive *at* these conclusions.

This highlights another problem with Mullins' position: whereas the major strength of organizational behaviour may lie in the extent to which it encourages an inter-disciplinary perspective on particular themes and issues, this can also be viewed as its major drawback. This is because inter-disciplinarity is encouraged by the intellectual focus upon a particular 'research problem' – in the case of organizational behaviour this is the nature, quality and effects of human action in organizational settings and how best to control them. The very essence of this approach is that the *object* of interest (organizations and organizational behaviour) take precedence over the context in which the object of interest arises, namely society. To take a medical analogy, it is a little like a doctor treating a broken leg without establishing how the break occurred. The broken leg *can* be treated without knowing how the injury came about, but the quality of treatment might be improved by the possession of such knowledge.

A third difficulty with the social-science-as-toolkit approach is that in the creation of organizational behaviour as a credible field of academic study its practitioners have relied heavily for validating their position on the claim that organizational behaviour is *vocationally relevant*, i.e. relevant to the extent that it can be used to manage organizations more effectively. This means that the problems and priorities of organization creators, leaders and managers have guided research activity, making it difficult to escape organizational behaviour's one-sided manipulative potential. Organizational behaviour as defined by most textbooks certainly pays lip service to the social context in which organizations function, to the conflict and inequality found in society, which means that different groups confront organizations differently. For the most part, however, as defined by its literature, organizational behaviour is primarily concerned with processes within the organization, which often means in practice excluding from the focus of study those external factors that bear on organizational forms and activities.

So far, then, some of the main 'downsides' of organizational behaviour have been identified. It is fair to say that the case has been somewhat exaggerated for effect. Organizational behaviour *has* developed its own critical traditions. Some writers are more frank than others. Moorhead and Griffin (1989, p. 763), for example, write:

> Some managers and many students...seem confused by what appears an endless litany of theories and by sets of contradictory research findings. They often ask, 'Why bother?'...Indeed, few absolute truths have emerged from studies of organizational behaviour.

Organizational behaviour has also been the focus of critique from those whose study of organizations is conducted from within the mainstream of other disciplines, notably sociologists and sociology (see Reed, 1992, for a good account of recent issues). It may seem heretical, but a worthwhile consideration to add to the foregoing is that of the validity of the knowledge produced by organizational behaviour.

It has already been noted that the validity of organizational behaviour knowledge is to some extent defined in terms of its vocational relevance to organizational leaders and managers and to the students of management who will eventually fill such positions. However, as Moorhead and Griffin imply in the quotation cited above, the findings of organizational behaviour research often elicit a 'so what' kind of response from organizational leaders. More often than not, the complaint is that social science studies are all very well in theory but of little use in practice. Managers live in a practical world: if they have a problem they may send for the accountant, the marketing manager, the purchasing director or even the personnel specialist. It is very rare to hear the call going out from the managing director's office to send for the 'organizational behaviourist'!

Further, confusion over the findings of research (and the failure to answer the questions it sets itself on occasions) means that in the simplest terms organizational behaviour can hardly argue too strongly that its justification is vocational relevance, for what evidence, *hard* evidence, exists for its vocational indispensability in the history of organizations? If anything, the work of the 'new management' writers such as Peters and Waterman (1982) suggests at one and the same time a recognition of the more definitely social and sociological in influencing organizational success *and* a crude cult of the personality, in that it is individual growth in the social context that is important to such success. The latter position may be somewhat paradoxical (and few sociologists will be happy with the assertion) but it is possible to read this literature as indicative of a *rejection* of much that has been claimed for organizational behaviour in terms of its purported legitimacy as the major intellectual vehicle for management in organizations.

A case for organizational behaviour?

The foregoing discussion may seem overly gloomy, but all is not lost! Organizational behaviour may be seen to be a victim of competing tensions – of seeking to be both 'relevant' to potential 'clients' (organizations and organizational leaders) and academically credible, i.e. to other academics. In many respects the academic development of organizational behaviour has led the subject away from its potential 'practical' value as greater intellectual sophistication has been achieved. Despite this, a strong orientation to managerial problem-solving has been retained by many exponents of organizational behaviour approaches to the understanding of industrial life.

One consequence of the maturation of organizational behaviour as a field of study has been the distillation of both competing and complementary approaches to the subject. This is not so much at the theoretical level (though it is certainly true that a theoretical pluralism exists within organizational behaviour) but at the level of how the subject is, for want of a better word, practised. These approaches very roughly correspond to the disciplinary interests of those who study behaviour in organizations. Crudely speaking, psychologists are interested in the nature of the behaviour of individuals within the organization, and sociologists with the social and cultural aspects of organizations and how they relate to the wider social order. Running parallel with these and other approaches is that of the managerialist school, which is more or less explicitly interested in attaining some synthesis of theoretical knowledge with a view to developing practical, vocational pay-offs. It is this approach that in the educational forum at least has prevailed when it comes to the teaching of organizational behaviour, and the approach that gives rise to the kinds of arguments discussed in the first part of this chapter.

The case *for* organizational behaviour derives from recognition of the limitations of this approach, in particular the slavish and mistaken desire evidenced by many of its key exponents to be 'vocationally relevant'. Organizational behaviour is by its very nature, *by definition*, vocationally relevant, by virtue of its attempts to apply social scientific knowledge and inquiry to behaviour in organizations. The term 'vocational relevance' has, however, acquired many meanings in recent years, not least that which equates (explicitly or otherwise) 'vocational relevance' with the necessary subordination of critique and scepticism to the maintenance of a *status quo* that is likely to find favour with potentially important audiences. Lennon (1990) found that, in the context of teaching social and organizational studies on hospitality management courses, concepts of vocational relevance were closely linked in the minds of academics and educational administrators to what industrial advisers to hotel management schools would find acceptable (a view prefigured by Deem, 1981, in the context of business education in general; see also Lennon and Wood, 1992).

The desire to satisfy – or pacify – audiences such as these by avoiding controversy is not in the interests of vocational or any other kind of relevance when it comes to either academic investigation or managers' engagement with the real world of business. Superficially at least, one thing demonstrated by new management writers such as Peters and Waterman (1982) is that controversy and creative tension are necessary and desirable features of organizational life. More to the point, large organizations at least are not (or at least they are very rarely) unified systems devoid of conflict, potential conflicts of interest, controversy and differences of opinion among various interest groups within them.

To take an example, Brymer (1991), among other commentators, urges the necessity of empowerment schemes as a means of improving customer service and productivity in hospitality organizations. The resistance of management to the introduction of empowerment schemes is seen as a problem – indeed as almost perverse – and something to be overcome. But what if managers are right to be sceptical of empowerment? There is little hard evidence in the hospitality industry context to suggest that the adoption of empowerment schemes is universally beneficial or necessary. Advocacy of new ideas is one thing, but advocacy of new ideas for their own sake or for the *potential* benefits they might bring is quite another, however sincere the motives.

More importantly, organizations come to be managed in certain ways not by accident but because those ways are perceived as being effective and appropriate by those who do the managing. One difficulty with the 'managerialist' approach to organizational behaviour is that, in seeking to be vocationally relevant, it has actively retreated from *being* relevant. Rather than seeking to tailor intellectual inquiry to the realities of particular organizational situations, much organizational behaviour theory and practice concentrates instead on seeking to arbitrate between the appropriateness of particular theories and concepts to these situations.

Stripped of the intellectual baggage of 'vocational relevance', as defined in this discussion, the value of organizational behaviour to the hospitality industry may be viewed as resting in the potential it brings for a genuine multi-disciplinary approach to studying what *actually* goes on in hotel and catering organizations. From such study, which will be necessarily pragmatic, drawing on a variety of concepts and disciplines, it should be possible to establish a much clearer picture of what is or is not an appropriate and effective way to understand and, if necessary, modify, industrial behaviour in organizations. This may necessitate facing up to some perhaps unpalatable truths from time to time: about pay and conditions of employment in the industry, about the nature of labour markets, and about the effectiveness of management by its own standards (without the help of organizational behaviour theorists). This approach at least goes some way to avoiding the delusions that are attendant on empty efforts to 'apply' inappropriate concepts to an understanding of behaviour in hospitality organizations, and may ultimately prove more intellectually and 'vocationally' relevant.

Discussion questions

1 Why should the notion of the social sciences as a managerial 'toolkit' be viewed with suspicion?

2 To what extent is organizational behaviour vocationally relevant to managers in hospitality organizations?

3 Identify examples of how organizational behaviour approaches can be used to solve real-life problems in hospitality organizations.

4 Is it fair to say that organizational behaviour as a field of study is constrained in its relevance because it embraces a too idealistic conception of its subject matter?

15 Some case exercises in organizational behaviour

This chapter contains a number of exercises designed to help readers explore some of the themes discussed in this book. The exercises are of varying complexity. Some adopt a conventional case-study approach but, while the case-study method is a valuable learning aid, human issues in organizations are often more immediate, entailing a substantial 'what if?' element. Dealing with people requires all organizational members – but especially managers – to draw on their commonsense and experience within some rational framework that can inform sensible action.

Role-play exercises

The American sociologist Harold Garfinkel is generally accepted as the pioneer of ethnomethodology – the study of the taken-for-granted assumptions, skills and behaviour that people use in their everyday interaction with others. These taken-for-granted aspects of interaction are, by definition, implicit and rarely recognized as important by social actors themselves or, if they are, they are labelled as 'commonsense' aspects of everyday life. To demonstrate the importance of these implicit interactional skills, Garfinkel conducted a number of informal experiments, the best known of which encouraged students to behave as if they were lodgers in their own homes and observe the disruption this caused to role relationships. Among other things, what Garfinkel was pointing to was the extent to which role expectations are taken on trust. People who appear to be occupying a particular role are expected to behave in certain ways. Thus as Wynne (1993, pp. 45–6) notes:

> When people enter hotels, all but the most seasoned travellers feel a certain amount of tension, because a hotel is not merely a place of rest and accommodation but is also a social setting of mutual rights and obligations. Here there are prescribed roles and prescribed scripts...An entrance into a luxury hotel is particularly fraught with tension, since, for most people, the environment is alien to their normal roles, routines and expectations

Role-playing exercises are an important component of employee and management development programmes in most organizations, and many of the exercises in subsequent sections of this chapter make use of the role-play method. The two exercises here are designed to sensitize users to this method, and reference should be made to Chapter 6, in particular the sections dealing with role sets and role perceptions, as well as earlier chapters on organization structure and design.

Case Exercise 1: Rationalization at an Impressionist Hotel

This case is partly based on events that occurred in a four-star chain-owned hotel in the early 1990s.

The Impressionist Hotel Group is a large multi-national chain that has recently opened a four-star property (the Impressionist Manet Hotel) in a large city in the North of England with a population catchment of several million within a 40-mile radius. The Manet is a new-build and enjoys a city centre location where six other chains also have hotels.

Catering to a business, convention and (overseas) tourist clientele for the most part, the Manet Hotel did better than expected business in the first 6 months of operation, and in the subsequent 3 months averaged 74 per cent occupancy and 54 per cent utilization of public restaurant and banqueting space. The cost of operative labour is believed by the general manager to have been pared to the bone, a view confirmed by the head office comptroller. The number of supervisory staff is small, and such staff in practice work large amounts of overtime, for which, as salaried workers, they receive time off in lieu. However, head office auditors, together with the general manager, have agreed that the unit's management structure is top heavy and that up to a quarter of the managerial staff must be released (made redundant). A chart showing the structure of the senior management team of the unit is shown in Figure 15.1. You are required to study the chart and:

(a)   Allocate the role of each managerial position to a member of your group.
(b)   Ask each member of the group to prepare within an agreed time limit a case for remaining on the management team.
(c)   Organize a group meeting where members can put their case for a specified time and then answer questions from other group members.
(d)   Subsequent to this, organize a secret ballot to establish who are least able to justify their contribution to the management team and effective running of the hotel.

The following points should be kept in mind throughout the exercise. First, the criteria by which each group member's contribution is assessed should be established *before* the start of the exercise and should exclude personal factors. Second, the assessment of contributions could be conducted in a variety of ways. For example, in addition to assessing a person across a variety of criteria, group members may in addition be asked to give a single absolute value for other members of the group. Results derived from these methods may then be compared for the purposes of establishing consistency in assessments. It should go without saying of course that no individuals should ever assess themselves.

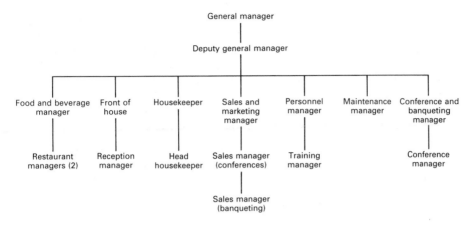

Figure 15.1   Management structure of the Manet Hotel

Case Exercise 2: The manager's morning

The following (edited) extract is from an interview with the general manager of a four-star city centre hotel. It is drawn from a research project into the work patterns of such managers and was conducted in the evening on a weekday during a particularly busy period for the hotel. Each study group member should read the extract and then, independently, list the roles played by the manager, distinguishing the formal from the informal (the interview in question had, as its major objective, an assessment of the range of tasks engaged in by the manager – the extract deals only with the morning period of the day in question). Having done this, group members should then compare their analyses and consider the following questions (it may also be useful for group members to refamiliarize themselves with the contents of Chapter 8 on management):

(a)   What relationship exists between the formal and informal roles performed by the manager?
(b)   Which roles might the manager have delegated (all other things being equal)?
(c)   What roles could only the manager have performed?
(d)   What 'role performances' could have been deferred because they might be deemed non-essential?
(e)   On the basis of the information supplied in the extract, what is the totality of the manager's role set on this occasion?

Extract

I had an early start this morning. The night porter rang me just after six to tell me that the breakfast supervisor and breakfast chef had not turned up for work. I told him to keep the night cook on and get one of the senior waitresses to supervise until I got there. It took me 40 minutes, and when I arrived, everyone was in a panic. There's a flu thing going round and two of the waitresses were off as well. We have a buffet-style breakfast operation but even so it's a big job and we were nearly full. My senior assistant lives in the hotel but had been working until 2.00 am, so I decided to leave him where he was. The night cook was in a state. She only really does sandwiches and snacks and had no idea how the breakfasts worked. The rest of the kitchen crew come in in stages and two of our young commis were there. I told the night cook that she would be of more use helping to ensure the restaurant was properly set up but she was too upset to work and thought I was getting at her. She usually has to get home to make her husband's breakfast – he's a nightworker too. I calmed her down and sent her home and then rolled my sleeves up. The commis were doing well, though they're only youngsters. To make matters worse, half way through the first hour deliveries started arriving, so I was receiving. Usually, I found out, one of the commis does this till the store clerk arrives, and I find that worrying because it is a bit unprofessional. While the bread and other baking was being offloaded, I did a spot check of the last week's orders and it all seemed OK.

I managed to get out of the kitchen when the normal crew arrived and went to help in the restaurant, just clearing up, you know, clearing tables and doing a bit of meeting and greeting. My assistant had arrived by this time and was dealing with a client who had buttonholed him at reception. A hall porter came to tell me that the client was demanding to see the manager and didn't think Jeff (the senior assistant manager) was coping too well. I went to have a look. It was some argument over the bill and Jeff had chosen to be awkward rather than just writing it off, so I dealt with that. Jeff asked me if I wanted him to do the cash check from last night so I could have a coffee, but I sent him to sort out the restaurant. I had some conference organizer arriving at 9.30. I usually like to sit with these people so they think they're getting personal attention but it's my conference and banqueting manager who does all the legwork. I didn't have time to deal with all the things I usually deal with before the appointment, including the morning mail. I needed to check the reservations for next week because my occupancy projections had to be in to head office.

I found out at this point that about fifteen people had called in sick but at least I had three of my managers in now. The trainee is a bit thick, though, so I really couldn't get him to do much, he needs watching constantly. The head housekeeper was moaning like mad because quite a few of the staff who had called in sick were hers and, to cap it all, half the morning's laundry returns were from another hotel, some sort of mix up, I don't know. I said I would look into it and ring up the company. By this time I just seemed to be being chased by everybody, so I went back to the office to meet Morag (the conference and banqueting manager) and the client – who was late. While we were waiting, I got Morag to run through our bookings for the next couple of weeks and then took a call from a colleague at our hotel up the road. He has a similar sickness problem, so I agreed to ask around and see if I could get any of our lot to go up there later in the day for a bit of overtime.

The client we had been waiting for finally turned up and was very fussy. It took an hour and a half, by which time I wasn't feeling too good myself but I had to do a check on all departments just to see if we were keeping our heads above water. I found that the night porter was still here helping with the rooms, so I gave him a hand with one or two and discussed his wife and children with him. The trainee was also around and had managed to break two table lamps in the rooms, so I sent him out to British Home Stores for some temporary replacements. I finally got some lunch, which I ate while dictating to my secretary (who only works mornings). That means all the mail will be a day behind. Still, Jeff had done the cash check from last night, so that was something.

Group and team exercises

The two exercises in this section are designed to help readers appreciate some of the processes in group and team working. Both are general exercises, i.e. not specifically related to the hospitality industry, and the first at least is also a test of general knowledge. At some point, reference to Chapter 7 may be helpful in understanding the motivations behind the case studies.

Case Exercise 3: Around the world

Each individual member of the study group should consider the under-noted pairs of letters and then, within a specified time limit (10 minutes is adequate), seek to generate the names of towns and cities of the world with each letter pair forming the first two letters of the placename. For example, CA might yield Canterbury (England and New Zealand), Canberra (Australia), and Cambridge (England, USA). The place name might comprise more than one word, but as long as the first word begins with the two letters indicated, this is permissible. The letters are:

AT	GE	MO	ST
BR	HE	NI	TO
CH	IS	OS	UT
DU	JA	PE	VA
ED	KU	QU	WE
FL	LO	RO	YO

Some method of arbitration of dubious responses should be laid down, then the individual responses should be marked, preferably by another member of the group. The study group should then be subdivided into smaller groups and the exercise repeated, using a second set of letters, as shown below. Here, each sub-group should work together. The scores for the groups should then be calculated, as should the average of all the individual scores for group members (from the first round). The second set of letters is:

AD	GR	MA	TR
BA	HA	NE	VI
CO	IN	OK	WA
DA	JE	PR	XA
EA	KA	RE	YA
FR	LA	SA	ZE

Two things should be noted at this point. First, while everyone should strive to maximize the number of responses, it might not be possible to get 100 per cent. Second, this exercise is conditioned by the letters given, but it is perfectly possible for groups to generate their own letter pairs and change the focus of the exercise. For example, generate sets of letters that then have to be 'matched' to film stars (or films themselves), books, authors, sports personalities and so on. The form of the exercise does not really matter, it is any differential between individual (and aggregate individual) performances and group performances that is important. The questions to be considered, once the exercise is completed, might include the following:

(a)   If there is a difference between individual and group performances, what might account for this?
(b)   In exercises like this, group performance is usually higher than the average of individual performances. If this is the case with the results obtained, explore reasons as to why this might be so and explore circumstances in which individual performance may be higher. If this is not the case, and group results are consistently lower than average individual scores for groups, seek to establish why this is the case.

Case Exercise 4: Desert disaster

This case is one of a popular series of 'what if?' exercises that require group skills to be developed within a specified time. You are in a party travelling from one town to another across a corner of the Sahara desert, part of a group on a 2-week adventure holiday organized by a specialist travel company. You are accompanied by a courier who was the last-minute replacement for the regular courier (he contracted influenza) and is normally employed in office duties, and a local driver.

Following a planned itinerary, which includes travelling 80 miles across the desert today, you are disturbed to find that after 35 miles the engine of the coach on which you are travelling begins to overheat. The driver decides to divert to an oasis at right-angles and to the north of your route, and some 25 miles from it. After travelling for 4 miles along this route, you encounter a sudden sandstorm, which causes an electrical fault in the coach and it catches fire. It is burnt out, leaving only a shell. As a result of this, the driver dies of a heart attack. Your party must stick together to improve chances of survival. Temperatures in the Sahara at this time of year vary from 120 degrees F at midday to below freezing at night. From the wreckage of the vehicle you have salvaged fifteen items. Ten of them must be selected and ranked in order of importance for your survival. Thirty minutes is allowed for you to reach a decision. The items are as follows:

(a)   A box of matches.
(b)   A barrel containing 4 pints of water for each group member.
(c)   One yellow blanket per person.
(d)   A machete.
(e)   An orange tent – with no poles.
(f)   Six plastic rubbish sacks.
(g)   One catering size tin of baked beans (10 lbs).
(h)   A flashlight.
(i)   A bottle of best brandy.
(j)   A book, *Lawrence of Arabia*.
(k)   A first-aid kit.

(*l*)　A bottle of salt tablets.

(*m*)　A compass.

(*n*)　Ten copies of yesterday's *Independent* newspaper.

(*o*)　Book of maps of the Sahara Desert, scale 1 inch to 5 miles.

The exercise should be progressed as follows. First, all individuals should rank ten of the fifteen items. Second, as a small group exercise, a consensus must be reached about the ten items chosen and their ranking. This means that the selection and ranking of the ten items must be agreed by each member of the group before it becomes part of the group's selection. You should try and observe the following guidelines in reaching your decision: (1) avoid arguing for your own individual judgements against those of your colleagues, (2) don't change your mind simply to avoid conflict, (3) do not support solutions to problems with which you cannot agree at all, (4) example differences of opinion as if they were helpful rather than limiting, and (5) constantly question your own initial ranking of the ten items.

The next stage is to check the group consensus against the answers given by the experts (listed at the end of the chapter, p. 209) and subtract the former from the latter to give a plus or minus value. These should then be summed to give a single figure. Generally speaking, this crude figure allows comparisons between smaller groups in the wider study group: the lower the sum of differences, the better has been the group performance. Having completed the exercise, group members should identify those processes that were important in reaching a consensus. To this end, it might be useful for each group to have an independent observer who does not participate in the exercise but instead makes notes on crucial areas, e.g. the nature of compromise and compromisers, leaders and the led, the basis of decision-making in the group, and crucial factors that lead to decisions being agreed.

Management

Much is taught about the theory of management on business study courses and there are a plethora of case studies written to support this learning. Many of these case studies tend to obscure the fact that in hospitality organizations the 'hands on' nature of management means that the problems commonly encountered by members of the management team are highly practical in nature. This is not to say, however, that managers at all levels of the organization do not have to deal with policy and strategic issues. Both cases are represented here, with the first exercise focusing on an unfortunate and unpleasant incident of the kind that might occur in any organization (the incident is based on events which actually occurred in a hotel of which the author has knowledge).

Case Exercise 5: Unpleasantness at the Corot Hotel

The night duty manager at the Corot Hotel, a four-star property belonging to the Impressionist Hotel Group and situated in the centre of a historic city in the North of England, is called to reception at 11.30 one evening by the night receptionist. The receptionist is greatly agitated and distressed, having experienced verbal abuse from a guest and been threatened with physical violence. The guest, who is standing nearby, is a young man in his early twenties, and is plainly intoxicated. The receptionist explains to the manager that the guest had asked for several bottles of wines and spirits to be sent to his room to allow him to entertain his female companion who is not staying at the hotel. The receptionist claims to have explained that it is not hotel policy to supply alcohol on these terms and reminded the guest that there was a mini-bar in his own room. The guest then allegedly became abusive and, in addition to the actions already described, smashed a vase of flowers that had adorned the reception desk. A few other guests are milling around in the foyer and looking on with interest by the time the manager arrives on the scene. One of these confirms the receptionist's account of events, though this guest has also been clearly drinking to excess. While speaking to the manager, the guest experiences a tirade of abuse from the young man.

Asking the perpetrator of these events to calm down, the manager suggests he returns to his own room, while explaining the hotel's obligation to provide for the comfort and well-being of all its guests. The young man, however, swings a punch at the manager, hitting him in the face. At this point, the guest's female companion, together with a night porter who has just returned to the hotel foyer after seeing guests to their rooms, restrains the young man. The night porter volunteers to ring the police, at which point the young guest starts shouting more abuse, revealing that he is the son of the hotel chain's managing director, although it is subsequently confirmed that he has booked into the hotel under a false name. Before collapsing in a stupor, he threatens to report the staff to his father.

The night manager decides to have the guest removed to his room and have him examined by the local doctor (who attends the hotel in emergencies). The former task is performed by the night porter, together with the young man's female companion, who is also given instructions to remain with the guest before, during and for some period after the doctor's attendance. The manager then calms the receptionist and, during the early morning, writes a report to the hotel's general manager (by this point the doctor has attended and judged that, though inebriated, the guest is unlikely to be in any danger beyond a colossal hangover when he awakes).

Early the following afternoon the night manager (who lives in staff accommodation in the hotel, as does the receptionist) is telephoned by the general manager's secretary and asked to attend a meeting in the GM's office at 6.00 pm. This meeting is also attended by the receptionist and night porter, together with the assistant manager for operations, who has responsibility for personnel matters in the hotel. The GM reveals that the young guest who had been the focus of the previous night's incident booked out at 11.00 am that morning. He had clearly contacted his father, however, as the managing director's personal assistant had telephoned to ask the GM for a full explanation of (in the words of the personal assistant) 'what appears to be the appalling treatment of a guest, shareholder and relative of a senior member of the company'. It has been indicated that the managing director will be contacting the GM at 9.00 am the next morning, 'after the managing director has had the opportunity to speak to his son in person'. The general manager is concerned to clarify the facts of the situation so as to prepare a suitable response. It is known that the managing director has a reputation for 'hiring and firing' and is very proud of his son.

As a small group exercise, discuss the above scenario, perhaps allocating the roles of the personnel gathered in the GM's office in order to play out possible responses, and agree what form the GM's response should take. Consider the possible attitude of the managing director and responses to it. After completing this sub-group exercise, come together with other sub-groups to report and analyse your recommendations. Make explicit the assumptions employed in arriving at your conclusions.

Case Exercise 6: The Leisure Corporation

The directors of X Leisure Corporation are being made aware that a number of problems in relation to their managers are beginning to emerge. Some of the problems are more conspicuous and quantifiable than others. Indeed some were predicted. They are the problems of success and expansion. The business plan forecast both expansion and change, but early signs of instability in the managerial labour force are making themselves felt. The figures from the field tell a story, but closer to home there is an 'atmosphere' at head office.

The Leisure Corporation has two operating divisions: a retail division (R) and a leisure division (L). Ten years ago the company sold its brewing interests to concentrate on retailing, and now has a chain of 200 off-licences and sixty sports and leisure stores in a region covering four counties. Four years ago the company bought a golf club and squash centre, which was the first step in the formation of a leisure management division. This division now manages ten golf clubs and fifty leisure centres. Only the original golf club is owned by the company.

The basis of the company is contract management. The business plan is to develop the R division by extending geographical expansion of the area and by purchases of smaller retail companies in desired locations. While sales have risen by an average of 7 per cent over the last 5 years, this trend is forecast to slow to 3–4 per cent. Volume has increased by 20 per cent per annum through the expansion plan.

The L division has grown in an opportunist way. The original plan was to go for only large sport clubs, but the explosion in leisure consumption has led the division into selling management expertise and discounted liquor to a wide variety of outlets. It is the variety that is beginning to give problems. The division includes former municipal baths with 'a bit of catering', 'a bit of a bar' and 'a fitness person', alongside multi-cinema and club facilities with more than a bit of a bar, and large sports venues and exclusive golf clubs with good restaurants. While the company operates with well-developed management systems, the profiles of the managers in L division are not focused. The variety of people, ranging from ex-hoteliers to ex-secretaries to ex-footballers, is leading to recruitment, training and promotion difficulties.

The prevailing wisdom has been that, as purchasing of liquor and sports goods is centralized and that central control sets budgets for each outlet, the type of manager and variety of types are simply not a problem. While accepted in R division, this point of view has always been viewed with scepticism in L division. Most of the company's in-house training schemes, run at their golf club, are concerned with training managers in the computer budgeting control system and central purchasing procedures. Shock waves had gone around the whole company when a large contract was nearly lost through the appointment of a poor manager. Only the 'drafting in' of an area manager saved the day.

The current organizational structure is as follows. R division is headed by an operations manager, who has under him two regional managers. The day-to-day control of the unit is by the area managers, who supervise between fifteen and twenty-five units. L division is headed by an operations manager, who has four area mangers – one covering golf clubs, one covering the four large multi-leisure clubs, and two covering the forty-six smaller leisure centres. Head office has five sections – the managing director, purchasing, finance and accounting, marketing and sales, property and legal. The heads of these sections report to the managing director.

The purchasing department was taken over from the brewery. It employs forty-five people, and is responsible for buying and issuing stores and distributing 85 per cent of the company's merchandise. There are eight 'buyers' – 'experienced drink tradesmen', who also 'buy in' promotional material from primary producers.

The functional role of the finance department is to process the weekly returns posted from the units. These returns consist of cash flow, revenue and stock positions. Plans for computerizing the accounting in the units so that they can connect directly with the head office computer system are at an advanced stage. The department includes a team of travelling auditors, whose role it is to spot-check stock and cash unannounced.

The principal functions of the personnel department are management recruitment, management training and the provision of a relief team of temporary managers. The marketing and sales department is a new and small department charged with getting new contracts for the L division, whereas the prime function of the property department is to secure leases for retail premises for R division. In addition, one man is employed as catering adviser to the operations manager of L division.

The various parts of the organization employ a variety of people. In purchasing the buyers are men and women around 40–50 with specialized knowledge, including wine experts, brewing chemists, and those with technological backgrounds. Beneath them come a small number of men and women aged between 24 and 30 acting as assistant buyers, stores controllers and computer technicians. All members of the personnel department are professional personnel managers, aged 38 to 40. The marketing and sales department comprises a group of young men aged 24 to 30, all with business and marketing qualifications. In property and legal there is a small group of young graduates qualified either in law or economics. Most have experience in property management.

In R division most managers, owing to licensing and insurance restrictions, are recruits over the age of 25. Most have no experience in the drinks trade. Ex-publicans are avoided. Ex-policemen are favoured. The typical modern recruits are a couple in their late twenties who have not yet entered the housing market.

In L division, unit management covers a wide range of backgrounds. The smaller ex-municipal leisure units are often managed by former local government employees, most of whom have a 'swimming' background.

The operational aspects of the organization can be summarized as follows. New units in R division are devised and planned by the operations managers in conjunction with the property, purchasing and personnel departments. The area manager selects the manager, but takes over responsibility a week before opening. New units in L division are obtained by the sales department in conjunction with the operations manager, catering adviser and area manager. The area manager does the tender in conjunction with the sales department. In other words, the area manager in L division plays a role in the total process.

The personnel department is focused on management recruitment for both divisions, and linked to operations through the maintenance of a number of relief managers, who are deployed from the centre at the request of area managers. This is a pressure point, and point of conflict when area managers try to target the relief to be permanent.

No organization is without politics. For example, in the Leisure Corporation, although the purchasing department was socially popular because of its constant 'tastings', the rest of head office thought it had too much clout. It was big, the oldest established department, and, most annoying of all, controlled almost all the assets. The purchasing department saw itself as the 'core' business. On the other hand, expansion was in L division and owed most to the efforts of the small sales team. A good informal relationship had built up between the young managers in the property department, who worked mainly for R, and the sales department, who worked for L. They looked at each other's figures and talked shop constantly. This had formed a liaison between the area managers in L and the property department. It is this liaison that informed Head Office generally of the pressures in the field.

The purchasing department seemed 'under-stressed'; the sales, personnel and property departments seemed 'under pressure'. This had been the way for some time and it was now a source of unfavourable comparison, which fuelled dissatisfaction with pay.

The following is an extract from a recent meeting in the company.

> 'Can you persuade him to stay?', Bill Smith asked the operations manager. 'No.'
>
> 'Another one gone then.' Jim Nichols, operations manager R division looked for comfort to his opposite number, Mike Brown of L division.
>
> 'I'm not going to be a Gofer for some disorganized branch manager, not at this salary – that was his parting shot.'
>
> All three were aware that they could no longer avoid looking at their management problems. The near loss of a big leisure contract was in all their minds, but now it was the problem of the area managers.
>
> 'I'm surviving on some young college boys – but even they are beginning to grumble about pay and not being able to get on with their job.'
>
> 'They're carrying the unit managers, not all of them but you know what I mean.'

'Finance say it'll be easier when they are on-line.' Mike and Bill looked
sceptical.

'We aren't getting the right calibre of manager.'

'The trouble is most of the units aren't big enough to carry assistant
managers, and those we have want to manage big units.'

'The job is one thing, Mike, but they aren't earning and we'll have to give
them more.'

'Hang on a minute', Smith, not wanting to go down on pay route so soon,
intervened, 'Is it just that they are covering their backs all the time?'

'No, sales are doing well and demanding more feasibility studies and
tenders. You just can't expect them to open new units and carry the problems
we have at the moment.'

Bill Smith thought for a moment, before summing up.

'You're saying they cannot do their job because of the shortage of good unit
managers and because they have to cope with so much new business. Is that
true?' He looked at Jim Nichols.

'It's not so much the new business as the shortages of managers and the
quality.'

'Add the new business with mine.'

Bill Smith sat back.

'Are we looking in the right place, it seems to me that we ought to be
addressing the problems of unit managers. If we can resolve those, we can
get a clear look at the area managers.'

Jim Nichols wasn't impressed – the problem of the area managers needed
urgent attention. His argument was that solving the recruitment problem
and waiting for the units to come on-line would simply take too long. Mike
Brown agreed the line couldn't be held too much longer, but conceded that
unit management quality was also a priority.

Finally, here, some consideration of the pay system and structure is
appropriate.

Unit Managers R division. The old brewery system of grading the units by
stock size was still in use. This produced just three types of unit. The salary
within grades was adjusted where accommodation was provided, and an
allowance for the spouse built in as a part-time employee. A bonus of 8 per
cent of the grade mid-point could be earned by reaching sale volume
targets set each year. The target usually called for an increase in turnover
of between 5 and 10 per cent.

Unit managers L division. The main influence here was the tender for the
contract. The effect was to keep all labour costs low. Despite 7-day operations, the management rates were usually low, particularly for the municipal leisure centres. Over time a rule of thumb grading system had been
worked out by the area manager and sales people.

Head office. The pay structure at head office has simply evolved. The
purchasing and finance departments were taken over from the old brewery
structure, but the other sections have been taken on board on the basis of
market forces as the company has grown.

Operations. R division pay structure has evolved from the pub system of
the brewery. L division's has been based on market forces in the contract
catering industry.

There are a number of current vacancies: one assistant buyer is required
at head office; R division requires three area managers, seventeen unit

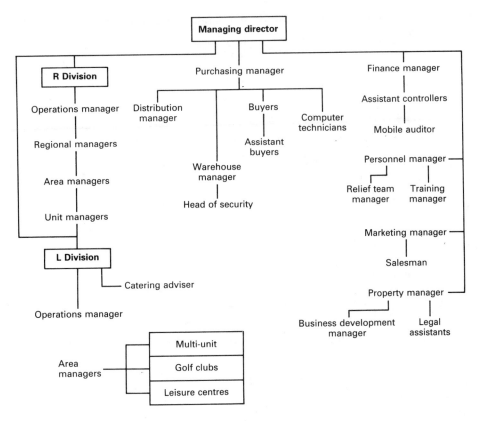

Figure 15.2 Organization chart of the Leisure Corporation

Field	S	Head office	S
R Division		(no HOD)	
Operations M	27–30k + c	Buyers	27–35k + c
Regional M	22–25 + c	Distribution M	25–27k + c
Area M	16–20k + c	Asst Controllers	18–22k + c
		Warehouse M	22–23k + c
		Assistant buyer	20–23k + c
L Division		Computer tech.	20–23k
		Salesmen	16–18k + c
Operations M	27–30k + c	Bus. dev. M	16–18k
Area M (golf)	20–22k + c	Mobile audit	18–20k
Area M (L)	16–20k + c	Legal asst.	16–20k
Catering adviser	20–23k + c	Training M	18–20k
		Relief team M	16–18k

Units
R Division (*a*) 7–9 k (live in) (*b*) 8–13k (*c*) 13–17k
L Division   Golf club 20–30k
          Leisure centre 11–17k

Figure 15.3 Salary structure of the Leisure Corporation

managers and a relief team of ten; and L division requires one area manager, one golf-club manager and eleven leisure-centre managers.

You are required to define:

(*a*)   The problems that exist now and will in the future.
(*b*)   Further information useful at this point.
(*c*)   What strategies you think appropriate to helping the company out of its difficulties.

You should accept the financial information as given. An organization chart is shown in Figure 15.2 and a current list of salary rates in Figure 15.3.

Leadership

As implied in Chapter 9, the concept of leadership is an elusive one: everybody has some idea of what leadership is but the opportunity to exercise leadership occurs in many different circumstances, few of which ever match any theoretical conceptualization of the phenomenon. The exercises in this section are designed to help readers of the text explore the nature of leadership further by analytic and interactive means.

Case Exercise 7: The nature of leadership

This exercise requires a number of small groups to conduct desk research. Each group should be allocated a particular type of leader to research, e.g. political leaders, captains of industry in general, leaders in the hospitality industry, and as many other categories as are deemed appropriate. By means of a library research exercise, each group should probe the backgrounds of two or three subjects in their chosen category and seek to determine any common factors in the subjects' backgrounds – in other words, account for determinants and influences that led to subjects achieving leadership positions. Note that it is not necessary for a chosen 'leader' to have been successful some or all of the time.

Once the research has been undertaken, the groups should come together to report back. The focus of the reporting should be the creation of a framework of factors that account for the leadership qualities of their subjects. Furthermore, in determining factors important to the development of these leadership qualities, the larger group should also seek to identify elements that detract from effective leadership in the make-up of their chosen subjects. To add another dimension to the exercise, the sub-groups could undertake to include in their sample at least one (agreed) successful leader and one unsuccessful leader.

Case Exercise 8: Leading for a decision

Certain core elements in the following case exercise are based on the real-life case that faced a small hotel company in the early 1980s. For reasons of confidentiality the name of the company and the case's donor must remain anonymous: the details have, in any case, been freely adapted.

The board of directors of Impressionist Hotels desires to build a new eighty-room, business-class hotel and leisure centre in or near a historic town some 30 miles to the west of London. All marketing and financial projections are favourable, and the leisure centre is regarded as a particularly important part of the development package, as the general area chosen for the development is not catered for by local authority or other private facilities and the hotel proposes to establish a leisure club for local residents. Three sites all within one mile of each other have been identified for the building project, and, even accounting for land costs, there is little to choose between them. However, some unexpected difficulties have arisen.

The choice of Location A would mean situating the development near a site of special scientific interest (which, however, is itself placed, somewhat ironically, a few hundred yards from a dual carriageway), and, though the company has given assurances that this will not be spoiled (and there is adequate road access), local environmental campaigners have organized considerable opposition to the proposal. They have the support of their local MP. Location A, though on the fringes of the town in question, is in a different parliamentary constituency to the town itself, and the MP is of a different political persuasion to the local council, which broadly supports the development. There are only three other hotels of any size in the town. Despite the opposition of the MP concerned, the council in the constituency in which Location A is to be found has indicated its willingness to consider any reasonable request for planning permission that protects the site of special scientific interest.

Location B is well within the town boundaries but has problems of its own. The land identified for the development is on the edge of a private housing estate served by a minor road. A major arterial roadway serving the town and points beyond constitutes the further boundary of the estate, leading to fears among residents that traffic to and from the hotel would increase as guests and users of the leisure facilities cut through the estate to reach the site.

Location C is on the edges of the 'Old Town' itself, in an area of Georgian streets and terraces that, though once residential, is now largely given over to offices. The area contains many listed buildings, and the proposed site of the hotel stands across a small park facing one of the principal streets that edge the district. As with Location A, there have been protests from environmentalists and heritage groups, despite assurances from the company that any development would necessarily be required to blend tastefully with the local architecture (a view qualified by the observation that the street in which the site of the proposed development is located already contains a number of twentieth-century buildings).

The board of directors has asked the company's senior projects director (SPD) to recommend the location that is least likely to damage the company's image. The SPD has, in turn, created four project groups. The first is chaired by the STD, and its purpose is to decide which of the three sites is most suitable. The purpose of each of the remaining three groups is to make a case for one of Locations A, B and C. Each of these groups is under the direction of a project officer. This method, the SPD believes, will best reveal the strengths and weaknesses of his own group's decision if each of the other three project groups is allowed to make a presentation.

The procedure is as follows. Each group should be allowed 15 or 20 minutes to prepare its case, which should be presented over a 5-minute period, with a few minutes at the end of each presentation for questions. The SPD's group should not, at this stage, indicate what decision it has arrived at. Having heard the evidence, the SPDs group should withdraw to consider if it has changed its mind about the most suitable location on the basis of the cases presented. A vote should then take place, with each group voting secretly for one of the locations. A group is not allowed to vote for its own location (and the SPD decision should still remain secret). There are three possible outcomes to this process – a majority in favour of the location that agrees with the view of the SPD's group; a majority in favour of a location that is at odds with it; and the possibility of a tie.

In the case of the last two, the SPD's group should once again decide if it intends to change its view on the basis of what it has heard. If not, then the SPD's group should make a presentation and a new free vote take place, but this time of all *individuals*. A simple majority in favour of one of the locations is all that is required this time.

Whatever the outcome, all participants should consider the processes they have gone through, addressing such points as (*a*) why consensus was achieved/not achieved; (*b*) why the SPD's group was supported/not supported; (*c*) to what extent the final decision was a function of argument over the known facts/force of personalities engaged in the exercise; and (*d*) what leadership qualities are required to reach a decision such as this?

Motivation

The purpose of these exercises is to encourage readers to consider, both individually and together with members of their study groups, the nature of motivation relative to the theories discussed in Chapter 10. Chapters 7 and 12 will also be of use for Case Exercise 10.

Case Exercise 9: Desires for life

Working alone, study the list of ten 'desires for life' below and then rank them on a scale of 1 (highest) to 10 (lowest):

- To be liked by others.
- A family of my own.
- The ability to afford consumer goods.
- To travel the world.
- To always be in love.
- A good job that is well paid.
- A large house in my preferred location.
- To be active in community life.

- To be respected for being good at my job.
- To gain recognition from others.

Having completed this part of the exercise, compare your rankings with a small sub-set of your study group and add together the score for each desire and divide by the number of people in the sub-set to reach a mean score for each item rated by the set as a whole. Each sub-set of the larger study group should then try to classify their (averaged) rank order of desires according to an agreed model of motivation discussed in Chapter 10. In addition, each set should attempt such a classification, using a different model.

At this stage, the larger study group should come together to discuss their rankings and subsequent classifications. Particular attention should be paid to obvious consistencies and inconsistencies in the rankings. To extend the basis of the discussion, the mean scores for each 'desire' from each group may be summed and an average for the whole group produced. With reference to the chosen model of motivation by which all sub-sets of the larger study group have classified the listed desires, proceed as follows:

(*a*) Identify how consistent such classifications have been, and discuss possible reasons for variations (perhaps age, gender, experience, background).

(*b*) Discuss how effective and realistic the model chosen as the 'common denominator' for all the sub-sets of the larger study group is as a means of understanding motivations.

(*c*) Relate this to other models of motivation used in the exercise to classify the listed desires.

(*d*) Consider to what extent the 'desires' comprise both need *and* want elements.

Case Exercise 10: Developing motivated jobs

The 140-room, three-star, city-centre Monet Hotel is part of the Impressionist Hotel Group. Its new general manager has recently returned from study leave, having completed a Master of Business Administration course. Before taking this study leave (sponsored by the company), she was general manager of a smaller property in the group. The new GM is keen, and has picked up many interesting techniques and insights from her course. She is, however, joining a crisis-ridden hotel, and is aware that executive management of the group regards her new post as something of a test.

The main problem facing the hotel is a high rate of labour turnover, which is concentrated in three main occupations – those of kitchen porter, waiting staff and room-cleaning personnel. The unit personnel manager has estimated rates of turnover of 50, 60 and 70 per cent respectively for the preceding financial year, at an average replacement cost of £430 per person. The personnel manager has, where circumstances permitted, conducted exit interviews with leavers. Interestingly, all the leavers have identified roughly similar reasons for their departure. These are shown in rank order as follows:

Kitchen porters
1   Boredom.
2   Nature of work.
3   Unsympathetic superior.
4   Poor equipment.
5   Better pay in job for which individual left the Monet.

Waiting staff
1   Poor and inadequate equipment in insufficient quantity for effective performance.
2   Better pay in job for which individuals left the Monet.
3   Long hours.
4   Intimidation by chefs.
5   Inadequate breaks from work.

Room-cleaning personnel
1   Too much work (too many rooms to be cleaned by a single individual).
2   Poor pay.
3   Unpredictable overtime requirements of management.
4   Poor and inadequate equipment.
5   Nature of the job.

The unit personnel manager sees many of these reasons as simply 'part of the reality of hotel life', but concedes that certain of the complaints listed by leavers are to a degree avoidable or may be ameliorated. The general manager conducts an inspection of the hotel over a 2-week period and collects and analyses relevant data, which include the following information:

1   The hotel's head chef has a long record of absenteeism because of ill-health.
2   The sous-chef is a young man and the Monet is his first post as deputy; he was appointed over the head of another, older, person, who had been with the hotel for 11 years.
3   While the capital equipment in the kitchen is adequate, movables have not been inventoried for 3 years.
4   There has been no inventory of crockery, cutlery and glassware in the restaurant for 2 years, and purchases during that period have been unsystematic – there is also evidence of loss through pilfering.
5   The previous general manager left all day-to-day decisions in the hands of departmental heads, and rarely played any part himself in the routine administration of the unit.
6   Authority structures in all departments are very traditional, and there is little adherence to standard company procedures as outlined in operation manuals.
7   Overtime rates have, in general, been paid across the hotel, but there have often been delays of up to 3 months between work performed and payment of overtime dues to employees.
8   The previous GM was resistant to the idea of employing large numbers of part-time and casual staff.

9   The head housekeeper has consistently been refused anything other than a nominal replacement budget for equipment.

10   Employees have usually been given very short notice of overtime requirements.

11   The morale of managerial and supervisory staff is variably low, and there are many established antipathies between senior personnel.

12   Local wage rates in similarly placed competitor hotels are 3–7 per cent higher than those paid to workers in the Monet: two fast-food chains have recently opened branches in the city centre, and a third is moving into the market in 6 months' time.

The new GM decides that, while in an ideal world these problems should be tackled holistically, her major priority is to increase labour stability in the hotel. She has asked you (working alone or as a group) to consider the available information and to:

(a)   Consider each occupational group in turn, specifying clearly and in brief what *immediate* measures might be taken to improve the motivation of staff and encourage them to stay with the hotel.

(b)   Identify key general issues that must be addressed to lend greater effectiveness to the measures outlined in (a) above, together with recommendations for action.

(c)   Propose general measures for increasing the motivation of all staff in the hotel.

Culture and empowerment

The exercises in the section are, in essence, analytic, and require small-group work.

Case Exercise 11: Mission and culture

Working in small groups, prepare for a multi-unit hospitality sector business a short organizational mission statement that clearly reflects the relation between the culture you wish to engender and the organizational goals that you propose. Having completed this task, groups should compare their finished documentation and then seek to identify specific policies that would need to be adopted by their organization in order to achieve the terms of the mission statement.

Case Exercise 12: Identifying elements of organizational culture

Using the college or college department of which they are members as an example, study groups should seek to identify the components of the organization's culture and assess how these relate to the organization's mission and its strategies for achieving goals. If possible, obtain a copy of the college's mission statement and use this as a basis for analysis, at the

The catering culture

UNDERPINNING the exciting developments in Forte Posthouse catering are a set of five cultural values (in an appropriate mnemonic) which drive the catering operation and provide the enthusiastic motivation for its staff.

At a basic level it states the how and why of the Forte Posthouse restaurant philosophy so visibly illustrated in the catering coaches development above and in the new Traders restaurant concept (see back page).

C   Consistency — ensuring brand standards and quality

H   Honestly offering — good value and quality to customers and staff

E   Enjoyment — ensuring guests and staff have fun

E   Empowerment — people matter and are empowered

R   Recognition — acknowledging the worth of an individual

S   Satisfaction — making sure that people want to return.

Figure 15.4   The catering culture of Forte Posthouse

same time identifying what might be an ideal model (from a student's point of view) of the organization's culture and mission.

Case Exercise 13: Hotels and organizational culture

Forte plc, the leading international hotel and hospitality company, has a tradition of quality linked to innovation. The Forte Posthouse brand of hotels throughout the UK comprises mid-market informal establishments whose aim is to offer 'Affordability, Accessibility and Availability' to business and leisure travellers and local non-resident diners. The Forte Posthouse brand has its own proactive commitment to the creation and maintenance of an organizational culture, which is articulated in a clear and precise statement of philosophy and is underpinned by the Forte Posthouse brand's desire to offer 'Britain's Warmest Welcome' to every customer. The statement of Forte Posthouse's cultural values is shown in Figure 15.4.

Study the Forte Posthouse statement of cultural values and:

(a)   Consider how *each* component might be elaborated by the addition of two further qualifying statements.

(b)   Putting yourself in the position of a marketing manager for a new chain of mid-price restaurants aimed at the youth market, devise your own statement of culture of similar style and clarity to that of the Forte Posthouse statement.

Human resource management

This final exercise requires readers to consider the elements that might go into a statement of human resource policy.

Case Exercise 14: Holiday Inn

In April 1992 the *Caterer and Hotelkeeper* trade magazine reported on the 'Excellence through people' initiative at the Holiday Inn, Leeds. It summarized the steps taken by the Holiday Inn's general manager to maximize the effectiveness of the hotel's staff. These included:

- A minimum one-day induction for all new staff (involving the general manager).
- All team members receiving departmental induction and being allocated a 'buddy' to work with for 2 weeks.
- All team members receiving a copy of the hotel's business objectives.
- The operation of an 'Employee of the Month' award.
- Creation of an active social committee to run social events and a staff newspaper.
- Monthly dinners with the general manager to discuss issues of mutual importance.
- A team appraisal scheme.
- Regular in-house training and development sessions.

Examine the above list and:

(a) Consider how each of the factors mentioned might contribute to (i) motivation, (ii) group cohesion, and (iii) team-building.
(b) Produce a short, concise human resource policy for a (hypothetical) hospitality *chain* that nevertheless embraces all the key elements to be considered in managing human resources across multiple-unit organizations.
(c) Outline ten key behavioural guidelines that general managers in a chain organization might observe in administering the human resource function.

Answer to Case Exercise 4: Desert disaster

The first thing to note is that you should stay with your vehicle – this will improve your chances of being found.
    The ten items to be selected, in order of importance, are the following:

1 Water – essential for survival but more will be needed.
2 Plastic bags for gathering water in the sand through condensation.
3 Can of beans for collecting and storing water.

4   Machete for opening can and digging holes for bags.
5   Tent – for shelter and as a signal for search aircraft.
6   Blankets – for wamth and signalling.
7   Flashlight for signalling.
8   Box of matches as firelighter for warmth and signal.
9   Copies of newspaper (for sun hats and fires).
10 First-aid kit.

The remaining items are considerably less useful:

11 Book of *Lawrence of Arabia* (you don't have a camel).
12 Maps – of too small scale to be of value and you are not going to move.
13 Compass – you are not going anywhere.
14 Brandy – potentially dangerous, as alcohol dehydrates the body.
15 Salt tablets – also dangerous in a dehydrated state and could make you more thirsty.

References

References marked with an asterisk thus * are to other organizational behaviour and related texts that are particularly valuable and useful to those confronting the subject for the first time.

Adams, J.S. (1965), 'Inequity in social exchange', in *Advances in Experimental Social Psychology, Vol. 2* (ed. L. Berkowitz), Academic Press, New York.

Advisory, Conciliation and Arbitration Service (ACAS) (1988), *Labour Flexibility in Britain*, ACAS, London.

Alderfer, C.P. (1972), *Existence, Relatedness and Growth*, Free Press, New York.

Anderson, G. (1992), Selection, in *The Handbook of Human Resource Management* (ed. B. Towers), Blackwell, Oxford.

Arnaldo, M.J. (1981), 'Hotel general managers: a profile', *Cornell Hotel and Restaurant Administration Quarterly*, **22**, pp. 53–6.

Aslan, A. and Wood, R.C. (1993), 'Trade unions in the hotel and catering industry: the views of hotel managers', *Employee Relations*, **15**, pp. 61–9.

Attewell, P. (1987), 'The deskilling controversy', *Sociology of Work and Occupations*, **14**, pp. 323–46.

Barrett, J. and Williams, G. (1990), *Test Your Own Aptitude*, Kogan Page, London.

Barron, P. and Maxwell, G. (1993), 'Students' perceptions of the hospitality industry: reality or chimera?', in *Proceedings of the Second Annual CHME Research Conference*, Manchester.

Baum, T. (1989), 'Managing hotels in Ireland: research and development for change', *International Journal of Hospitality Management*, **8**, pp. 131–44.

*Bennett, R. (1991), *Organizational Behaviour*, Pitman, London.

Berger, F. and Vanger, R. (1986), 'Building your hospitality team', *Cornell Hotel and Restaurant Administration Quarterly*, **26**, pp. 82–90.

Blake, R.R. and Mouton, J.S. (1964), *The Managerial Grid*, Gulf, Houston.

Bowey, A. (1976), *The Sociology of Organizations*, Hodder and Stoughton, London.

Braverman, H. (1974), *Labor and Monopoly Capital*, Monthly Review Press, New York.

*Brown, R.K. (1992), *Understanding Industrial Organizations: Theoretical Perspectives in Industrial Sociology*, Routledge, London.

Brown, M. and Winyard, S. (1975), *Low Pay in Hotels and Catering*, Low Pay Unit, London.

Bryman, A. (1992), *Charisma and Leadership in Organizations*, Sage, London.

Brymer, R.A. (1979), 'Stress management for management stress', *Cornell Hotel and Restaurant Administration Quarterly*, **20**, pp. 61–9.

Brymer, R.A. (1991), 'Employee empowerment: a guest-driven leadership strategy', *Cornell Hotel and Restaurant Administration Quarterly*, **32**, pp. 58–68.

Bryon, M. and Modha, S. (1991), *How to Master Selection Tests*, Kogan Page, London.

*Buchanan, D. and Huczynski, A. (1985), *Organizational Behaviour: An Introductory Text*, Prentice-Hall International, London.

Burns, T. and Stalker, G.M. (1961), *The Management of Innovation*, Tavistock, London.

Burton, C. and Michael, N. (1992), *A Practical Guide to Project Management*, Kogan Page, London.

Butler, S. and Skipper, J. (1981), 'Working for tips', *The Sociological Quarterly*, **22**, pp. 15–27.

Byrne, D. (ed.) (1986), *Waiting for Change*, Low Pay Unit Publications, London.

Chitiris, L. (1988), 'Herzberg's proposals and their applicability to the hotel industry', *Hospitality Education and Research Journal*, **12**, pp. 67–79.

Chivers, T.S. (1973), 'The proletarianisation of a service worker', *Sociological Review*, **21**, pp. 633–56.

Clark, M. (1993), 'Communication and social skills: perceptions of hospitality managers', *Employee Relations*, **15**, pp. 51–60.

*Clegg, S. and Dunkerley, D. (1980), *Organization, Class and Control*, Routledge and Kegan Paul, London.

Comission for Racial Equality (1991), *Working in Hotels*, Commission for Racial Equality, London.

Commission on Industrial Relations (1971), *The Hotel and Catering Industry, Part 1: Hotels and Restaurants*, HMSO, London.

Crompton, R. and Sanderson, K. (1990), *Gendered Jobs and Social Change*, Unwin Hyman, London.

Croney, P. (1988), 'An investigation into the management of labour in the hotel industry', MA thesis, University of Warwick, UK.

Dann, D. (1990), 'The nature of managerial work in the hospitality industry', *International Journal of Hospitality Management*, **9**, pp. 319–34.

Dann, D. (1991), 'Strategy and managerial work in hotels', *International Journal of Contemporary Hospitality Management*, **3**, pp. 23–5.

Deal, T.E. and Kennedy, A.A. (1982), *Corporate Cultures: The Rites and Rituals of Corporate Life*, Addison-Wesley, Reading, Mass.

Deem, R. (1981), 'The teaching of industrial sociology in higher education: an exploratory analysis', *Sociological Review*, **29**, pp. 255–371.

Dronfield, L. and Soto, P. (1980), *Hardship Hotel*, Counter Information Services, London.

Drucker, P.F. (1954), *The Practice of Management*, Harper and Row, New York.

*Drummond, K.E. (1990), *Human Resource Management for the Hospitality Industry*, Van Nostrand Reinhold, New York.

Dyer, W.G. (1986), *Culture Change in Family Firms*, Jossey-Bass Inc., San Francisco.

Evans, M.G. (1970), 'The effects of supervisory behaviour on the path-goal relationship', *Organizational Behaviour and Human Performance*, May, pp. 277–98.

Ferguson, D.H. and Berger, F. (1984), 'Restaurant managers: what do they *really* do?', *Cornell Hotel and Restaurant Administration Quarterly*, **25**, pp. 26–36.

Fiedler, F.E. (1967), *A Theory of Leadership Effectiveness*, McGraw-Hill, New York.

Fiedler, F.E., Chemers, M.M. and Mahar, L. (1976), *Improving Leadership Effectiveness: The Leader–Match Concept*, John Wiley, New York.

French, J.R.P. and Raven, B.H. (1959), 'The Social Bases of Power', in *Studies in Social Power* (ed. D. Cartwright), University of Michigan Press, Ann Arbor.

Gabriel, Y. (1988), *Working Lives in Catering*, Routledge and Kegan Paul, London.

Gardner, K. and Wood, R.C. (1991), 'Theatricality in food service work', *International Journal of Hospitality Management*, **10**, pp. 267–78.

Goffman, E. (1959), *The Presentation of Self in Everyday Life*, Doubleday Archer, New York.

Guerrier, Y. (1987), 'Hotel managers' careers and their impact on hotels in Britain', *International Journal of Hospitality Management*, **6**, pp. 121–30.

Guerrier, Y. and Lockwood, A. (1989), 'Core and peripheral employees in hotel operations', *Personnel Review*, **18**, pp. 9–15.

Guest, D. (1992), 'Human Resource Management in the United Kingdom', in *The Handbook of Human Resource Management* (ed. B. Towers), Blackwell, Oxford.

Hales, C. (1987), 'Quality of working life: job redesign and participation in a service industry: a rose by any other name?', *The Service Industries Journal*, **7**, pp. 253–73.

Hales, C. and Nightingale, M. (1986), 'What are unit managers supposed to do? A contingent methodology for investigating managerial role requirements', *International Journal of Hospitality Management*, **5**, pp. 3–11.

*Handy, C. (1975), *Understanding Organizations*, Penguin, Harmondsworth.

Hayter, R. (1993), *Careers and Training in Hotels, Catering and Tourism*, Butterworth-Heinemann, Oxford.

Herzberg, F. (1968), 'One more time: how do you motivate employees?', *Harvard Business Review*, January–February, pp. 53–62.

Herzberg, F., Mausner, B. and Snyderman, B. (1959), *The Motivation to Work*, Wiley, New York.

Hotel and Catering Training Board (1987), *Women in the Hotel and Catering Industry*, Hotel and Catering Training Board, Wembley.

House, R.J. (1971), 'A path–goal theory of leadership effectiveness', *Administrative Science Quarterly*, September, pp. 321–39.

House, R.J. and Mitchell, T.R. (1974), 'Path–goal theory of leadership', *Journal of Contemporary Business*, Autumn, pp. 81–98.

Howe, L.K. (1977), *Pink Collar Workers*, Avon, New York.

Hughes, H.L. (1986), *Economics for Hotel and Catering Students*, Hutchinson, London.

Hyman, J. (1992), 'Training and Development', in *The Handbook of Human Resource Management* (ed. B. Towers), Blackwell, Oxford.

Ineson, E.M. and Brown, S.H.P. (1992), 'The use of biodata for hotel employee selection', *International Journal of Contemporary Hospitality Management*, **4**, pp. 8–12.

Ishak, N.K. and Murrmann, S.K. (1990), 'An exploratory study of human resource management practices and business strategy in multi-unit restaurant firms', *Hospitality Research Journal*, **14**, pp. 143–55.

Johnson, K. (1978), 'Personnel matters: an overview or an oversight?', *Hotel, Catering and Institutional Management Association Journal*, January, pp. 21–3.

Johnson, K. (1981), 'Towards an understanding of labour turnover?', *Service Industries Review*, **1**, pp. 4–17.

Johnson, K. (1985), 'Labour turnover in hotels – revisited', *The Service Industries Journal*, **5**, pp. 135–52.

Jones, P. and Davies, A. (1991), 'Empowerment: a study of General Managers of four star hotel properties in the UK', *International Journal of Hospitality Management*, **10**, pp. 211–17.

Kelliher, C. and Johnson, K. (1987), 'Personnel management in hotels: some empirical observations', *International Journal of Hospitality Management*, **6**, pp. 103–8.

Knight, K. (1976), 'Matrix Organizations: a review', *Journal of Management Studies*, May, pp. 111–30.

Kottak, C.P. (1978), 'Ritual at McDonald's', *Natural History Magazine*, **87**, pp. 75–82.

Lawrence, P.R. and Lorsch, J.W. (1967), *Organization and Environment*, Harvard University Press, Cambridge, Mass.

Lennon, J.J. (1990), 'Social Science in Hotel and Catering Degree Education', M.Phil. thesis, University of Strathclyde, UK.

Lennon, J.J. and Wood, R.C. (1989), 'The sociological analysis of hospitality labour and the neglect of accommodation workers', *International Journal of Hospitality Management*, **8**, pp. 227–35.

Lennon, J.J. and Wood, R.C. (1992), 'The teaching of industrial and other sociologies in higher education: the case of hotel and catering management studies', *International Journal of Hospitality Management*, **11**, pp. 239–53.

Ley, D.A. (1980), 'The effective General Manager: leader or entrepreneur?', *Cornell Hotel and Restaurant Administration Quarterly*, **21**, pp. 66–7.

Likert, R. (1961), *New Patterns of Management*, McGraw-Hill, New York.

Likert, R. (1967), *The Human Organization*, McGraw-Hill, New York.

Locke, E.A., Feren, D.V., McCaleb, V.M., Shaw, K.N. and Denny, A.T. (1980), 'The relative effectiveness of four methods of motivating employee performance', in *Changes in Working Life* (eds K.D. Duncan, M.M. Gruneberg and D. Wallis), John Wiley, London.

Lockwood, A. and Guerrier, Y. (1989), 'Flexible working in the hospitality industry: current strategies and future potential', *International Journal of Contemporary Hospitality Management*, **1**, pp. 11–16.

Lockwood, A. and Jones, P. (1984), *People and the Hotel and Catering Industry*, Cassell, London.

Lowe, A. (1987), 'Small hotel survival – an inductive approach', *International Journal of Hospitality Management*, **7**, pp. 197–224.

Lucas, R. (1991), 'Remuneration practice in a Wages Council sector: some empirical observations on hotels', *Industrial Relations Journal*, **22**, pp. 173–285.

Lucas, R. (1993), 'Ageism and the UK hospitality industry', *Employee Relations*, **15**, pp. 33–41.

Lundberg, C. and Woods, R.H. (1990), 'Modifying restaurant culture: managers as cultural leaders', *International Journal of Contemporary Hospitality Management*, **2**, pp. 4–12.

Macaulay, I.R. and Wood, R.C. (1992), *Hard Cheese: A Study of Hotel and Catering Employment in Scotland*, Scottish Low Pay Unit Publications, Glasgow.

Macaulay, I.R. and Wood, R.C. (1992a), 'Hotel and catering employees' attitudes towards trade unions', *Employee Relations*, **14**, pp. 20–8.

McClelland, D. (1961), *The Achieving Society*, Van Nostrand Books, Princeton, NJ.

McGregor, D. (1960), *The Human Side of Enterprise*, McGraw-Hill, New York.

McGregor, D. (1966), *Leadership and Motivation*, MIT Press, Boston

Mars, G., Bryant, D. and Mitchell, P. (1979), *Manpower Problems in the Hotel and Catering Industry*, Gower, Farnborough.

Mars, G. and Mitchell, P. (1976), *Room for Reform*, Open University Press, Milton Keynes.

Mars, G. and Nicod, M. (1984), *The World of Waiters*, George Allen and Unwin, London.

Maslow, A.H. (1943), 'A theory of human motivation', *Psychological Review*, **50**, pp. 370–96.

Medlik, S. and Airey, D. (1978), *Profile of the Hotel and Catering Industry*, Heinemann, London.

Mintzberg, H. (1973), *The Nature of Managerial Work*, Harper and Row, New York.

Mitchell, B. (1989), Biodata: using employment applications to screen new hires', *Cornell Hotel and Restaurant Administration Quarterly*, **29**, pp. 56–61.

*Moorhead, G. and Griffin, R.W. (1989), *Organizational Behaviour*, Houghton-Mifflin, Princeton, NJ.

Mullins, L. (1992), *Hospitality Management: A Human Resources Approach*, Pitman, London.

Nailon, P. (1968), 'A Study of Management Activities in Units of an Hotel Group', M.Phil. thesis, University of Surrey, UK.

Nailon, P. (1978), 'Tipping – a behavioural review', *Hotel, Catering and Institutional Management Association Review*, **2**, pp. 231–43.

Nebel, E.C. and Stearns, G.K. (1977), 'Leadership in the hospitality industry', *Cornell Hotel and Restaurant Administration Quarterly*, **18**, pp. 69–76.

Orwell, G. (1933), *Down and Out in Paris and London*, Penguin, Harmondsworth (1986 reprint).

Ouchi, W.G. (1981), *Theory Z: How American Business Can Meet the Japanese Challenge*, Addison-Wesley, Reading, Mass.

Paterson, E. (1981), 'Food Work: maids in a hospital kitchen,' in *Medical Work* (eds P. Atkinson and C. Heath), Gower, Farnborough.

Peters, T.J. and Waterman, R.H. (1982), *In Search of Excellence: Lessons from America's Best-Run Companies*, Harper and Row, New York.

Pine, R. (1987), *Management of Technological Change in the Catering Industry*, Gower, Farnborough.

Plumbley, P.R. (1985), *Recruitment and Selection*, Institute of Personnel Management, London.

Porter, L.W. and Lawler, E.E. (1968), *Managerial Attitudes and Performance*, Dorsey Press, Homewood, Ill.

*Pugh, D.S. and Hickson, D.J. (1989), *Writers on Organizations*, Penguin, Harmondsworth.

Randlesome, C. (1990), 'The Business Culture in the United Kingdom', in *Business Cultures in Europe* (eds C. Randlesome *et al.*), Butterworth-Heinemann, Oxford.

Reed, M.I. (1992), *The Sociology of Organizations: Themes, Perspectives and Prospects*, Harvester Wheatsheaf, London.

Reyes, J.P. and Kleiner, B.H. (1990), 'How to establish an organizational purpose', *International Journal of Contemporary Hospitality Management*, **2**, pp. 26–9.

*Riley, M. (1991), *Human Resource Management: A Guide to Personnel Practice in the Hotel and Catering Industry*, Butterworth-Heinemann, Oxford.

Riley, M. (1991a), 'An analysis of hotel labour markets', in *Progress in Tourism, Recreation and Hospitality Management, Vol. 3* (ed. C. Cooper), Belhaven Press, London.

Riley, M. (1992), 'Functional flexibility in hotels – is it feasible?', *Tourism Management*, **13**, pp. 363–67.

Riley, M. and Turam, K. (1988), 'The career paths of hotel managers: a developmental approach', in *Proceedings of the International Association of Hotel Management Schools Symposium*, November, 1988, Leeds, UK.

Ritzer, G. (1992), *The McDonaldization of Society*, Pine Forge Press, London.

*Robbins, S.P. (1992), *Essentials of Organizational Behaviour*, Prentice-Hall International, London, 3rd Ed.

Robertson, I.T. and Makin, P.J. (1986), 'Management Selection in Britain: a survey and critique', *Journal of Occupational Psychology*, **59**, pp. 45–7.

*Rose, M. (1988), *Industrial Behaviour*, Penguin, Harmondsworth, 2nd Ed.

Roy, D. (1952), 'Quota restriction and goldbricking in a machine shop', *American Journal of Sociology*, **57**, pp. 427–42.

Salaman, G. (1986), *Working*, Tavistock, London.

Saunders, K.C. (1981), *Social Stigma of Occupations*, Gower, Farnborough.

Saunders, K.C. (1985), *Who is your Kitchen Porter?*, Middlesex Polytechnic Research Monographs, London.

Saunders, K.C. and Pullen, R.A. (1987), *An Occupational Study of Room-Maids in Hotels*, Middlesex Polytechnic Research Monographs, London.

Saunders, P. (1990), *Social Class and Stratification*, Routledge, London.

Schein, E.H. (1985), *Organizational Culture and Leadership: A Dynamic View*, Jossey-Boss, San Francisco.

Sepic, F.T., Mahar, L. and Fiedler, F.E. (1980), 'Match the manager and the milieu: testing the contingency model', *Cornell Hotel and Restaurant Administration Quarterly*, **21**, pp. 19–22.

Seymour, D. (1985), 'An occupational profile of hoteliers in France', *International Journal of Hospitality Management*, **4**, pp. 3–8.

Shamir, B. (1978), 'Between bureaucracy and hospitality – some organizational characteristics of hotels', *Journal of Management Studies*, **15**, pp. 285–307.

Shamir, B. (1981), 'The workplace as a community: the case of British hotels', *Industrial Relations Journal*, **12**, pp. 45–56.

Shaner, M.C. (1978), 'The nature of hospitality managers: an inquiry into personal values', *Cornell Hotel and Restaurant Administration Quarterly*, **19**, pp. 65–9.

Shortt, G. (1989), 'Work activities of hotel managers in Northern Ireland: A Mintzbergian analysis', *International Journal of Hospitality Management*, **8**, pp. 121–30.

Singh, R. (1992), 'Human resource management: a sceptical look', in *The Handbook of Human Resource Management* (ed. B. Towers), Blackwell, Oxford.

Slattery, P. (1983), 'Social scientific methodology and hospitality management', *International Journal of Hospitality Management*, **2**, pp. 9–14.

Snow, G. (1981), 'Industrial Relations in Hotels', MSc thesis, University of Bath, UK.

Sternberg, L.E. (1992), 'Empowerment: trust vs. control', *Cornell Hotel and Restaurant Administration Quarterly*, **33**, pp. 69–72.

Stone, G. (1988), 'Personality and effective hospitality management', in *Proceedings of the International Association of Hotel Management Schools' Symposium*, Leeds.

Tanke, M.L. (1990), *Human Resources Management for the Hospitality Industry*, Delmar, Albany, NY.

Teare, R., Adams, D. and Messenger, S. (1992), *Managing Projects in Hospitality Organisations*, Cassell, London.

Thomas, K. (1976), 'Conflict and conflict management', in *Handbook of Industrial and Organizational Psychology* (ed. M. Dunnette), Rand McNally, New York.

Thompson, P. (1989), *The Nature of Work: An Introduction to Debates on the Labour Process*, Macmillan, London.

Thompson, P. and McHugh, D. (1990), *Work Organizations: A Critical Introduction*, Macmillan, London.

Towers, B. (1992), Introduction to *The Handbook of Human Resource Management*, Blackwell, Oxford.

Tuckmann, B.W. (1965), 'Developmental sequence in small groups', *Psychological Bulletin*, **63**, pp. 384–99.

*Tyson, S. and Jackson, T. (1992), *The Essence of Organizational Behaviour*, Prentice-Hall International, London.

Umbreit, W.T. (1986), 'Developing behaviourally-anchored scales for evaluating job performance of hotel managers', *International Journal of Hospitality Management*, **5**, pp. 55–61.

Umbreit, W.T. (1987), 'When will the hospitality industry pay attention to effective personnel practices?', *Hospitality Education and Research Journal*, **11**, 3–14.

Umbreit, W.T. and Eder, R.W. (1987), 'Linking hotel manager behaviour with outcome measures of effectiveness', *International Journal of Hospitality Management*, **6**, pp. 139–47.

Vroom, V.H. (1964), *Work and Motivation*, John Wiley, New York.

Watson, T.J. (1980), *Sociology, Work and Industry*, Routledge and Kegan Paul, London.

Weaver, T. (1988), 'Theory M: Motivating with Money', *Cornell Hotel and Restaurant Administration Quarterly*, **29**, pp. 40–5.

Whyte, W.F. (1948), *Human Relations in the Restaurant Industry*, McGraw-Hill, New York.

Whyte, W.F. (1949), 'The social structure of the restaurant', *American Journal of Sociology*, **54**, pp. 302–10.

Wood, R.C. (1988), 'Against Social Science?', *International Journal of Hospitality Management*, **7**, pp. 239–50.

*Wood, R.C. (1992), *Working in Hotels and Catering*, Routledge, London.

Wood, R.C. (1992a), 'Deviants and misfits: hotel and catering labour and the marginal worker thesis', *International Journal of Hospitality Management*, **11**, pp. 179–82.

Wood, R.C. (1992b), 'Hospitality industry labour trends: British and international experience', *Tourism Management*, **13**, pp. 297–304.

Wood, R.C. (1992c), *Food for Thought: A Study of Hotel and Catering Workers' Enquiries to the Scottish Low Pay Unit*, Scottish Low Pay Unit Publications, Glasgow.

Wood, R.C. (1993), 'Status and hotel and catering work', *Hospitality Research Journal*, **16**, pp. 3–15.

Wood, R.C. (1994), 'Hotel culture and social control', *Annals of Tourism Research*, **21**, pp. 65–80.

Woods, R.H. (1989), 'More alike than different: the culture of the restaurant industry', *Cornell Hotel and Restaurant Administration Quarterly*, **30**, pp. 82–97.

Woodward, J. (1958), *Management and Technology*, HMSO, London.

Woodward, J. (1965), *Industrial Organization: Theory and Practice*, Oxford University Press, Oxford.

Worsfold, P. (1989), 'Leadership and managerial effectiveness in the hospitality industry', *International Journal of Hospitality Management*, **8**, pp. 145–55.

Wynne, J. (1993), 'Power relationships and empowerment in hotels', *Employee Relations*, **15**, pp. 42–50.

Index